PRAYING

Reflections on 40 Years of Solitary Conversations with God

JOHN PIIPPO

WESTBOW
PRESS®
A DIVISION OF THOMAS NELSON
& ZONDERVAN

WestBow Press books may be ordered through booksellers or by contacting:

WestBow Press
A Division of Thomas Nelson & Zondervan
1663 Liberty Drive
Bloomington, IN 47403
www.westbowpress.com
1 (866) 928-1240

ISBN: 978-1-5127-3735-6 (sc)
ISBN: 978-1-5127-3737-0 (hc)
ISBN: 978-1-5127-3736-3 (e)

Library of Congress Control Number: 2016905718

Cover art by Gary Wilson

Print information available on the last page.

WestBow Press rev. date: 04/14/2016

DEDICATION

To Linda
F.S.L.

CONTENTS

ACKNOWLEDGMENTS

My thanks to the many who have helped me discover a life of praying and assisted me in reading preliminary drafts of this book.

To Dr. Tom Finger of Northern Baptist Theological Seminary for asking me to teach a class on Prayer in Northern's M.Div. program.

To Dr. Leah Fitchue for inviting me to teach on prayer and spiritual transformation at Palmer Theological Seminary and Payne Theological Seminary.

To my students in the Baptist Student Center at Michigan State University for supporting and suggesting ways of incorporating praying into our community life together.

To John and Ruth Peterson, and Dr. John Powell, whose influence on me goes beyond what words can express.

To Dr. John Hao of Faith Bible Seminary for inviting me to teach prayer and spiritual formation.

To Don Follis for support and encouragement in my writing and teaching.

To the small group in Sioux Falls, South Dakota, who read my manuscript and made several helpful suggestions and encouragement.

To my friend Steve Wamburg and my brother-in-law Grady Hauser who helped me think about ways to approach publishing this book.

To my parents and Linda's parents, who were living examples of praying people.

To the many people who have invited me to teach on prayer at churches, conferences, and in seminars.

To my co-laborers in Holy Spirit Renewal Ministries, who have supported and encouraged me in so many ways.

To Redeemer Fellowship Church, my beloved church family, who are a great, praying people. Thank you for your support.

To the Elders of Redeemer Fellowship Church for speaking into my life over the years we have been together.

To Gary Wilson of Redeemer Fellowship Church, for your beautiful, creative book cover.

Finally, and most importantly, to my beautiful wife Linda. Thank you for your constant loving partnership, your dedication to praying, and your supportive presence. I would never have come this far without you.

INTRODUCTION

When I was a little boy my mother would tuck me into bed and pray a prayer with me. It went like this: "Now I lay me down to sleep, I pray the Lord my soul to keep. Guide me through the starry night, and wake me up when the sun shines bright. God bless mommy and daddy, Johnny and Michael, and mummu and äiti and pappa."

Michael is my brother, and the last three are Finnish words for my two grandmothers and surviving grandfather. Every night, for many years until my mother probably thought I was too old for this, she would sit on my bed and we prayed these words together. Thus a river bed where prayers flow was formed in my soul that remains to this day. Even through years of prayerlessness as an adolescent, the prayer bed remained. When I turned 21 it filled with water and began to flow again. This book is about what happened to me when the waters of praying returned.

In addition to my mother's influence, two events stand out. The first was when I graduated from Northern Baptist Theological Seminary. It was the spring of 1977, and my theology professor, Tom Finger, asked me: "What class do you think we need in our theology department?"

"We need a class on prayer," I responded.

Tom said: "I want you to teach it."

Me: "But I need a class on prayer. I'm in no shape to teach others how to do what I need so badly."

Tom convinced me to teach the class on prayer. I believe it was the largest class at the seminary that semester. My main assignment was for students to pray a half hour a day, every day. This forced me to do it. I was not going to teach the class and confess that I didn't have time for this. This pressure was good for me. It was a first installment in my praying life. I began to pray a half hour every day. God encountered me in some of those prayer times, but I felt a lot of my praying was out of duty rather than relationship.

God knew I needed something more, and it was given to me in 1981. A friend of mine, John Powell, gave me a copy of Richard Foster's *Celebration of Discipline*. This became one of the few books I have read that actually moved me to action. I knew I had to back off my busy activity and reconnect with God in a life of deeper praying.

Motivated by Foster's book, I began a new journey of extended times of praying. I will never forget that first day! We were living in East Lansing, Michigan. I drove to a county park carrying my Bible, spiritual journal, and a copy of *A Guide to Prayer for Ministers and Other Servants*.[1] I found a field where there was an abandoned rusty old tractor. I climbed up and sat on the tractor seat. I remained there for four hours.

At first I remember thinking, "What am I doing here, 'doing nothing'?" I could be xeroxing or getting stuff done!"

It was a struggle to pray that day. To pray is to be in relationship with God, and I was having a hard time knowing how to respond. I loved God, but apparently not enough to spend a lot of focused time with him.

That long prayer-afternoon on the tractor was the dawning of a deeper prayer life. It was a watershed moment where the deep waters of my heart began to flow in a different direction.[2] I was led to meditate on Psalm 139:23: "Search me, O God, and know my heart; test me and know my anxious thoughts." On that day something different happened. I felt like God was saying to me, "John, allow me. Allow me." I responded, "Yes, God. Search me and test me." Then God said, "I've wanted to, but I need you to be still." I was. God did. And I wrote

[1] *A Guide to Prayer for Ministers and Other Servants*. Nashville: Upper Room Press, 1983.
[2] I used *A Guide to Prayer for Ministers and Other Servants* for two years as my devotional guide.

and wrote pages in a journal that had been mostly blank. In the act of praying God met me and began to bring healing to my agitated spirit. My deeper praying life was born.

This is a book about *praying*. You won't learn much from a book on prayer if you don't spend time praying, and praying in a certain way. In the same way you won't learn much about food by reading books but not eating. Praying is superior to prayer as eating is superior to food.

I distinguish 'praying' (the verb, in the continuous tense) from 'prayer' (the noun). "Praying" denotes an activity; "prayer" refers to a concept or idea. The concept is important, but means little if the activity is not engaged in. In this sense praying is more important than "prayer."

This book is a partial record of my experiences and reflections on a life of praying. Since that God-encounter on a tractor I have spent countless hours praying, and recording over three thousand pages of journal entries. My journals contain words from God spoken to me, experiences I've had, and biblical, theological, and philosophical reflections on the act of praying. My hope is that God would meet you in these pages and anoint you with a praying life.

1

WHAT IS PRAYING?

In 1977 I taught a course on prayer at Northern Baptist Theological Seminary in its Master's program. My main assignment for the students was to pray thirty minutes every day for twelve weeks. I knew that, in a course on prayer, students had to engage in actual praying. To *not* pray in a prayer class would be like taking a swimming class and never getting in the pool.

A few students objected to this assignment. Instead of actually praying they wanted to read books and write papers on prayer. How absurd!

You'll learn more about prayer by actually praying than can be gotten from a book. I'd rather talk with my wife Linda than read a book about her. I prefer sitting on the beaches of the Caribbean Sea more than reading about it. I'll take eating Gino's Chicago Pizza over looking at photos of it. Better to taste and see for myself than read about how good it tasted to others.

Eugene Peterson expresses it like this:

> I want to do the original work of being in deepening conversation with the God who reveals himself to me and addresses me by name. I don't want to dispense mimeographed hand-outs that describe God's business; I want to witness out of my own experience. I don't

1

want to live as a parasite on the first-hand spiritual life of others.[1]

You are beginning to read a book. Thank you. But above all, pray.

Praying: A Definition

What is praying? *Praying is talking with God about what God and I are thinking and doing together.* This is the best definition of *prayer* I have ever heard.[2]

Praying is communicating with God about The Mission. In praying I meet with my Commander and receive my marching orders.

In praying I experience comfort, healing, deliverance, and rescue. I receive encouragement. I am told that I am loved. I get corrected and directed, which calls for obedience. I find out what God wants from me and what he wants me to do.

This definition or praying ups the ante in my life. It makes following Jesus more exciting and more real. God really does expect me to follow him. This gets practical whenever I hear God call my name and say, "John, I want you to do/go/say _____."

Praying is, as Martin Luther King Jr. said, a "conversation with God." It is a dialogical give-and-take, between God and me.

Praying Within the Big Dance

Since 1981 my extended praying day has been Tuesday. On Tuesday afternoons I go alone to a quiet place, away from distractions, and talk with God about what we are thinking and doing together. Solitary praying is one-on-one, God and I, for several hours.

---

[1] Eugene Peterson, *The Contemplative Pastor: Returning to the Art of Spiritual Direction*, Kindle Locations 175-178. Grand Rapids: Eerdmans, 1989.
[2] See Dallas Willard, *The Divine Conspiracy: Fulfilling God's Kingdom on Earth*, 243. San Francisco: Harper Collins, 1998.

As I meet with God I carry certain core beliefs with me. They are the following[3]:

1. *God exists.* God is real. There is a God. God *is.* Without this, praying is an illusion. In the act of praying I am keeping company with the all-knowing, all-powerful, all-loving, necessarily existent (everlasting; without beginning or end), personal agent who created and sustains all things. This is no small appointment I have!

2. *God is a personal being.* God desires relationship. The Christian idea of God as a Trinity makes sense of God as essentially relational. God, in his being, is three relating Persons in One.[4] God, as a Three-Personed Being, makes conceptual sense of the idea that God *is* love. Everlastingly, the Father has been loving the Son, the Son has been loving the Spirit, the Spirit has been loving the Father, and round and round in the Big Dance.[5] To pray is to accept God's invitation to the Big Dance.

3. *God made me.* For what? For relationship with him. God desires relationship. He made me for such a partnership as this. When I pray I am living in the heart of God's desire for me.

4. *God knows me.* In praying God's Spirit searches me out. God is aware of my deepest thoughts and inclinations, many of which are beyond me. God knows me better than I know myself. This would be devastating, were it not for the fact that...

5. *God loves me.* God, in his essence, *is* love. Therefore, God cannot not-love. This is good news for me! As I put 4 and 5 together I'm singing "Amazing Grace" accompanied by tears of gratitude and joy.

---

[3] A "belief" is a statement or proposition I affirm or find true.

[4] I confess I very much like William Young's *The Shack* on Trinitarian theism.

[5] I get "Big Dance" from the Greek word *perichoresis. Peri* means "to go around" and *choresis* means "to sing and dance; choral and choreography." *Perichoresis* means to "dance in a circle." Early Christians coined this word to describe the Trinitarian being of God as an everlasting circle dance of love.

6. *God desires me to love and know him in return.* God has called me into a reciprocal relationship. Between God and me is a give-and-take.

This is where praying comes in. To pray is to enter a loving-knowing relationship with God.

When I talk with God I often begin by asking, "God, is everything all right between you and me?" This is the "Search me, O God" moment. Then I listen. If God reveals something that's breaking relationship with him, I confess it. It then becomes God's delight to forgive me. God loves doing this because God *is* love. God desires to heal anything that breaks relationship.[6]

In praying, I talk to God. I express my love to God. I voice concerns to him. I don't hesitate to ask for myself if my request feels kingdom advancing. This is called "petitionary prayer." I meet some who feel weird about asking for themselves. That feeling is not from God.

I also pray for others. This is called "intercessory prayer." All these kind of things and more are what happen when I talk with God.

In praying I listen to God. When God speaks to me, I write it down. I keep a spiritual journal, which is a record of the voice and activity of God to me. In this way I remember the things God says to me. God's history with me is more precious than material things and accomplishments.

I have found that God has much to say to me today. I take "This is the day the Lord has made" literally. Today is the day of encounter for me.

God has plans and purposes for me, which have to do with his kingdom and his righteousness. I seek these two things in the first place. Then God will add all good things unto me.[7]

---

[6] God's grace is amazing but it's not cheap. It will cost something to be in relationship with God. This does not surprise me, since there is a cost involved in real relationship with anyone. Love is sacrifice. There are no exceptions to this.

[7] "Good" equals the kind of things God values, such as love, honor, reconciliation, joy, peace, and real, authentic relationship.

There is no formula for this because praying is relationship with God. Praying cannot be programmed. No two dialogues are the same. Praying is a movement, not an institution.

There is more to prayer as relationship than the things I have shared above. Yet there are essentials that apply to any strong relationship: listening, understanding and being understood and, of course, love.

I have such things in mind, residually in the background of my soul, when I am praying.

Praying in Solitary Community

Solitude is not the same as loneliness. Solitude is getting alone with God, which is not a lonely experience since someone is with me ("Emmanuel"). Solitude with God is fruitful, organic, growing, and experiential.

In praying my heart is moved from loneliness to solitude, from restlessness to restfulness. The praying person is gathered in the welcoming wings of God. I am sheltered beneath those wings, alone in fellowship with the Father, Son, and Spirit. Many times I have known what it is to be-with God while going alone to pray. This is an experience of the dissolution of desolation supplanted by the warmth of consolation.

Solitary praying is communal. It happens in community with the Triune God.

Praying Is an Environment

My '99 Ford van had 170,000 miles on it. It was rusting out, required constant attention and care, had doors that no longer worked, and needed a brake job. Being unsafe to drive, Linda and I wondered how much more money we should pour into this thing.

We talked together with God about this. We prayed. It seemed clear we were to get rid of the old van and purchase a reliable car that would last a long time. God told us that. God directed us in what to do.

Praying means thinking and living in the presence of God. Praying is a God-soaked environment, a divine culture. Praying is a vast space inhabited by God's presence. Praying is a dwelling-with. In the praying environment much is given to me in the *much-ness* of God with me.

Thinking and living in a praying-environment brings discernment. Answers to questions like "What should I do?" are found in God's presence. His presence is the place where I am to think and live.

To Pray Is to Have a Spiritual Life

Henri Nouwen said, "A spiritual life without prayer is like the Gospel without Christ."[8] His analogy is appropriate because Jesus had a spiritual life, right? At the heart of the spiritual life of Jesus is that *he prayed*. If Jesus prayed, how can I claim to follow him if I am "too busy to pray"?

Praying is at the center of a spiritual life. A prayerless person has little or no Jesus-kind-of spiritual life. Saying this will not motivate people to pray. It might produce guilt, but guilt is a poor motivator.

Still, the standard must be lifted up in our watered-down, relativistic religious world. If I, as a pastor, stood in front of my church family and said, "I don't have time to meet with God in prayer, but I've got some cool things to share with you today," they should relieve me of my duties.

To have a praying life *is* to have a spiritual life. This is good news for all who actually pray. Praying people see prayer as essential to the Jesus Movement. In praying I am part of the Movement. To pray *is* to engage in the Mission. In praying I get my marching orders. My praying personhood becomes an instrument of righteousness in the hands of Almighty God.

---

[8] Nouwen, *The Only Necessary Thing: Living a Prayerful Life*, New York: Crossroad, 32.

Praying Is Knocking On the Door of the Sanctuary of the Heart

The human heart[9] is like a home. The heart is a dwelling place designed for God. When my heart was constructed, the architect and builder was God. In the secret place, I was knit together in the image of God. I was made by God, and for God to be present in me. My purpose is to host the presence of God in the home that is my heart. I am a portable sanctuary hosting the presence of God.

If I place my trust in God, this will happen. Jesus said, in John 14:23, "All who love me will do what I say. My Father will love them, and we will come and make our home with each of them."

I am a Jesus-truster, and Christ, the "hope of glory," has gone house hunting and found me. He lives within, by his Spirit. The gateway into this inner place is praying. Praying knocks on the door of the heart sanctuary where God dwells. When I knock in prayer, God opens. God will never *not* respond to conferencing with me.

Conferences with God are not mere business meetings. Imagine a planning meeting where the lofty CEO interrupts, calls you out, and says, "I love you." He cares for you! Doing business with God is like this. I know it from experience.

In the history of Christian spirituality many have drawn on the John 14:23 image of the human heart as the place where God makes His home. One famous example is Teresa of Avila's *Interior Castle*. The heart, writes Teresa, is a castle containing many mansions. "The door of this castle is prayer."[10]

Enter into the inner sanctuary of the heart today.

Praying Is an Education

In Dostoevsky's *The Brothers Karamazov* Father Zossima offers this counsel on prayer:

---

[9] By "heart" I mean the same as "spirit." See, e.g., Dallas Willard's *The Renovation of the Heart* as a treatise on spirit-formation.

[10] Teresa of Avila, *Interior Castle*, Kindle location 353. New York: Dover, 2012.

Young man, be not forgetful of prayer. Every time you pray, if your prayer is sincere, there will be new feeling and new meaning in it which will give you fresh courage, and you will understand that prayer is an education.[11]

Here are some takeaways from this quote for me:

- To pray is to learn praying. We learn more about prayer by actually praying than by reading about prayer.
- To pray is to learn about God. An intimate education in the being of God is gained in a life of praying. We learn things about God by praying that we cannot learn by reading about God.
- To pray is to grow in discernment regarding the ways of God. Praying teaches us the distinction between deciding and discerning.
- To pray is to learn to hear the shepherding voice of God. In a life of praying we learn discipleship.
- To pray is to gain and feel the heart of God. To pray is to grieve and rejoice with God. Praying educates us in sorrow and joy.
- To pray is to learn trust in God. To pray *is* to trust. I cannot authentically pray without trust-jumping into the arms of God.
- To pray is to gain an education in obedience. Where there is disobedience, the prayer life screeches to a grinding halt. In the obedience that emerges from the act of praying trust grows, hence prayer grows and flourishes.
- The praying person graduates with a PhD in patience.

Praying Is the Soul of Religion

"Prayer is the very soul of religion"
Auguste Sabatier

What Sabatier means is something like this: those who pray are true believers in God. People who pray live out of the center of their

---

[11] Fyodor Dostoyevski, *The Brothers Karamazov*, New York: MacMillan, 339.

Jesus-faith. Praying is the *nephesh*, the *psuche*, the inner fire, of the God-relationship.

Praying tends the fire burning in the depth of my soul.

Praying Is an Act of Protest

One result of habitual praying is that God removes unrighteous anger from my heart. God lifts the chip off my shoulder. He softens the edge of my attitude. He lowers the elevation of my proud altitude. He forms his heart of compassion in me for my enemies. He frees me from the prison cell of hatred, and releases me to love in ways I have never done before.

This is not a theory, but an empirical, existential reality. Linda has seen the results. I am a better husband as Christ is more deeply formed in me. I get changed. Much of this happens as I am praying.

In praying, I am clay on a potter's wheel. I am not the shaping agent of my own transformation. God is. At times I can *feel* his hands on me.

This is praying as an act of resistance to the common, unholy structures of the world, which demand conformation to their will. To pray is to protest against the hate-filled standards of culture. In solitary praying, I am protesting against a world that wants to shape my heart into its forms of destruction, hatred, manipulation, competition, suspicion, defensiveness, and war.

In praying, I give witness to God whose love is all-healing and all-embracing. I protest against the world by declaring, "Hands off me!"

Praying Is Subversive Activity

Real praying transcends the kind of prayer some people "don't have time for." Praying establishes the rule of God in my heart, and in my circumstances. Praying dethrones ungodly powers that want to reign over me.

In this way, praying is subversive. Praying is an "open act of defiance against any claim by the current regime."[12] Praying disestablishes manmade hierarchies, subordinating all things to the rule of God.

Praying is revolutionary activity whereby I revolt against pretenders to the throne. Praying is a revolution against the kingdom of this world as I meet with the true Lord of heaven and earth.

In the act of praying, I join forces with the underground movement, the "Society of Seeds Growing Secretly" that subverts this world's false ideologies.

Praying people assault and endanger the powers of darkness.

Praying and the Grand Invasion

I have built solitary praying into my life. Like DNA shapes my physical being, praying becomes the DNA of my spiritual self. It *is*, more and more, my life.

I do this because Jesus prayed, in solitude. I am one of Jesus' followers. Therefore, as he goes, I go.

Such singular focus is a challenge in our APP-addicted world.[13] In 1961, before the Age of App, Howard Thurman wrote that "The fight for the private life is fierce and unyielding. Often it seems as if our times are in league with the enemy."[14]

Thurman saw our world as a "great huddle" of people who are inwardly desolate, lonely, and afraid. To combat this he advised us to find "ever-creative ways that can ventilate the private soul without blowing it away, that can confirm and affirm the integrity of the person in the midst of the collective necessities of our time."[15]

---

[12] Eugene Peterson, *The Contemplative Pastor*, Kindle Locations 104-106

[13] See, e.g., *The App Generation: How Today's Youth Navigate Identity, Intimacy, and Imagination In a Digital World*, by Howard Gardner and Katie Davis. New Haven and London: Yale, 2013.

[14] Howard Thurman, *A Strange Freedom: The Best of Howard Thurman on Religious Experience and Public Life*, 21. Boston: Beacon, 1998.

[15] Ib., 22

These cultural, collective necessities mitigate against the deeper life by forcing their fearful, urgent, task-ordering on us. They shape human hearts into purposeless, vacuous "doings." This herd-like busyness inoculates the soul against what Thurman called "the Grand Invasion" of the presence of God.

The flesh defends itself against the Grand Invasion. But our spirit gradually feels at home with God, in the place where he and I meet. Life becomes private without being self-centered. The solitary praying person comes to their senses, and thus to themselves. When I began meeting with God I found myself. The Grand Invasion had begun.

When Prayer Changed

N.T. Wright, in *Paul and the Faithfulness of God*, states that, with Paul, the Jewish idea of prayer changed in a radical Reformation-like way. Ben Witherington notes this and comments:

> As it turns out, the real radical Reformation did not take place shortly after Luther (and in reaction to him). No, it happened in the first century when Paul revamped the whole symbol system of early Judaism. When someone reorients and reinterprets things like Temple, Territory, Torah, Prayer, Family, Battle etc. then they are messing with the vital parts of an ancient religion, not merely its thought world, but its praxis.[16]

Paul the Jewish Christian reframed praying. No longer need one pray at set times of the day, in set geographical places, or facing in a certain direction. No longer need praying be memorized or recited. In Paul the idea of a fixed, set prayer is diminished. Now we can, and should, pray whenever (without ceasing), wherever, and however, as

---

[16] Ben Witherington, "Wright's Paul and the Faithfulness of God – Part Fourteen," http://www.patheos.com/blogs/bibleandculture/2014/03/02/wrights-paul-and-the-faithfulness-of-god-part-fourteen/

guided by the Spirit. This is a major modification of ancient Jewish monotheistic praying, not to mention the modification of the Shema.

Therefore, praying...

- need not be at set times of the day
- need not have some special body posture or position
- need not be in some special location
- does not involve formulas
- is to be engaged in any time and all the time
- is addressed to the Father, through the Son
- is Spirit-enabled

The historical Jesus-event unleashed praying into a deeper, more intimate relationship with God, giving us greater freedom in how we can come to him.

3. In the name of Jesus Christ and by the power of His blood, I cancel all lies and deception that have been directed against my life, the lives of my family, the church family, (name whatever else the Lord puts on your heart.). Lord, forgive me for believing lies I have accepted as truth and the deception that has shaped my life at this time. Break off and remove all spiritual evil attached to them, and speak again your Truth. May I know the difference now between your Truth and the lies of people and the Enemy (Satan). Thank you Lord. Bring back all that was intended but was not received or lived out because of the lies and deception. Restore your purpose in my life and the lives around me. Thank you Lord. Holy is Your Name.

4. A prayer of redistribution.

"Lord Jesus, in Your strong Name and by the power of Your Blood, whatever burdens (emotional, mental, spiritual, financial) I've been carrying that have not been blessed by You, please remove them now. I release to you every person and their emotional content that I have called mine; that I have been carrying that has not been blessed by You to carry. Rearrange my pack and put only in it the burdens that You want me to carry. Let me know the difference in weight from what I was carrying and what you are allowing me to carry now. Forgive me for any assumptions I have made in my decision making. Remove any spiritual debris that has hindered my walk with you in any way because of those decisions. "All that evil leave and go to the feet of Jesus!" Lord, restore all that has been expended in trying to carry all these things myself. Your yoke is easy and Your burden is light."

Spiritual Warfare Prayers

Prayers of Forgiveness

Prayers of Praise

Prayers of Blessing – Praying blessing over someone is praying God's fullest intent on that person's life.

1. In the name of Jesus Christ and by the power of His blood, I cancel (or Lord, cancel) all ungodly ties and bonds between me and _____ (name the person or group). Remove any thing that is not of you from this relationship. All evil in this relationship leave now and go to the feet of Jesus and do what He says. Anything that is of you in this relationship, O Lord, plant deep in my heart and let it be revealed through my actions.

2. In the name of Jesus Christ and by the power of His blood I cancel all curses, pronouncements, and judgments made against me by any person, knowingly or unknowingly, especially by _____ (name the person).

I cancel all curses, pronouncements, and judgments made by me against any person, knowingly or unknowingly; especially toward _____ (name the person).

Cancel all the effects of gossip on my life and the lives of others. All that evil leave and go to the feet of Jesus. Lord loose all blessing into my life and the lives of others that have been held back because of those things. Thank you Lord.

The corrections of discipline are the way
of/to Life!

Boasting in weakness...

David before Nathan re: Uriah

2

PRAYING AND THE NATURE OF GOD

Late at night Linda and I stepped out of our house to view the promised Perseid meteor shower. We stood in the darkness that enveloped our yard. She leaned into my arms, and I held her as we looked at the perfectly clear, starry sky. I have never gotten over the feeling of wonder and awe and smallness that comes when I look into the vastness of space. I wanted us to see just one meteor together. We waited and waited, until it finally came, streaking across the black canopy.

On the following night, the Perseid shower happened again. I got a chair and sat beneath the stars, for a long time. The early evening sky was clear, the humidity was low, the temperature was warm, and I had childlike expectancy in my soul.

My experience with God is like this. As I meditate on this stunning creation, I am given insights into the being of God. In God there is a greatness, and a perfection, that dwarfs the cosmos.

God's hugeness concerns his essential attributes, which are omniscience, omnipotence, omnibenevolence, atemporality,[1] nonphysicality (hence omnipresence), and all of which are ascribed to a necessarily existing (everlasting; without beginning or end) being.

---

[1] An excellent discussion about God's relationship to time is found in *God and Time: Four Views*, by Gregory Ganssle and Paul Helm. Downers Grove: Intervarsity, 2001.

This God who loves me, and invites me to communicate with him, is beyond comparison. When I survey God's wondrous analytic predicates, my praying life is transfigured. To consider God, the great Subject of my prayers, is to pray differently. In this chapter I will share some things I have learned about prayer as it relates to the nature of God.

Prayer Is Original Research About God

"Parasite"– *a person or thing that takes something from someone or something else and does not do anything to earn or deserve it.*[2]

I need my own prayer life, not yours (if you have one). It's wonderful that spiritual giants like Martin Luther, Mother Teresa, and the apostle Paul prayed. I can learn from them. One thing I have learned from praying people is that *I* must take much time to pray. The prayer lives of the great saints mean little if I am too busy to pray.

I must "do the original work of being in deepening conversation with the God who reveals himself to me and addresses me by name."[3] I need to testify out of my own experience, lest I be rendered inauthentic. I cannot be a parasite living off the experiences of others. I must taste for myself, and see that God is good.

Real praying is non-parasitic. The insights of others are helpful, but personal revelations are better, more inspiring, and more convincing. I can learn from others about God, but I learn more about God from God himself.

In praying, I am engaging in original research about God. I address and am addressed by an all-powerful, all-knowing, all-loving, personal agent who is non-physical and everlasting. I can't get that living like a parasite on another person's spiritual skin.

---

[2] Mirriam-Webster Dictionary, http://www.merriam-webster.com/dictionary/parasite.

[3] Eugene Peterson, *The Contemplative Pastor*, Kindle Locations 175-178.

Praying to an All-Powerful God

If you believe in a God who created the universe, then it should be unproblematic to believe this God is powerful enough to address your struggles.

God is omnipotent. God can do everything that is possible to do. Does this mean God can create a rock so heavy he can't lift? Or a burrito so hot he can't hold? Or a god more powerful than himself? No. These are all logical nonsense questions, and variations on this nonsense non-statement: *There is an all-powerful being that is not powerful enough to do some things.* That is self-contradictory.

The idea that an all-powerful being is not strong enough to do some things is a logical contradiction, like "square circle," or "married bachelor." It's not that square circles are hard to find or difficult to conceive. Square circles *cannot* exist and *cannot* be conceived.[4] It's the same with "limited all-powerful being," or "all-powerful being who is unable to change me."

I sometimes hear a person say, "Some people cannot change." Or, "My spouse will never change." But that can't be right. It is logically possible to change, and God can do all things that are logically possible. To think that some people cannot change denies the all-powerfulness of God. If God made a universe out of formlessness and void, then surely God can change a person whom he has formed. If God created all that exists, then surely God can speak into that existence.

To pray is to enter into dialogue with an Omnipotent Being. God is an Almighty, Loving, Personal Agent who is more than capable of addressing our struggles. Acknowledging this creates confidence to bring all things to him, in prayer. God is able to effect transformation and change, in me.

---

[4] "Cannot be conceived" means: cannot be thought of; i.e., one cannot form a mental image of "square circle" because such a thing is a logical impossibility.

Praying To An All-Knowing God

God knows everything that can be known. God is omniscient, all-knowing.

Nothing is unknown to God. You cannot hide from him. This is good, because God is loving. All of you and all of me is seen and known by God.

> You have searched me, LORD,
> and you know me.
> You know when I sit and when I rise;
> you perceive my thoughts from afar.
> You discern my going out and my lying down;
> you are familiar with all my ways.
> Before a word is on my tongue
> you, LORD, know it completely.
> You hem me in behind and before,
> and you lay your hand upon me.
> Such knowledge is too wonderful for me,
> too lofty for me to attain.[5]

For some it is bad news that God is all-knowing, because he sees our moral and spiritual misdeeds. But others, like David, are in awe of God's omniscience. David sings:

> Such knowledge is too wonderful for me,
> too lofty for me to attain.[6]

Why be thankful for God's omniscience? I can think of two reasons. The first is: God's omniscience is wonderful.

I had an appointment with my eye doctor. It was a follow-up to do another series of tests on one of my eyes. "Why do I need a follow-up?"

---

[5] Psalm 139:1-5
[6] Psalm 139:6

I asked the doctor? "As a precaution on possible problems in the future," he replied.

I allowed my eye to be searched out by my doctor's more-knowing eyes. He is excellent at what he does. He purposes my well-being. If there is a problem, we need to know so it can be treated.

I am grateful for my eye doctor's superior knowledge, combined with his care for me. In the same way I thank God for his all-knowingness, combined with his all-lovingness towards me. God, knowing all things, is the Ultimate Diagnostician. As I submit to him I feel his lovingkindness. When God sees failure in me his objective is not to condemn, but to restore, renew, and transform me. How wonderful this is!

A second reason to be grateful for God's omniscience is: God's omniscience is lofty.

When I was a doctoral student at Northwestern University I took Reginald Allen's graduate seminar on Aristotle's *Metaphysics*. I'll never forget the first day of class. There were eight of us waiting for him. He walked into the seminar room carrying the *Metaphysics*, and began teaching. The astounding thing was that Dr. Allen knew the entire Metaphysics by heart (or close to it), in Greek![7]

As he taught he walked slowly around the classroom, rarely opening the book. I've had classes where a professor is not so awe-inspiring, and the students challenged him or her. Not so in Dr. Allen's class. No one on the planet knew Aristotle (and Plato, Allen's specialty) better than he.

Occasionally, another Northwestern professor would drop in on our class, sit quietly, and take notes on this brilliant professor. One day - to my shock and awe – the philosopher E.M. Curley[8] sat next to me. I think I said nothing in class that day!

In Dr. Allen's class I saw and experienced human brilliance. Such knowledge is too wonderful for me, too lofty to attain. But when I think of God and *his* omniscience, *nothing compares*. I only have weak

---

[7] Dr. Allen taught in Northwestern's Philosophy department and Greek language department.

[8] E.M. Curley might be the world's greatest scholar in the philosophy of Spinoza.

analogies to comprehend this. Shall I fall on my face and not look up? Shall I forget trying to understand and just worship? Does not God have to seriously dumb down the conversation so I can comprehend even a bit of it? In the presence of God, I have mostly questions, not answers.

How can it be that Omniscient God invites *me* to pray, to speak to him, to listen to him? Yet he does.

When I pray I address an All-Knowing Being, and am in awe.

Praying to an All-Loving God

To pray is to confer with an omni-being whose attributes include omniscience (all-knowing = knows everything that can be known), and omnipotence (all-powerful = is able to do all things that can be done).[9]

It is important to remember just Who calls our name and to Whom we are speaking. We pray to a being who knows all things that can be known, and who is able to do all logical possibilities. The appropriate emotions are awe, worship, thanksgiving, and love.

All this would be terrifying if God was not all loving (omnibenevolent). But he is. God *is* (*esse*) all-loving. The essence of God *is* to love. Because God's essence is love, God cannot not-love. God cannot, essentially and in principle, despise me. Others may, but God cannot. I may hate myself, but God never does.

All God's actions towards me are love. I have 3500 pages of journal entries attesting to the love of God in my life. My record is but one small, brief, moment among billions of lives past, present, and future.

Because God is love, the only fear I need experience is awe. I find it an awesome privilege to be invited by God into his earth-shattering presence. Thank God that he is love or I would be destroyed!

God *is* love. The idea of God as a Trinity of persons-in-relationship makes conceptual sense of this. Love is a relational reality. Love requires an "other." God is a Three-Personed Being of Otherness in essential,

---

[9] An all-knowing being knows all logical possibilities. An all-powerful being is able to do all that is logically possible.

metaphysical, unitive relationship. When I pray, I am invited into this everlasting love community.[10]

When we pray to God it's far bigger and greater than we could even begin to imagine. Even those with the deepest praying lives fail to fully fathom the dimensions of God's love.

Praying to an Everlasting God

When I pray, I address an all-powerful (omnipotent) being. I am known by an all-knowing (omniscient) being. I am spoken to by an all-loving (omnibenevolent) being. I am conferencing with a necessarily existent (everlasting) being.[11]

God cannot not-exist. Existence is of God's essence. God has an ontological stability nothing else has. Intellectual recognition of God's stability breeds stability in me.

God's everlastingness means he never began to exist and will never cease to exist. God never came into being, because God IS.

When Moses asked God, "Who are you? What is your name?", God responded with a form of the verb "to be." "God said to Moses, "I AM WHO I AM. This is what you are to say to the Israelites: 'I AM has sent me to you.'"[12]

God said, essentially, "My name is *I IS*."

I'm not forcing Greek philosophy on the Hebrew text. The Hebrew word *hayah* is hard to translate. It could mean, "I will be who I will be." *Hayah* is a form of the verb "to be." God is BEING. God is Is-ness, *par excellence*.

No wonder God has no fear. Nothing could ever, in principle, harm God. God is a rock, except infinitely more solid.

---

[10] See John chapters 14 and 15.

[11] To refer to God as necessarily existent speaks of the aseity of God. "Aseity" is a put-together of *a* (from) + *se* (oneself).

[12] Exodus 3:14

The contingent, praying human addresses the everlasting, quite-secure Person. I gain confidence and strength to think that such a God loves me as well. Realizing this, who wouldn't have time to pray?[13]

Praying to a Non-physical God

Physicalism is the belief that all facts are physical facts. Many intellectual atheists today are physicalists. Physicalism, hence atheism, has its problems.[14] It is unable to account for consciousness and free will. On physicalism, such things do not exist, which I find absurd.[15]

Not all atheists are physicalists. See, for example, NYU philosopher Thomas Nagel's *Mind and Cosmos: Why the Materialist Neo-Darwinian Conception of Nature is Almost Certainly False*.[16] Nagel's point regarding consciousness is that a physicalist (materialist) view of the natural world not only fails to account for consciousness, but *positively excludes* it. Nagel sums his book up by saying that the physical sciences, as wonderful as they are, cannot - in principle - "provide the basis for an explanation of the mental aspects of reality as well — that physics can aspire finally to be a theory of everything."[17]

---

[13] Occasionally I hear someone who thinks they have come up with a trick question ask "If God made the universe, who made God?" The answer, of course, is that this is a nonsense question. For if God is necessarily existent than God never began to exist. Only things that begin to exist have a cause. God is a Uncaused Being (in this sense akin to Aristotle's metaphysically necessary "Unmoved Mover."

[14] See, e.g., Stewart Goetz and Charles Taliaferro, *Naturalism,* Grand Rapids: Eerdmans; and Robert Koons and George Bealer, eds., *The Waning of Naturalism,* New York: Oxford.

[15] See, e.g., J. P. Moreland's critique of physicalism in *The Soul: How We Know It's Real and Why It Matters*. Chicago: Moody Publishers, 2014); *Consciousness and the Existence of God: A Theistic Argument:* New York and London: Routledge, 2008.

[16] Nagel, New York: Oxford, 2012

[17] http://www.nytimes.com/2013/02/07/books/thomas-nagel-is-praised-by-creationists.html?pagewanted=all&_r=0

I believe (and reason) that non-physical realities (like consciousness and free will) exist.[18] Among the set of nonphysical realities is God. God is an immaterial, therefore non-physical, Being. This has implications for how we pray.

Since I am made in God's image, there are things about me that are God-like. John Calvin, at the beginning of his *Institutes of the Christian Religion*, wrote that "No man can survey himself without forthwith turning his thoughts towards the God in whom he lives and moves; because it is perfectly obvious that the endowments which we possess cannot possibly be from ourselves."[19]

I have a soul, a mind, consciousness, and free will. I am not a purely physical thing. In this sense I am like God. This is the point that connects me to God. Just as God transcends physical reality, so do I. When I pray, I do so as an image-bearer. This is where I stand in relation to God. J.P. Moreland writes: "An entity can stand in certain relations and not others depending on the sort of thing it is."[20]

I, and you, and all persons, are a certain sort of thing that is inherently non-physical. "I" cannot be reduced to mere matter. When I pray, my non-physical spirit interacts with the non-physical God. God is not limited by physical constraints, therefore neither am I (think of Paul, praying while in prison chains).

Contemplative Prayer Is Revelatory of the Being of God

In the history of Christian spirituality, meditation is distinguished from contemplation. Meditation is ruminating on the thoughts and truths of God; contemplation concerns the *visio dei*, the beholding of God. In contemplation there is a God-encounter. Meditation can birth revelation; contemplation *is* revelation.

---

[18] For deep thinking on the possibility and reality of nonphysical abstract objects, see Paul Gould, ed., *Beyond the Control of God? Six Views on the Problem of God and Abstract Objects*, New York: Bloomsbury Academic.

[19] Quoted in J.P. Moreland, *The Recalcitrant Imago Dei: Human Persons and the Failure of Naturalism*, 4. London: SCM, 2009.

[20] Ib.

Henri Nouwen says that "the practice of contemplative prayer is the discipline by which we begin to see God in our heart."[21] Note: *we* begin to see God. This is participation in divine self-recognition.

This is the language of Trinitarian theism, exemplified in John chapters 14 -17. This is Jesus' prayer that we would be one, as he and the Father are one. Jesus' words on "oneness," and Paul's words on "inness," bespeak unitive experience. In contemplative praying God is up close and intimate.

Meditation escorts us into God's presence. Contemplation is intimate, abiding, God-connectedness. Jesus invites us into the Big Dance of Father-Son-Spirit. We fellowship with God and are empowered within the perichoretic union.[22]

Contemplative prayer is revelatory of the being of God. I have experienced this, many times over the past four decades.

> Go to pray, seeking God.
> Do this as a lifestyle.
> Have much time for this.
> He will reveal himself to you.

Our Concept of God Makes a Praying Difference

A year ago at Redeemer we preached through the biblical book of 1 John. At the heart of John's letter is his concern that some of his readers are walking in darkness, saying they have no sin when they really do, and thus deceiving themselves. John's redemptive strategy is to bring the concept of God's character as light, purity, and righteousness, to center stage. This makes all the difference in our struggle against our inner corruption.

---

[21] Nouwen, *The Only Necessary Thing: Living a Prayerful Life*, 35

[22] Perichoresis – ancient Christians described the Trinitarian being of God as an everlasting circle dance of relationship. Peri – "around"; choresis – from which we get "choral" and "choreography."

Recent empirical research supports this.[23] Prayer seems effective in combating psychological challenges, such as relieving anxiety. The level of effectiveness is connected with the person's concept of God.

Baylor University sociologist Matt Bradshaw received a Templeton Grant to study this, and published his findings in the journal Sociology of Religion - "Prayer, Attachment to God, and Anxiety-Related Disorders Among U.S. Adults."[24] Bradshaw found that people who viewed God as loving and supportive, and prayed with this idea of God in mind, displayed fewer symptoms of anxiety-related disorders — such as irrational worry, fear, self-consciousness, dread in social situations and obsessive-compulsive behavior — than those who prayed but did not expect God to comfort or protect them.

Perceived characteristics of God - such as loving, remote, or judgmental - affect the relationship between prayer and mental health.

For the praying person, what we think of God makes a difference.

In Praying, Think of God's Goodness to You

God is good. In his very being. In his essence.

To confess this is to attribute the quality, or property, of "goodness" to God.

"Goodness" is an essential, not contingent, attribute of God. Contingent properties are attributes a thing has, but which are not essential to being that thing. An essential attribute is a property something has which is essential to that thing, and without which that thing would not be what it is.

For example, it is essential that a "cup" has the property of "holding liquid." A cup that does not hold liquid is not a cup. A "cup" cannot not hold liquid. But the color of the cup is a contingent property. Color does not make a cup a cup.

---

[23] See "Sociologist: Our concept of God impacts the power of prayer, affects anxiety-related disorders." https://baptistnews.com/faith/item/29092-sociologist-concept-of-god-impacts-power-of-prayer

[24] http://socrel.oxfordjournals.org/content/75/2/208.abstract

God cannot not be good. God *is* good, in his essence. Because of this, all that issues forth from God is good. Whatever God creates is good. God's words are good. God's commands are good, and for our well-being.[25]

Belief in the essential goodness of God is deeply rooted in Judeo-Christianity. Once recognized and experienced, it occasions the human response of thanksgiving. Thanksgiving is the natural and logical response to the experienced goodness of God.

We see this in a verse like 1 Chronicles 16:34: "Give thanks to the LORD, for he is good; his love endures forever."

As you are praying today think of God's goodness. To you. And be thankful.

Learned Ignoramuses Praying to an Omniscient God

I remember, as an undergraduate in the early 1970s, reading Jean-Paul Sartre's novel *Nausea*. One of my favorite philosophy teachers, Michael Gelven, recommended it to me. Gelven really knew his existentialism. I was attracted to atheistic existentialism's themes of meaninglessness and absurdity in light of the absence of God.[26]

Even though I had recently come to believe in God, I was convinced the atheistic existentialists had it right about life's "meaning," in light of God's non-existence. If God did not exist, then everything is morally, and amorally, possible (since there are no objective moral values).[27]

Existentialists like Sartre and Kierkegaard, reacting to Hegelian-type rationalism, emphasized the limits of human reason. Human reason, on atheism, has serious, big-time epistemic limitations.

---

[25] With this we avoid Plato's famous "Euthyphro Dilemma." See especially William Lane Craig's discussions on this. For a thorough response to the Euthyphro Dilemma see David Baggett and Jerry Walls, *Good God: The Theistic Foundations of Morality*. New York: Oxford, 2011.

[26] My attraction was not to atheistic existentialism, but to the rationality regarding the logical outcomes of a godless universe. If I were an atheist I would think like this.

[27] Philosophical atheists from Nietzsche to, more recently, Joel Marks have reasoned that, on atheism, morality does not exist.

We see this in one of *Nausea's* characters, the "Self-Taught Man." This "autodidact" spends his life in a library, with the goal of reading all the books, in alphabetical order. By doing this, he believes he can learn all there is to know. But this is foolish meaninglessness, since he spends a lifetime reading, but never gets past the letter 'A'. His failed attempt to know everything is absurd, as is life for Antoine Roquentin, the main character of *Nausea*.

One of my many encounters with my own ignorance came on a trip to my favorite bookstore in the world, the Seminary Co-op Bookstore at Chicago Theological Seminary, adjacent to the University of Chicago. I've spent hours there lavishing before a feast of theological and philosophical texts. There is a lot of learnedness in that place, and I wanted to partake of all of it!

On this Day of Greater Revelation of Self-ignorance in the bookstore, I had an "Antoine Roquentin" experience.[28] I looked at all the books, old and new, and knew that, among these thousands of academic texts, I had read perhaps 1% of 1% of 1% of them. Before me I saw a table with new publications, all containing recent research, and fresh reasoning. Of them, I had tasted none.

I felt ignorant.

I am.

We are.

Philosopher Jose Ortega y Gasset once called scientists "learned ignoramuses." He wrote:

> Previously, men could be divided simply into the learned and the ignorant, those more or less the one, and those more or less the other. But your specialist cannot be brought in under either of these two categories. He is not learned, for he is formally ignorant of all that does not enter into his specialty; but neither is he ignorant, because he is 'a scientist', and 'knows' very well his own tiny portion of the universe. We shall have to say that

---

[28] I experienced a mini-Nausea come-over, not full-blown existential angst.

he is a learned ignoramus...a person who is ignorant, not in the fashion of the ignorant man, but with all the petulance of one who is learned in his own special line.... That state of 'not listening', of not submitting to higher courts of appeal which I have repeatedly put forward as characteristic of the mass-man, reaches its height precisely in these partially qualified men.[29]

We are all learned ignoramuses. Epistemically, we're all partially qualified. And that, I am certain, is an understatement. We may have moments when we feel we know much. Those moments are delusions.

Not one of us knows everything, sees everything, or understands everything. We don't come close, right? But God does. "For the eyes of the LORD range throughout the earth to strengthen those whose hearts are fully committed to him."[30]

Praying and a Revelation of Three Gaps

Musician and worship songwriter Misty Edwards has a simple lyric in her song "Finally I Surrender" that repeats, "You are God, I am man, You are sovereign."[31] It's important to keep this in perspective. It affects the way we pray. I understand that God is all-knowing; I am a learned ignoramus.[32] God is all-powerful; my powers are meager and dwindling, even as I type. God is all-loving; I still have hatred within. Thus, I receive the counsel of C.S. Lewis, who wrote that the true Christian must keep their nostrils constantly attuned to the inner cesspool.[33]

In praying, I confront three gaps between myself and God. These are an Ability Gap, an Epistemic Gap, and a Benevolence Gap (which includes a Grace Gap and a Mercy Gap). Where there is a gap, there is a distance to be traversed.

---

[29] Says Jose Ortega y Gasset, *The Revolt of the Masses*. New York: Norton, 1932.
[30] 2 Chronicles 16:9.
[31] From the album *Relentless*.
[32] Philosopher Jose Ortega y Gasset described intellectuals as "learned ignoramuses."
[33] In C.S. Lewis, *Letters to Malcolm: Chiefly on Prayer*, 98. New York: Mariner, 2012.

When I was in London I rode on "The Tube," London's subway. At every station, before getting on board, a sign reads, "Mind the Gap." When it comes to you and God, mind the Gap. Remember the vast qualitative gap between yourself and God. This reduces pride, arrogance, and entitlement. It prevents you from praying things like, "I thank you, God, that I am not like that other person," implying that God and you are moral equals.

To pray is to enter the full light of God and confess, "I am human, and you are God." I am not someone who occasionally makes a mistake, and God is not someone who once in a while forgives. I am a sinner, and God is love.[34]

Approach praying with the idea that God is God, and you are not.

Praying Is Considering

On January 28, 2014, the high temperature in Southeast Michigan was 2°F. My son Josh works nights at Chrysler. He got off work at 4 AM, and his car wouldn't turn over. I bundled up and went out into -10°F weather, and we jumped the car.

The drive home was frigid, windless, lonely, and dark. A large, thin, crescent moon dangled like an icicle in the eastern sky. Looking at it, I had an epiphany. The Biggest of Big Questions jump-started my spirit: *Why is there something rather than nothing? Why does anything exist at all?*[35]

That this universe in all its starry glory *is* coheres with my theistic worldview quite well. It ramps up my cosmological wonder. "I look up at your macro-skies, dark and enormous, your handmade sky-jewelry, Moon and stars mounted in their settings. Then I look at my micro-self and wonder, Why do you bother with us? Why take a second look our way?"[36]

---

[34] See Henri Nouwen, *With Open Hands,* 54. Notre Dame: Notre Dame, 1972.

[35] See Jim Holt, *Why Does the World Exist? An Existential Detective Story.* New York and London: Liveright: 2013.

[36] Psalm 8:2-4, from Eugene Peterson, *The Message: The Bible in Contemporary Language.* Colorado Springs: Navpress, 2002.

All of this is prayer. *When I <u>consider</u> your heavens, the moon and the stars...*

To pray is to attend. To behold. To contemplate. To ponder. To wonder.

Praying is considering.

3

PRAYING AS RELATIONSHIP WITH GOD

Praying is being-in-relationship-with God. As a relationship, it is not a religious duty that one *has* to do. I communicate with Linda not because I "have to," but because I love her. To talk and listen to her merely out of duty would signal a strange, unsatisfying marriage. If prayer is but a transaction, it becomes "an occasional and awkward exercise with little connection to life."[1]

How I communicate with Linda when no one is around signals how I view her and our marriage. In the same way my relationship with God is best seen, if it could be, behind closed closet doors, when I'm not sermonizing or making public appearances.

God is a Person. Within God's Trinitarian being there is relationship. We are God's children. Parents desire relationship with their kids. Praying is a main way of being in relationship with God.

In this chapter I'm sharing thoughts I have about how praying looks, in relationship with God.

Praying Is Trusting, Not Controlling

One of my favorite TV shows in the 1960s was "The Outer Limits." I remember the opening scene when the show took over control of everything. A calm, detached, obviously-in-control voice said,

[1] Philip Yancey, *Prayer*
, Kindle Locations 844-845. Grand Rapids: Zondervan, 2006.

There is nothing wrong with your television set. Do not attempt to adjust the picture. We are controlling transmission. If we wish to make it louder, we will bring up the volume. If we wish to make it softer, we will tune it to a whisper. We can reduce the focus to a soft blur, or sharpen it to crystal clarity. We will control the horizontal. We will control the vertical. For the next hour, sit quietly and we will control all that you see and hear. You are about to experience the awe and mystery which reaches from the inner mind to... The Outer Limits.

I remember watching and, just to be safe, changing channels (we only had 3 at that time!) to verify that I, and not this totalitarian voice, was really controlling things.

Part of me likes being in control, and fears being out of control. I can control the channel I'm watching, as long as you trust me with the controller. But I have learned that, in actuality, I don't control much in life.

One of life's great delusions is that we control many things. Yet most of what we experience in life is beyond our governance. We don't control the weather, the expanding universe, or the microbiome that colonizes our body space. We don't control the foxes that live in our backyard, the sparrows that come to our feeders, or the bug I just saw in my family room. We don't control the outcome of our DNA, or the laws of gravity. I place my fingers on my wrist and check my heart rate, which I have little control over. I program my phone to remind me of the coming meeting with you, but I do not control you. I cannot control the hearts and minds of other people.

I am not in charge of 1% of 1% of 1% of all that is happening within, and without. To embrace the illusion of control is to live in falsehood.

Conversely, I am controlled by many things. I am subject to the weather, the expanding universe, the colonizing microbiome, my DNA, global warming, and life's circumstances.

Addictive behaviors may control me. I am a slave to anything that controls me. Anything I cannot repeatedly say "No" to, controls me. Clinical psychiatrist Gerald May writes:

> Loss of willpower is especially important for defining the difference between the slavery of true addiction and the freedom of sincerely caring about something or of choosing to satisfy simple desires. If you find yourself saying, "I can handle it," "I can stop it," or "I can do without it," try to perform a very simply test: simply go ahead and stop it. *Do without it.* If you are successful, there is no addiction. If you cannot stop, no amount of rationalization will change the fact that addiction exists.[2]

In a world where I control little, and am subject to many things, what can I do?

What I am not to do is: try to control the essentially uncontrollable. This leads to bad outcomes, especially in relationships. We may frantically attempt to control others, but this produces unhappy friends, children, co-workers, and lovers. There are no happy campers in the world of a controller.

What I must do is *trust.* I must trust God. Trusting God is the antidote to the futility of control. One way to trust is to pray. "In the act of prayer, we undermine the illusion of control by divesting ourselves of all false belongings and by directing ourselves totally to the God who is the only one to whom we belong."[3]

Pray to be free of the illusion of control. Abandon yourself to God, trusting him.

---

[2] Gerald May, *Addiction and Grace*, 28. Emphasis mine. San Francisco: Harper, 1988.

[3] Henri Nouwen, *The Only Necessary Thing: Living a Prayerful Life*, 39

Praying Is Better than Books About Prayer

Reading books about prayer and the spiritual life is no substitute for an actual life of dwelling in the presence of God, just as reading books on swimming is not the same as jumping in the water and doing it. Yes, God can meet me while reading a book about prayer. But a good book on prayer will send me to my knees, like a good book on the ocean sends a person looking for a boat. Eventually I must put the book down, lift my head, and lock eyes with the Great Lover of My Soul.

If I have time to read a book about prayer, then I have time to pray. The two are different. The Person is greater than the book about the Person.

What is this inner thing that wants to read about the prayer rather than engage in it? Why complain about no time for prayer, when I refuse to take the opportunities I get to pray? Why don't I lay my media down and go to that lonely non-wired place to talk with God?

Lay this book down, and have some deep conversation with God.

Normal Christian Experience Includes a Conversational Relationship with God

The biblical story of Philip provides a good example of how evangelism happened through the early church.[4] It happened the Jesus way. Which was:

1. Hear from God.
2. Obey.

That's how Jesus did it. Peter did it that way. So did Philip the evangelist. By logical extension, so should I. Which means: no evangelism program is needed. No method or technique is required. I must simply stay "in the Vine." Keep in relationship. Get my directions from God.

---

[4] See Acts 21:8; Acts 6; Acts 8. Philip was one of the "7," to be distinguished from the "12" in Acts 1:13.

In one of our Sunday morning worship times, I asked people to share an example of hearing *directionally* from God without knowing what the outcome would be. A number of testimonies went like this.

1. God told me to _____.
2. I obeyed.
3. God showed up and was with me.

I hear from God regularly. Many of my friends hear from God, too. For some this sounds like boasting, and for others it sounds like mental illness. It is neither. All of Jesus' "sheep" can hear his voice.[5] Hearing God is part of the normal Christian life. This is another experience of Emmanuel, God with me. It's about relationship and friendship with God.

In our desacralizing, disenchanted Western culture, this sounds bizarre. It helps to realize that concepts like "bizarre," "strange," and "normal" are functions of one's prethematic, mostly-non-reflected-on worldview. "Normal" Christian experience includes having a conversational relationship with God. This is called "prayer."[6]

God has much that he wants to say to you today. Conversation with him is part of your normal Christian experience.

Kindling a Dark Night in My Soul

Before I went to teach in Kenya, some Redeemer friends gave me a gift for my trip. It was a Kindle. One of my first Kindle purchases was St. John of the Cross's *Dark Night of the Soul*. I'd read it before, but wanted to soak in it again.

What does St. John mean by the "dark night of the soul?" He does not mean "going through a hard time." Rather, his is a type of

---

[5] John 10:27
[6] See especially Dallas Willard, *Hearing God: Developing a Conversational Relationship with God*. Downers Grove: Intervarsity, 1993.

nondiscursive epistemology.[7] For example, in the Prologue to *Dark Night* John writes:

> In darkness and concealment, my house being now at rest. In the happy night, when none saw me, Nor I beheld aught, without light or guide save that which burned in my heart. This light guided me more surely than the light of noonday to the place where he (well I knew who!) was awaiting me – A place where none appeared. [8]

These poetic words anticipate what is to come. The soul moves toward God, who is known in "darkness." The "lights" of the senses, reason, and logic, are left behind. For John this is necessary, since God cannot be adequately known via human powers of experiencing and knowing. As this "dark knowing" happens, he calls it a "happy night." One's "house" is at rest.

This is dark knowledge. Such knowledge is relationally (not metaphysically) unitive, as the distance between knowing subject and sought-after Object is removed. Concerning religious epistemology, *Dark Night* expresses a mystical vision of what it means to know God.

While praying in the darkness of my physical and intellectual limitations, God illuminates my soul with his humanly unknowable presence.

---

[7] Nondiscursive epistemology – knowledge that cannot be discoursed about (in Paul Ricoeur's sense of experience that contains a "surplus of meaning." See Ricoeur, Interpretation Theory: Discourse and the Surplus of Meaning.

[8] St. John of the Cross, *Dark Night of the Soul*, Prologue 423-32. Westminster, Maryland: Dover, 2003. *Dark Night* is essentially a worship document and an epistemic document. We might refer to it as an Epistemology of Worship.

The Focus of Praying Is Not Prayer

The focus of praying is not prayer itself, but God. James Houston says, "this is absolutely basic to prayer, but it is easy to forget in today's world."[9]

Praying is like a sign. A sign is not self-referential, but about something else; viz., that to which it points.

Using another simile, praying is like using a tool. Tools have specific purposes extending beyond themselves. This is important to know. I inherited some of my father's tools, but have no idea of what many of them are for. His unused tools hang on display in our garage. This might look impressive, but tools are not meant to be gazed on. Like, "Look at all these tools - aren't they cool?"

Like a tool, praying is something to be used. I use prayer to communicate with God. I am not to pray simply because I can, or because it's my religious thing to do. Prayer is my response to God's interest in me, and his love for me. "To pray is to become aware that God's Spirit lives within us. Through prayer, we explore a deeper and more intimate relationship with God."[10]

Jeremiah 29:13 says, "You will seek me and find me when you seek me with all your heart."

In true praying I find God.

That is the point of the whole thing.

Praying and the Relation Ship

I love calling people to a praying life. I receive little persecution for this. "Prayer" sounds so innocuous and non-threatening. But there is resistance. Most Christians, to include pastors, lack a significant praying life.[11]

---

[9] James Houston, *The Transforming Power of Prayer: Deepening Your Friendship with God*, 34. Colorado Springs: Navpress, 1996.

[10] Ib.

[11] By "significant praying life" I mean the kind of "as usual" praying life of Jesus. Early in the morning, as usual, Jesus went to a lonely place and there he prayed. By "pastor" I refer especially to Western pastors.

Is it too much to ask for thirty to sixty minutes of time with God, each day of the week? The truth is, this asks too little. If I, as Linda's husband, only talked with her a few minutes a day, or not at all, then I have a weak marriage. Use this as an analogy for the Bride of Christ, and the implication is the same. Some churches are weak because they are composed of prayerless people and prayerless leaders.

I'm not interested in judging people. This is a report from the front. I have had *many* pastors and people confess prayerlessness to me.

Praying thirty to sixty minutes a day can kick-start a *relation ship* with God. Relation ship. A ship of relations. A community of people in close, abiding connectedness to Christ, and therefore to one another.

This little match is capable of lighting a lasting, unquenchable fire. Is it possible? I know it is. I have seen it happen in the lives of many people.

I see it now, happening in me. I am in a love-relationship with my Redeemer, no longer struggling to "find time" with him, because he has become my great love.

I see myself, in community, sailing forward on the Relation Ship.

Praying and My In-Christ Status

As a Jesus-follower, my spiritual status is being "in Christ." This is not dependent on how I *feel* about things. My "in Christ" status is independent of circumstances. This describes the intimate God-relationship I have, in Jesus. To pray is my response to this already-existing relationship, rather than an attempt to connect with God. *I am in Christ and already connected.*

Praying is not a means to establish relationship with God. Rather, it is a way of responding to God's nearness, whether I can sense it or not.[12]

Jewish scholar Abraham Heschel says that this is not something we achieve. "It is a gift, coming down to us from on high like a meteor, rather than rising up like a rocket. Before the words of prayer come to

---

[12] See Philip Yancey, *Prayer*. Kindle Locations 955-956

the lips, the mind must believe in God's willingness to draw near to us, and in our ability to clear the path for His approach. Such belief is the idea that leads us toward prayer."'[13]

I am praying "in Christ," within the already established connection.

Real Praying Knows from the Inside

After I die, should someone pick up my copy of *Through the Year With Thomas Merton*, they would conclude, "He read it. And read it through again and again." That would be correct. My copy is falling apart from use.

I read Merton because he had this deep, thick, organic praying life. Over many years. In the garden of Merton's praying heart, it was always spring. His praying was chronic, never yielding to the growing media circus of our shallow culture. Merton detached from the media. In praying he met God, and was led to the wellspring of life.

August 28, 1990. That's the date I bought the book, inscribing it inside the cover. It became one of my companions, along with the Bible, and other writers who know prayer from the inside. Real praying knows from the inside, from much personal experience.

Merton heard the voice of God, and matured in discernment. Only the experienced discern. Discernment is a way of being studied by God. When I read the Scriptures, I not only study them, but am studied by them. When this happens, I pray the Scriptures. In them, I am confronted by the One who is beyond me, yet comes to me. In and through the Bible, I am known. And then, on rare occasions, someone who knows praying wider, longer, higher, and deeper than I, opens their arms to me through the pages of a book. Like Merton, who prayed much, and gained inside knowledge about God. I find myself drawn to praying through his writings.

This life-of-praying thing is an inside job, available to all who grow weary of the outside world's pseudo-sophia, and want the real thing.

---

[13] In Ib.

Solitude Is the Place of the Great Encounter

Henri Nouwen writes that "Solitude is the place of the great struggle and the great encounter— the struggle against the compulsion of the false self, and the encounter with the loving God who offers himself as the substance of the new self."[14] What does Nouwen mean by this?

First, solitude is being alone with God. I can have interior solitude, even when others are around. True interior solitude is a condition of the heart. It is cultivated and developed as I take time, without the presence of other people, alone in the presence of God.

Second, solitude is the place of the "great struggle." This struggle is "against the compulsion of the false self." This is the self that has come out of the kingdom of darkness. The false self is life-denying, controlling, manipulative, fearful, defeatist, and condemning. In solitude, especially as I practice it, these unloving voices make the experience crushing. In my busyness I have covered them up. In my solitary unbusyness, voices of darkness step onto the stage of my soul and recite their lines.

Third, solitude the place of the Great Encounter. Here I meet the loving God who offers himself as the substance of the new self. God names me, and says, "You are my beloved child." *In the God-encounter nothing surpasses this.*

In solitude my false self is burned away by the purging fires of loving holiness. My soul is forged into the joyous freedom of Christlikeness.

Solitary Unbusyness with God

Today I've been able to get away and get alone with God. I've prayed for some things, and listened for his voice. I've written in my journal notes that are from God, for me. All this restores, renews, and refreshes me.

I get away often and meet with God. So did Jesus. It was his custom to go alone to meet with the Father. If Jesus needed to do this, who am I not to, since I am one of his followers. It is very, very good to do this. It's good for God, for me, for Linda, for my church family, and the

---

[14] Henri Nouwen, *The Way of the Heart*. New York: Ballantine, 1981.

world. The world benefits when I pray. Nothing but life and goodness come from much time spent alone in God's presence.

The simple truth is that God is God, and I am not. God is omnibenevolent, I am not. God is omniscient, not I. God is omnipotent, I am neither omni nor potent.

My effectiveness for Christ and his kingdom is directly proportional to my solitary unbusyness in relationship with the One who is God.

I Meet with God in Stillness of the Heart

I'm wrapping things up on my laptop, packing my Bible and journal, and going out for 3-4 hours to pray. I have done this on every Tuesday for the past 40 years.

I'm going to a quiet place where I won't be disturbed.

I'll slow down in my spirit.

I'm going to get silent. And still. It is in stillness that my Lord and I meet.

"Be still... be not rushed... cease striving... and know that I am God."

What is most needed today, in the followers of Jesus, is to take blocks of time and be silent. Silence is needed to break free from a world that godlessly wants to grip us and squeeze Jesus out of us

To be held firmly in God's grip requires breaking free from the grip of the world. In the silence of my heart and mind, I am held by God. Going alone to pray, now, with these last strokes of my laptop's keys, has become the wellspring of my life.

In Praying I Bring My Ignorance to God

It's OK to express doubts to God in the act of praying. I *should* do this, as I have them. Otherwise the conversation is inauthentic and unreal. I have doubts and questions. This is the paradox of intimacy. The closer we get to someone or something, the more we know. The more we know the less we know. This raises new questions.

In praying, I sometimes argue with God about the dubitable. God can handle this. I complain to God, like the psalmist did. I bring my massive ignorance to the throne, and entrust it to God. This helps me as "doubts take on a different cast as I get to know the Person to whom I bring them."[15]

God doesn't freak out when we doubt. But it is weird to have doubt, and pray as if the doubt is nonexistent.

In praying I can, and ought, to be real with God. God is all-knowing; I am not. God loves me, so any fear I have of God is unfounded.

God gives permission to bring my entire being to him in praying, including the vast fog of my unknowing.

Praying and the Presence Motif

New Testament scholar Gordon Fee writes:

> The Holy Spirit is none other than the fulfillment of the promise that God himself would once again be present with his people... The Spirit is God's own personal presence in our lives and in our midst; he leads us into paths of righteousness for his name's sake, he "is working all things in all people," he is grieved when his people do not reflect his character and thus reveal his glory..., and he is present in our worship, as we sing "praise and honor and glory and power" to God and to the Lamb.[16]

Fee calls this "the Presence Motif." This is the interpretive key to the book of Exodus. In Exodus the people are seeking the experiential presence of God. They follow God's tangible presence through the wilderness. The experiential reality of God's presence strengthens, comforts, and encourages them.

Experience, not theory, breeds conviction. It is one thing to talk about God and his love and power. It is quite another thing to encounter and experience the Living God. There is knowing from the outside, as

[15] Philip Yancey, *Prayer,* Kindle Locations 729-731
[16] Gordon Fee, *God's Empowering Presence.* Grand Rapids: Baker, 2009.

an observer "knows about" something, and inside knowledge gained from personal experience. When it comes to relationships, the latter is better.[17]

The Jesus-story has always been about this. Knowing Scripture is good, but the goal of existence is not to know Scripture. Scripture points beyond itself, intending to bring us into a living, knowing, and being-known relationship with God. What I need is the real presence of God, not a theory or doctrine about it. Things like God's love, grace, and mercy, are essentially experiential realities of the God who is with me, not theoretical postulates.

I am told that the Spirit deluges our hearts with these things. Romans 5:5 says that "hope does not put us to shame, because God's love has been *poured out into our hearts* through the Holy Spirit, who has been given to us."

In the act of praying the Spirit escorts me into the dwelling place of God's presence.

In Praying I Can Bring More of Me to God

The best spiritual place to be with God is in full transparency. God knows what's in me anyway, so why not bare it all?

But why reveal myself, if God already knows me fully, inside and out? The answer is: this God-thing is about a relationship, not a ritual. God loves me, and wants me to trust him. Relationship requires my response.

We see this in a parent-child relationship. The good parent knows much about their child. The child is not aware of this. If the child steals something, the most fruitful spiritual response will be for the child to come forth on their own, rather than being exposed by their parents, even if the parent already knows. The parent wants the child to *trust them*.

In a similar way, God desires that I bring my entire self before him. This is how I learn to trust that God will always be truthful and loving towards me, and has his best interests in mind when it comes to me.

---

[17] See C.S. Lewis, "Meditations In a Toolshed," in *God In the Dock*, for a nice illustration of these two kinds of knowledge. Grand Rapids: Eerdmans, 1972.

When it comes to other people, I am voluntarily vulnerable. I don't bare my entire soul to just anyone. I cannot be fully transparent before most people, for they are not God. I can't trust that their response to me will be loving and truthful. Truly, there are only a handful of people I can be entirely open before.

On top of my trusting list is Linda. Certain qualities in her allow me to trust her with my deepest self.

- She loves me.
- She never condemns me.
- She's not out to "get me."
- She never tries to control me.
- She is forgiving (because she, like me, has been forgiven much).
- She speaks truthfully to me (no game-playing or manipulating).
- She champions my spiritual being - she wants Christ to be more deeply formed in me.

I discovered this in her before we got married. If she has changed. it's that she's gotten even better at this. But my wife is not God. God is safer and better than either of us. Therefore, in times of praying, I have learned to trust God, and expose more of myself to him.

Praying Is Gaining Access to the Power of God

I meet many people, including pastors and Christian leaders, who struggle to find time to pray. My seminary teaching tells me that 80% of North American and European pastors don't have much of a prayer life.[18] Why not? I think the reasons for this are:

- They don't know what prayer is. Or...
- They know what prayer is but do not really believe it. Or...
- Their material prosperity allows "no time to pray" and creates the illusion of not needing to pray. Or...

---

[18] By "much of a prayer life" I mean the kind of praying life Jesus had, who, as was his custom, went out in the morning to lonely places and prayed.

- Their lives have become so cluttered with many things to "do" that they have little time for just "being" with God.

If prayer is what it claims to be, then someone who truly believed in prayer *would* pray. Why? Because praying is talking with *God*. God and I are to be doing things together.

God and I, dialoguing!!![19] Are you kidding me?! If this is real, only a fool would *not* pray. If this is *not* real, then you won't see me praying, even in a foxhole.

Dallas Willard writes: "*Prayer* is God's arrangement for a safe power sharing with us in his intention to bless the world through us"[20] In praying, I interact with God. God shares power with me. Pause at the enormity of this. Who in their right mind would not have time for this?

As I respond to prayer, God empowers me with his power to bless the world. That would be cool and helpful, if only it was true.

Sometimes I read things like this and feel guilty. OK. But guilt feelings mean nothing if action does not follow. Where there is unbelief, there is no action. Guilt without action is equivalent to confession without repentance.

The sign that I believe in prayer is that I pray, a lot. What I need is *belief*. Belief must be cultivated in me. God will not simply download belief into me. The way to increase in belief is to choose a life of praying.

I learn prayer by praying. I keep praying, and discover unbelief morphing into belief. Then, I find time for praying.

Unveiled Praying

In the act of praying, I not only listen *to* God, I listen *with* God. In praying, I am not listening to some distant voice, but a voice that lives in me.

The Hope of Glory resides inside. He dwells in the home that is my heart. He knows me, intimately, into-me-seeing. To pray, therefore, is to dwell in the presence of God with all I have and am: with...

---

[19] I'll give this three exclamation points, one for each member of the Trinity.

[20] Dallas Willard, *Knowing Christ Today*. New York: HarperCollins, 2009.

...my fears and anxieties,

…my guilt and shame,

…my greed and anger,

…my joys, successes, aspirations and hopes,

…my reflections, dreams and mental wandering,

…and, most of all, my people, family, friends and enemies,

…in short, all that makes me who I am.

In praying *I* come into God's presence. All of me. With God. I allow God to speak to every corner of my being. "This is very hard since we are so fearful and insecure that we keep hiding ourselves from God."[21]

My tendency is to only show God the parts of myself that are more presentable. This makes my praying selective and narrow. "And not just our prayer but our self-knowledge, because by behaving as strangers before God we become strangers to ourselves."[22]

In 2 Corinthians 3:12-18 Paul writes:

> Therefore, since we have such a hope, we are very bold. We are not like Moses, who would put a veil over his face to prevent the Israelites from seeing the end of what was passing away.… *But whenever anyone turns to the Lord, the veil is taken away.* Now the Lord is the Spirit, and where the Spirit of the Lord is, there is freedom. And we all, who with unveiled faces contemplate the Lord's glory, are being transformed into his image with ever-increasing glory, which comes from the Lord, who is the Spirit.

To authentically pray, I must turn toward the Lord with an unveiled mind, heart, and soul. As I pray, God at times lifts the veil off my face and sees-into-me. Thomas Merton comments: "The Spirit is given to me, the veil is removed from my heart, that I reflect "with open face" the

---

[21] Ib.

[22] Ib., 83-84

glory of Christ. It would be easy to remain with one's heart veiled, and it is not by any wisdom of my own, but by God's gift, that it *is* unveiled."[23]

God allows me the choice of living veiled or unveiled, even though he sees behind the veil. This is an act of his grace. He won't force himself on me, but invites me to be voluntarily vulnerable. Just that thought makes me *want* to remove the veil over my heart when I come to God.

I can choose to keep my heart veiled before God, but this will make life harder. I then fake it before God. I become an actor, and acting is hard work.

To live unveiled before God is freedom. Unveiled living is the gateway to my experience of God's love, mercy, and grace. It becomes my foundation for holy living. It is the portal to contemplation of God.

As I turn my heart to God, in praying, I allow him to lift the veil.

Praying in My Desperate Circumstances

While she was imprisoned in Auschwitz, a young Jewish girl, Etty Hillesum, kept praying. She experienced "an uninterrupted dialogue with God." Hillesum writes: "Sometimes when I stand in some corner of the camp, my feet planted on Your earth, my eyes raised towards Your Heaven, tears sometimes run down my face, tears of deep emotion and gratitude."

She non-theoretically knew evil, and said, "I want to be there right in the thick of what people call horror and still be able to say: life is beautiful. Yes, I lie here in a corner, parched and dizzy and feverish and unable to do a thing. Yet I am also with the jasmine and the piece of sky beyond my window."[24]

Hillesum concluded, "For once you have begun to walk with God, you need only keep on walking with God and all of life becomes one long stroll — a marvelous feeling."[25]

Etty Hillesum prayed in a morally barren place. There, she had God-encounters and epiphanies. God met her within the circumstances

---

[23] Thomas Merton, *A Year with Thomas Merton*, 23. New York: HarperCollins, 2004.
[24] In Philip Yancey, *Prayer*, Kindle Locations 936-940.
[25] Ib.

of horrendous evil. There is no place, no environment, where God will not be found, in the act of praying. Nothing can separate us from the loving presence of God.

Don't cease praying in your desperate circumstances. "I will fear no evil" takes on new meaning when you know he is with you.

Heart-Silence Is a Key that Opens the Heart of God

"True silence is a key to the immense and flaming heart of God."
Catherine De Hueck Doherty[26]

In 1990 I went with Linda, Dan, and Josh, to Singapore, to teach at Assemblies of God Bible College. I taught two courses over a twenty-day period. One of them was my Spiritual Formation and Prayer course.

The college was located in the heart of Singapore, near the historic Raffles Hotel. Every class day I sent my Chinese students out to pray for an hour. I told them to find a quiet place outside of our building, and meet alone with God. Stepping outside our classroom, we entered the crowded streets of busy, downtown Singapore. I decided to pray in the lobby of the Raffles. This was where many great writers once stayed, including Ernest Hemingway and Somerset Maugham.

The lobby was beautiful, and a beehive of activity. In the center of this bustling buzzing, my heart was still. And silent. Years of stillness and silence had built into me a capacity to focus, to attend to one thing.

A silent and still heart is a receptive heart. In this quiet, inner place, is where I most often hear the voice of God. In stillness God is known.[27]

Heart-silence is the key that opens me to the immense, flaming heart of God.

---

[26] In Richard Foster, *Sanctuary of the Soul: Journey Into Meditative Prayer*, Kindle Location 148. Downers Grove: Intervarsity, 2011.
[27] Psalm 46:10 – "Be still, and know that I am God."

If I Pray, God Will Use Me

From 1981-1992 I was the American Baptist Campus Minister at Michigan State University. One of my predecessors was Roger Palms. Upon leaving MSU, Roger became editor of Billy Graham's *Decision Magazine*.

Once Roger and his wife came back to campus, and joined Linda and I for dinner. I was fascinated by the experiences Roger had, traveling all over the world with Billy Graham. I asked a question: "Tell me - what is Billy Graham really like?"

"Here," replied Roger, "is how I see Billy. We were on a crusade in another country. I was looking for Billy. Someone told me he was in a church building. I went to the building, looked everywhere, but could not find him. I went into the church's sanctuary, and walked to the front. There was Billy lying face down on the floor, before the altar, praying. *That is what Billy Graham is really like.*"

"No wonder," I said, "that God really uses him!"

If you have a praying life, expect God to use you.

Praying Lives on a Fearless Trust in God

"Like a child that takes a leap into Daddy's strong arms,
we need to have that same fearlessness that characterizes
trust. Prayer lives on this fearless trust in God."[28]
James Houston

What if you have a hard time trusting? What if you were raised in a home that lacked love, and you felt worthless?[29] If that's you, recall that God's love for you came before you loved him. God, not you, took the initiative. 1 John 4:10-11 says: "This is love: not that we loved God, but that he loved us and sent his Son as an atoning sacrifice for

---

[28] James Houston, *The Transforming Power of Prayer: Deepening Your Friendship with God*, 65.

[29] This was *not* my childhood experience.

our sins. Dear friends, since God so loved us, we also ought to love one another."

Much-loved children love much. The more we internalize that we belong to God because he first loved us, the more we will be able to love and trust him.

This is the entrusted life, which causes praying to be safe and joyful. I am loved. I belong. I can share all of my life with God.

In praying, I am trusting the God who loved me in the first place.

Covenant Praying as Being Welded to God

To make a "covenant" is to vow allegiance to a person, for better, for worse, in sickness and in health, 'til death do us part. A covenant vow is more than saying words. Actions follow true covenanting. Certain actions establish and reinforce a covenant.

A covenant is different from a contract. A contract is like sticking two post-it notes together. One of them can pull away from the other, without damage being done. But a covenant is like welding two pieces of metal together. The properties of each are infused into the other.

When Jesus said "What God has joined together, let not anyone tear asunder," the Greek word for "joined" literally means "welded." New Testament scholar R.T. France says "It would be hard to imagine a more powerful metaphor of permanent attachment."[30] A covenant is a welding, done by God, the Master Welder.

One sign that a person has made a heart-covenant with God is that they have a praying life. Real praying is covenant-making activity. Praying is a way of saying, "'til death do my God and I join forever." Praying is an expression of everlasting super-weldedness to God.

Ps. 57:7 expresses the confession of a covenant heart:

> My heart, O God, is steadfast,
> > my heart is steadfast;
> > I will sing and make music.

---

[30] R.T. France, *The Gospel of Matthew*. Grand Rapids: Eerdmans, 2007.

And from The Message[31]:
> I'm ready, God, so ready,
>> ready from head to toe,
>> Ready to sing, ready to raise a tune!

This is commitment-language. Praying welds my heart to the heart of God.

Praying and Feelings

I'm going out to pray today. I've been doing this Tuesday afternoon prayer time for four decades. I'm going to meet with God, not to get some experience. My *raison pour prier* is not to get thrills. That would be using God, right?

I am not expecting certain feelings to arise as I pray. My praying life is not dependent on *feeling* God, but on *the reality of God-with-me* whether I feel him or not. In praying I do not need to ask for more of God, since God is fully present to me, in toto.

My *feelings* about God's presence or absence are real, but irrelevant to the *fact* of God's presence with me. Any feelings I experience are important, but are not necessarily indicative of the reality.

Experiencing God is vital. Feelings will come. I welcome and embrace them, but they are not the goal of my praying life.

> As I am praying I give thanks for however God chooses
> to love and touch me. And, for his presence, whether I
> feel it or not.

Praying and Self-Divestment

Praying is collaborative, kingdom activity. God is up to something today. I am part of it.

---

[31] Eugene Peterson, *The Message.*

Praying isn't praying if I come to God expecting him to validate my plans and purposes. The idea is to hear from God about what he is doing, receive direction as to what I am to do, and act on that knowledge. "Prayer is the act by which we divest ourselves of all false belongings and become free to belong to God and God alone."[32]

In praying I self-divest, so as to be abandoned to God. Self-divestment brings God's investment in me.

I Need to Hear from a Praying Person

I need to hear from people who are not "too busy to pray." I don't need to hear from someone who "believes in prayer," but can't find the time for it. Non-pray-ers are disconnected people. They have nothing to say to me.

I don't need another theoretician, because theory without experience equals unfamiliarity. I need fellowship with people who have actual experience, who don't talk about praying as much as they actually pray.

Experience, not theory, breeds conviction. The kind of person I need to hear from does original research in the life of praying. I need witnesses who know God, allow God access to the depths of their being, and who are able to guide me into God's beautiful kingdom.

Such people have taught me many things. They pray. They speak. I listen. I even listen to their theories, if they are praying people. This is because there is an asymmetric relationship between praying and prayer-theorizing. Out of a deep prayer life, I theorize. Then I reflect biblically, theologically, and psychologically on my experience with God, especially in times of praying.

This is a whole-being activity. Hence, it is authentic and relevant.

Praying connects heart and mind, logic and emotion, will and passion. Praying permits the Holy Spirit to dispense life and power that penetrates to every corner of my being.

---

[32] Henri Nouwen, *The Only Necessary Thing: Living a Prayerful Life*, 39.

Praying affects our entire being. Praying people are profoundly affected people. I need to hear from praying people, those voices of experience who have gone before me.

Praying People Abandon Themselves to the Will of God

As a praying person, I must abandon myself to the will of God. If this is not true, then "prayer" is a monologue led by myself, full of sound and fury, signifying nothing transcendent.

Real praying seeks God, not self. "Self" is what I want to be rid of; God is who I must be found in.

The beauty of this is that, once I set my own plans and ego aside and release myself into the being of God, I get found by God. Here is where my true self emerges.

In abandoning myself to God I find myself, and who I was always meant to be. My subhumanity morphs into true humanity. This even changes my prayer life.

Dwelling Praying Grows Deep Roots

A praying person is in a process of continual change. The change is into greater and greater Christlikeness.[33] To pray is to be changed, because I cannot consistently dwell in God's presence and remain the same.

"Praying," in the Jesus Way, is different from what I call "McPrayer[34]," which effects little transformation. McPraying breeds non-relationship, and the "I'm too busy to pray" disease. Real praying, on the other hand, is dwelling, abiding prayer, as an ongoing, intimate relationship with God. Pray*ing*. A verb in the continuous tense. Ongoing prayer.

Success in the kingdom of God demands dwelling praying. This is a deep, rich, profound relational reality with God. Dwelling praying

---

[33] Galatians 4:19; Romans 12:1-2

[34] I coined the term "Mcprayer" to mean short prayers offered while multitasking, distinguishing it from extended times of solitary praying, so as to argue for the essential primacy of the latter in the development of a praying life.

deepens my experience and knowledge. Dwelling praying strengthens my heart, soul, and mind. People who pray this way grow deep roots into the soil of God's kingdom.

Our real strength comes from our prayer lives. As a person prays, so they are. I feel that my ministry of preaching and counseling flows from my fervent praying.

From deep-rooted praying comes life and ministry.

Praying as Abiding and Fruit-Bearing

I attended a great weekend conference, with wonderful worship and inspiring speakers. Now, the conference is over. What do I do? The answer is: continue to live my life attached to Jesus, the True Vine.

There is an old pear tree in my back yard. Every spring it buds. Every fall its fruit is plentiful and delicious. Sometimes branches fall off the tree. I pick them up and burn them. I am not expecting unattached branches to produce fruit. No matter how hard an unattached branch strives to produce fruit, it will not, because it cannot. All its striving is in vain.

But if the branch is attached to the tree, striving is not needed for fruit-bearing. Does a pear work hard to become a pear? Not at all. What must it do? Simply stay connected. If a branch is connected to a pear tree it will produce pears, just as surely as *If it rains, then the ground gets wet.*

When the big, exciting conference is over, what do I do? The answer is what I have been doing for the past forty years. *Dwell. Remain. Abide. Connect with Jesus.* Jesus has told me, "I will not leave you as orphans; I will come to you.... On that day you will realize that I am in my Father, and you are in me, and I am in you."[35]

I may be sitting alone in a chair typing these words, but I am not orphaned. Do not mistake equating the now-presence, activity, and power of God with exhilarating conferences. God can show up at a conference. God can also show up while I am wearing pajamas sitting in my living room. Actually, I think I would experience more of God

---

[35] John 14:18, 20

at the conference if I daily experienced his presence in my living room. And, by the way, God's presence - wherever encountered - is awesome and earth-shattering.

As a Jesus-follower, I am told that the Father, Son, and Spirit have come and made their home in me.[36] I am a portable sanctuary who hosts the presence of God. When I left the big conference God came with me.

How good is this for me, now? To begin with, God is God - everlastingly. The omnipotent, omniscient, omnibenevolent, everlasting God is here, now. As I connect with him, he gives me his peace and joy.[37] He calls me "friend."[38] As I abide in him, I can expect to do the kind things Jesus did, with the kind of heart by which He did it. Christ, the hope of glory, is in me![39] I am in awe.

I will be fruit-bearing..., *now*. Jesus did not say, "If you attend the conference you will bear much fruit." He did say,

> I am the vine; you are the branches. If you remain in me and I in you, you will bear much fruit; apart from me you can do nothing.... If you remain in me and my words remain in you, ask whatever you wish, and it will be done for you. This is to my Father's glory, that you bear much fruit, showing yourselves to be my disciples.[40]

Fruit-bearing. Fruitfulness. That is what my Jesus-life is about. Trying harder to bear fruit won't work, just as the budding pear-flower in my back yard is not working hard to achieve pear-ness.

Does this mean I do nothing? No. It means what I *do* comes out of my dwelling-relationship with Christ. I must stay tight with him. I hear his voice. He calls me to take part in The Movement. In my obedience I work to the glory of God. My "doing" comes from my

---

[36] John 14:23
[37] John 14:27; 15:11
[38] John 15:15
[39] Colossians 1:24-29
[40] John 15:5-8

"being" (dwelling). In this way, my "doing" is authentic and relevant. Any disconnected-doing is inauthentic, irrelevant, and mere striving.

God has much for me today. Abiding in Jesus is my constant, current joy.

It's all about The Relationship.

Connectedness *now* is the key to the outpouring of the Spirit, upon me.

A main way of connecting and abiding is praying.

All Relevant "Doing" Comes from Abiding Praying

Much of what I *do* comes out of my prayer life. My d*oing* comes from my *being*, not vice versa. All relevant "doing" comes from abiding in Christ.

Relevant doing is called *obedience*. Doing for doing's sake is non-obedience.

"Obedience" has the Latin root *audere* in it, from which we get our English word "audio." Obedient doing is audio-relevant. It comes from listening. This happens as I pray. In praying, I listen. When directed, I am to *do*. Take note that listening precedes doing.

Resist "doing things for God" without consulting God first. Baptizing your doings in prayer without being led by God to do those things is to move without God. This is not good. Consider these prescient words from Thomas Merton:

> There are men dedicated to God whose lives are full of restlessness and who have no real desire to be alone. Interior solitude is impossible for them. They fear it. They do everything they can to escape it. What is worse, they try to draw everyone else in to activities as senseless and as devouring as their own. They are great promoters of useless work. They love to organize meetings and banquets and conferences and lectures. They print circulars, write letters, talk for hours on the telephone in order that they may gather a hundred people together in a large room where they will all fill

the air with smoke and make a great deal of noise and roar at one another and clap their hands and stagger home at last, patting one another on the back with the assurance that they have all done great things to spread the Kingdom of God.[41]

I am praying to be saved from this kind of stuff, from doing for doing's sake.

Undissipated Prayer

To be dissipated is to be scattered, scatterbrained, scatterhearted. This can happen to the self. We can be spread out like a thin layer of Saran wrap over the minutia of life.

The issue of personal and corporate identity is the crisis of our time. We are an identityless people. Our culture makes T.S. Eliot's "hollow people" look like the paragons of self-discovery.[42]

The more we lose focus, the more the self dissipates. Our identity gets dissipated among a lot of things that do not have the value we think we see in them. We get lost in all the world's stuff. Our being tends towards equilibrium in the liquid solutions of life.

Things disappoint and sicken us once we get what we have desired. It's not life's failures that disappoint us, but life's achievements and successes, since once acquired we come to see they do not fulfill us in the way we imagined they would.

The result is that the dissipated, flat-as-a-pancake self, becomes less and less in its never-satiated quest to be more and more. The inner life blurs together.

What is needed is the discovery, or rediscovery, of selfhood. This can be found in a life of praying. In praying, the self is oriented to the true north of the being of God. In praying, God gathers the scattered fragments of self and clays them into an undissipated whole.

---

[41] Thomas Merton, *New Seeds of Contemplation*, 83. Boston and London: Shambala, 2003.
[42] T. S. Eliot, "The Hollow Men." http://allpoetry.com/The-Hollow-Men

In the dedicated act of praying, we are pieced back together, and restored to our first love, which is Jesus.

In praying we realize, experientially, that our identity lies fully "in Christ."

Praying as Unbroken Relationship with God

It's seven AM in Monroe. I wake up, put on my bath robe, come downstairs, and notice I am praying. I am thanking God for being awake and alive, and for this day that he has made. I did not make a conscious decision to pray. I am simply talking with God. Is this the "unceasing prayer" life Paul was talking about? Perhaps.

A life of unceasing prayer grows out of a disciplined life of choosing to pray. I have been choosing to set aside praying time for over forty years. On this day, a Tuesday, I will pray for three to four hours. This has been my habit for decades.

This discipline is the fountain of my spiritual life. It has produced the experience of an ongoing prayer-relationship with God. Praying has become DNA. My default heart-setting is dialed to: praying.

I think it's like this. When I sing a song I like over and over, the melody and words get inside me. In a way, the song becomes me. I wake up humming the melody. Praying is like that for me.

The progression is:

I choose to pray.

I discover the beauty of the Relationship.

Praying becomes me, comprehensively.

This is good because Scripture calls us to live a comprehensive life of praying. We read:

"Pray without ceasing"
1 Thess. 5:17

"Rejoice in your hope, be patient in tribulation, be constant in prayer"
Rom. 12:12

"Pray in the Spirit at all times in every prayer and supplication"
Eph. 6:18

"Continue steadfastly in prayer, being
watchful in it with thanksgiving"
Col. 4:2

"Do not worry about anything, but in everything
by prayer and supplication with thanksgiving let
your requests be made known to God"
Phil. 4:6

"Continually offer a sacrifice of praise to God, that
is, the fruit of lips that confess his name"
Heb. 13:15

Jesus spoke of our "need to pray always and not to lose heart"
Luke 18:1

Here is the possibility of living in constant, unbroken relationship with God. My spiritual life becomes seamless. The disciplined praying life leads to unceasing praying.

Praying Is Where Beholding Is Birthed

C. S. Lewis writes:

> Say your prayers in a garden early, ignoring steadfastly the dew, the birds and the flowers, and you will come away overwhelmed by its freshness and joy; go there in order to be overwhelmed and, after a certain age, nine times out of ten nothing will happen to you.[43]

---

[43] C. S. Lewis, *The Four Loves*, 21-22. Orlando, Florida: Harcourt, 1988.

I read these words a long time ago and they stayed with me. The idea is that true praying is about meeting with God, not about being blown away by God's creation.

I consistently find the following to be true: the more I take time to meet with God and pray, the more I am stunned by the beauty of God's creation. The consistent act of praying gives me eyes and ears to see and hear the world differently. Instead of looking, I behold.

In long-praying "the world loses its opaqueness and becomes transparent: that is, the world of experience starts pointing beyond itself to the luminous Source of wisdom and understanding, to the translucent realm of the Spirit of God."[44] What has been hidden from ordinary, secular life becomes visible through praying eyes.

I don't need to travel far to behold God's glory in his creation. It's in my backyard. It's in the park down the street, and in the skies above. It's in the wintry pine trees waving outside the window of my upstairs office. This is the handiwork of God, pointing me back to him again, and again.

First, I will pray.

This is where I am given eyes to see, and ears to hear.

Beholding is birthed in me in the act of praying.

Seek First God's Presence, Not God's Presents

Many years ago a man verbally abused me in a church meeting. He hurt me in front of others. I did not hurt back. The following Sunday morning he came and asked me to forgive him. I was glad for this, until he added, "I have to ask you to forgive me, because if I don't, God won't give me my blessing."

My gladness was short-lived. None of this was really about God, or me. This man was using both of us for his own selfish prospering.

For the pure-hearted follower of Jesus God himself is their great reward, not what God can give them. The idea is not to control circumstances by using God, but simply to love him. Seek first God's

---

[44] Henri Nouwen, *Spiritual Formation: Following the Movements of the Spirit*, Kindle Locations 408-410. New York: HarperCollins: 2010.

kingdom and righteousness, for its own sake. Love the Lord your God with all your heart, *simpliciter*. Love God for who God is, not for what God can give you.

"Our contentment lies not in his presents but in the presence of the One whose presents they are."[45] In your praying, seek God for who he is, not for what he can give you. Seek his face, not his hand; his presence, not his presents.

In Praying Don't Dishonor the Relationship

Anger has three objects:

1) self
2) others
3) God.

I understand one and two, but three is hard to swallow. It seems disrespectful, and whiny-immature, to be angry with God. But it happens, and is recorded in the Psalms.

Like...

Why, O LORD, do you stand far off?

Why do you hide yourself in times of trouble?

How long, O LORD? Will you forget me forever?

How long will you hide your face from me?

My God, my God, why have you forsaken me?

Why are you so far from helping me, from the words of my groaning?

O my God, I cry by day, but you do not answer; and by night, but find no rest.

There's more.

Of course, my life is not all one long lament. But I see, in the Psalms, an unhidden heart. A non-faking soul. And a God who listens to it all. I can come to God just as I am. I bring my complaints to him, because pretending to smile while I'm dying inside is disrespectful.

---

[45] Dallas Willard, *Hearing God*, 60.

I dishonor the God Relationship if I do not bring my whole heart to him in prayer.

Praying: When the Requirement Became a Relationship

Many years ago I was counseling a marriage where the woman wanted, more than anything, for her husband to co-partner with her in a life that follows Jesus. This hope was in her heart before they were married. He promised he would do this. He went to church services with her, prayed with her, and they talked about their common faith.

When they got married, it all changed. He stopped talking with her, and stopped worshiping God.

She felt desperate. He worried she would leave him because he didn't keep his promises. So he promised again, this time in front of me, that he would go after a Jesus-guided life. She trusted again.

Less than a year later he was spiritually adrift. He made promises, created expectations, and broke them. She was taken in by a faith-relationship that was never really there. He got religious just to get her. Love for Jesus was in his mouth, but not his heart.

When my recent Spiritual Formation class at Payne Theological Seminary ended, I assigned students to get a prayer life, and report to me on their progress. Will they continue praying? Some will not. Even though they told God they would, before the entire class. I know this, from experience.

Some will. They will be like me and others who got a God-given prayer life years ago, and have been immersed in the intimate God-relationship for years.

That is my hope and prayer for each of my students.

I am praying that my course requirement will become a relationship.

The Purpose of Praying Is to Know God

When I instruct seminary students or pastors to pray, I counsel them not to do church work, or sermon preparation, during that time.

I say to them, "You are going to pray because *you* need God. Anything less than this, and "prayer" is really about you, instead of God."

Prayer is not another self-help technique to make life easier. It is not the secret to happiness. It's not a key to getting things from God. Its core is about knowing God. Because, as Philip Yancey has said, "I need God more than anything I might get from God."[46]

This makes sense to me. Real praying is a give-and-take *relationship* with God. God will give of himself to me in the praying relationship, but he will not be used.

In a life of praying, knowledge is a two-way street. I grow in personal knowledge of God, and I am searched out and known by God.

Praying and Belovedness

In the prayer-relationship there is a divine searching-out of my heart. This is one reason some people don't pray. They are afraid of what God will expose inside of them. Praying uncovers and discovers us.

In my early days of serious praying, one thing God showed me was that I was too concerned about what other people thought of me. When I received complements, I held them too tightly. Sometimes, depending on who it was and how it was expressed, negative criticism spiraled me into self-hatred. Even now, when it comes to affirmation and criticism, I have not fully arrived at some kind of equanimity and contentment.

But I know the solution. It is: to find my worth in Christ. I am, to God, of unsurpassable worth. I am loved by God.

If I did not regularly spend time one-on-one praying with God, I would lose sight of this, and be a spiritual and emotional disaster. I would crave affirmation and seek it out. My pastoral care of people would be skewed by my need to be praised, and my fear of being blamed. Only as I experientially know my worth in Christ am I then free to love others as Christ does.

Today I am reminded that I am one of the Lord's beloved children. I praying, I heard the voice of God saying, "John, I love you."

---

[46] Philip Yancey, *Prayer*, Kindle Locations 1039-1040.

Praying as Quantity Time with God

Praying is being in relationship with God. In praying, God engages me, and I, him. This is me and God, connected in the perichoretic union.

A praying person is in a love-relationship with God. She is a bride, syncing with her bridegroom. This is why the idea of "a little quality prayer time with God" is dysfunctional.

One reason marriages fail is because courtship habits and being together for long periods of time stops. What is needed, in prayer as well as marriage, is *a lot of time*, "quantity-time," together. Brief together times will lack quality without ongoing quantity-time.

Quantity-time with God has certain characteristics. Spend lots of time with God, in certain ways. Such as: focusing, listening, opening your heart towards God, worshiping, thanking, meditating, and contemplating.

In praying, I am attending to God. *Being* with God. A lot.

Praying and Suffering in the Fields of God's Grace

Paul writes, in Romans 5:1-5:

> [1] Therefore, since we have been justified through faith, we have peace with God through our Lord Jesus Christ, [2] through whom we have gained access by faith into this grace in which we now stand. And we boast in the hope of the glory of God. [3] Not only so, but we also glory in our sufferings, because we know that suffering produces perseverance; [4] perseverance, character; and character, hope. [5] And hope does not put us to shame, because God's love has been poured out into our hearts through the Holy Spirit, who has been given to us.

Everyone who trusts and places their faith in Christ is "justified." Correctified. Straightened out. Placed on the straight path of life. Made right with God. From this it follows that followers of Jesus have peace with God. I am brought into relationship with God. This is the Jewish idea of *shalom*.

Shalom is a robust, physical concept. The image is of two hands meeting in a handshake, of two persons who were enemies coming together in an embrace. I was once God's enemy,[47] as sin caused me to fall short of his glory. But now, the atoning sacrifice of Christ on the cross has reconciled me to God. I am brought into God's presence, not as a result of my good performance or lack thereof, but by his grace.

If I am to have a praying life, I must keep the following in my heart and mind: *God loves me.* Period.

By placing my faith in Christ, I gain access into the fields of God's grace. "Grace" is a kind of "sphere which the believer enters and stands within. The image may be of a weak person who is able to stand up and withstand whatever life brings through the divine power and love of God."[48]

As a Jesus-follower, I stand in these gracious fields *now*. I have been made right with God, brought into *shalom* with my Maker, and stand in his garden of realities. To comprehend this is "the beginning of something so big, so massive, so unimaginably beautiful and powerful, that we almost burst as we think of it."[49] This is what I was created for; viz., to host the presence of God.[50]

There is more. Reconciliation to God is not only for the sake of one-to-one relationship. God is enlisting us in working for his kingdom. This will bring new, different problems, and suffering of a certain kind. My trials are not for nothing, but for the cause of God's Kingdom and the Gospel.

Suffering as a Jesus-follower who is engaged in the Mission is not meaningless, as an atheist's suffering ultimately is. The purpose of life is not to avoid suffering and achieve happiness (God is not a utilitarian

---

[47] Romans 5:10

[48] Ben Witherington, *Paul's Letter to the Romans: A Socio-Rhetorical Commentary*, 134. Grand Rapids: Eerdmans, 2004.

[49] N.T. Wright, *Romans for Everyone*. Louisville: Westminster, 2004.

[50] See C. S. Lewis's beautiful "The Weight of Glory," in *The Weight of Glory and Other Addresses*. New York: HarperCollins, 1980.

ethicist). I go *through* suffering, *through* the valley of the shadow of death. In suffering I have real hope, and boast of it.

What I boast of, in praying, affects how I suffer. Some boast in their wisdom, strength, and riches.[51] Such personal accomplishments have limited therapeutic value when one is hurting. Ultimately, in death, they fail us. But because I trust Christ, have been made right with God, am in *shalom* with my Maker, and stand in the fields of his grace, suffering looks, and is, different.

How I pray looks different, too. When my son David died at birth, and his twin brother Joshua was fighting for his life, Linda and I looked at each other and said, "How could anyone go through this without Christ?" In that difficult, dark valley, we not only stayed with Jesus, but strengthened our resolve to do so. At such times, personal trophies mean nothing. One can only glory ("boast") in the hope of the glory of God.

Suffering with Christ forms endurance. Character is developed.[52] The Greek word Paul uses for character is *dokimos*. This word describes the fiery purification of precious metals. God redeems my suffering, and uses it to burn away all that is peripheral in my life in order to establish his moral and spiritual being and glory within me. As this happens, I finally find where I belong, to be with him. Because of this, I have hope. Eschatological hope. Which means: future hope.

The first biblical verse that stood out to me when I turned to Jesus at age twenty-one was Romans 8:18: "I consider that the sufferings of this present time are not worth being compared to the glory that will be revealed to us." Today, over four decades later, these words come to me, and mean more than they ever have. I have placed all my eggs into this basket of hope. This profoundly affects how I pray.

One existential reason for the hope I have is this: God's Spirit has poured out His love for me into my heart. My verification for this is first-person subjective experience. The words "pour out" are used in

---

[51] Jeremiah 9:23-24

[52] See David Brooks, *The Road to Character*, for stories of how character is formed through trials and limitations. New York: Random House, 2015.

the Bible to describe a rainstorm's deluge of water. God's love does not come as a meager trickle, but as an outpouring. I have experienced this.

The language of God's love is pure, and experiential. It is not a bad thing to intellectually acknowledge that, "Yes, I know, God loves me." But love is not essentially an intellectual thing, though it includes that. God's love, real love, is a visceral, experiential, encountered reality. The fact of God's love, poured into every Jesus-follower, is undeniable. A love-outpouring is something that is felt. It is needed when walking through the dark valley of despair.

I pray for the Outpouring, as I kneel in the fields of God's grace. I pray for a fresh rain-deluge of the love of God, flooding the fields where I am with the One who has made all things right, between myself and he.

4

PRAYING IS CONFERENCING WITH GOD

A praying person has, by definition, space to pray, because praying *is* getting together with God and conferring.

Praying needs a conference room to meet in. That room is my heart, where God makes his home.[1] In the act of praying, a roomy space exists within, where God and I meet to discuss the profound matters of his kingdom.

Praying, as Martin Luther King, Jr. believed, is conversation with God.[2] In the act of praying I converse with God about what *both of us* are thinking and doing together.

Praying is mutually collaborative conversation. In praying, God and I confer about The Mission.

I have attended many large-event conferences. At some of them, God has met me in significant ways. This has been good. But I am not waiting for the next conference to come around. I confer with God now, today, this moment. The conference doors are open. I enter in. I'm sitting with the Main Speaker at the God Conference.

This happens now. Greg Boyd, in *Present Perfect*, writes:

---

[1] See John 14:23 – "Jesus replied, 'Anyone who loves me will obey my teaching. My Father will love then, and we will come to them and make our home with them.'"
[2] See Lewis Baldwin, *Never to Leave Us Alone: The Prayer Life of Martin Luther King Jr.*. Minneapolis: Fortress, 2010.

"God is the God of the living, not the God of the already-past or the not-yet-present. He's the great "I AM," not the great "I was" or the great "I will be." He's been present in every moment in the past, for which we can be thankful, and he'll be present at every moment in the future, which gives us great hope. But he's *only* alive and active now, in the present - which is, once again, the only thing that's real."[3]

God, the great I AM, is present to my experience *now*. This encourages me to pray. Praying is now-conferencing with God. *This moment.* My God and I, meeting together.

Many of the most life-changing, spiritually formative times for me have been when I've conferred with God, one-on-one. Just God and I. As wonderful as some conference speakers are, God is better.

The God-conference is happening today.

Cost of admission: $0.

Main speaker: God. (He's very good.)

Break-out sessions: me and God.

Praying takes me into God's Conference Room. In this chapter I share some things I have learned from attending many God Conferences.

Attend the Solitary God-Conference

I have been privileged to speak at several conferences and retreats for pastors and Christian leaders. I am always grateful for the opportunity to do this. Folk wisdom says the person who teaches gets more out of the event than the students. There's truth in this. God gives personal takeaways when I'm the teacher. I get spoken-to, by God. I receive new insights that stay with me. I take notes on myself. And, being with colleagues in ministry instructs and enriches my life.

---

[3] Greg Boyd, Present Perfect: Finding God In the Now, 15. Grand Rapids: Zondervan, 2010.

I've also attended gatherings for pastors and leaders, as a non-presenter. When I'm there, I want to have open ears to what God is saying to me, through others.

But as good as these events are, the beating heart of my God-encountering spiritual life remains solitary praying times. As Luke 5:16 says, *Jesus often attended the Solitary God Conference and prayed.*[4] Therefore, as a follower of Jesus, I do the same.

Sadly, there are Christians "who have spent a great deal of time and money traveling the world "chasing God" at various revivals, all the while missing what God was doing—and what God wanted to do—in and through their own lives."[5] They seem to view the Big Conference as more pregnant with God's presence than the present moment. If they fail to find God presently, it's not clear to me that they will find God at the big event.

I can't depend on the coming conference that is still weeks away. I need God, today. Now. Presently. The good news is that God's presence is available to me, 24/7.

Assume God is doing something in you, now.

Assume God has something to tell you as you pray, today.

Praying and the Inborn Desire for God

I've taught philosophy courses at our local community college for over 15 years.[6] I report to you that, in adolescents today, the metaphysical impulse has not gone away.

When my philosophy students are introduced to some of life's Big Questions they are interested, even captivated. Some, who are unimpressed with the Entertainment Church or the Relevant Church,

---

[4] Translation mine. From "Jesus often withdrew to lonely places and prayed."
[5] Greg Boyd, *Present Perfect: Finding God in the Now*, 135
[6] I teach philosophy at Monroe County Community College, Monroe, Michigan.

open their eyes, ears, and hearts to Big Question discussions. The mostly unfulfilled, inner-Pascalian abyss opens wide.[7]

The psychiatrist Gerald May, in his amazing book *Addiction and Grace*, observed that "after twenty years of listening to the yearnings of people's hearts, I am convinced that human beings have an inborn desire for God. Whether we are consciously religious or not, this desire is our deepest longing and most precious treasure."[8]

Religion is not going away. The inner longing for something more is intrinsic to humanity. The human heart is a throne wanting to be occupied, and our world has many pretenders to it. It is the place of deepest desiring. Because I am "made in God's own image, God will find a way to fulfill that deepest longing. Prayer is that way."[9]

Praying is Inter-asking

N.T. Wright believes that "we are people who live at the interface between God's world and the life of this present world. We are people who belong in that uncomfortable borderland. We are called to stay at this post even when we have no idea what's actually going on."[10]

To stay at this post is to be a praying person. Praying is the act of interfacing this world with the kingdom of God. Praying is a relationship occurring where heaven and earth intersect.

In conversational praying, I confer with God about what we are doing together. This viewpoint radically changes a traditional view of prayer as *only* "petition," or "asking." Instead of sending prayer requests up to heaven, heaven meets earth in the place and act of praying. Praying includes asking, but is more than that. It is interacting. Praying is inter-asking.

---

[7] I'm not as sure as James K.A. Smith is (via Charles Taylor) that the "abyss" Pascal talks about is mostly relegated to history. See Smith, *How (Not) To Be Secular: Reading Charles Taylor*, on three levels/stages of secularization in American culture. Grand Rapids: Eerdmans, 2014.

[8] Gerald May, *Addiction and Grace*. I've read this book three times!

[9] Philip Yancey, *Prayer*, Kindle location 237.

[10] N. T. Wright, *After You Believe: Why Christian Character Matters*, Kindle Locations 4725-4727. New York: HarperCollins, 2010.

As you pray you interface with the Maker of heaven and earth. This is important. We are given the location of the God-conference, which is: the intersection of heaven and earth. Praying is the place where God and humans meet. Prayer is the point where God and I converge. The moment of praying is when the rule of God (the "kingdom of God") invades this present darkness.

Real praying is when this happens. For example, Colossians 1:9 reads: "For this reason, since the day we heard about you, we have not stopped praying for you. We continually ask God to fill you with the knowledge of his will through all the wisdom and understanding that the Spirit gives..." Here, Paul prays for the Colossian Jesus-followers. This has been called "intercessory prayer." To "intercede" means: to come between. The word "intersection" is helpful here.

The intersection of Telegraph Road and M-50 is one mile north of our church building. If a person's car stalls in the middle of this intersection, will their car be on Telegraph Road, or on M-50? The answer is: both. This is because, in this intersection, the properties of Telegraph Road and the properties of M-50 are shared, or are the same.

Set theory, in mathematics, illustrates this. Imagine two sets representing realms of experience: Set A (the realm of God), and Set B (earthly reality). Set A equals the being of God; viz., all God's attributes, God's desires (God's will), and God's character. Set B equals the Colossian Jesus-followers (and, by extension, Jesus-followers today).

Now imagine that these two sets overlap, or intersect. Intercessory praying happens at the intersection of God's reality and my reality. In Colossians 1:9, Paul kneels at the intersection of A and B, the place where heaven intersects with earth. In that place he asks God to bring heaven to bear on the earthly existence of the people he is interceding for.[11]

> Praying people are "intercessors," kneeling before
> God in the place where heaven intersects with
> earth, where God interacts with humanity.

---

[11] Think of the Lord's Prayer here.

5

PRAYING AND LISTENING

When I was teaching in Singapore, Linda and I were introduced to a young Chinese woman who wanted to meet with us. She told us that her father had only spoken one sentence to her, in her entire life. The result was self-punishing. Surely, she thought, her father must not love her.

How sad it would be if God did not speak to us. I have discovered that he does, and has more than one sentence to share with me. God and I communicate.[1]

Communicating in relationship is a two-way street. There is speaking, and there is listening. Most of my early praying was speaking. I would pour out my heart to God, say "Amen," and be on my way. It's hard to listen when you are the only one doing the talking.

Years of praying have changed this for me. If anything, listening now predominates over speaking. I think listening is an acquired skill. I have learned to listen to God. Once the ability to listen takes hold, it changes everything about praying. The one who learns to listen now has "ears to hear."

I expect to hear from God. I am certain God has much to tell me. Jesus said to his disciples that his sheep hear his voice. I apply this to myself. After all, I am one of Jesus' disciples, too. How disappointing to think that God might have nothing to say to me!

---

[1] Dallas Willard's *Hearing God* makes the strongest biblical case for this.

God is not like the unloving father who spoke virtually nothing to his daughter. Instead, God speaks to us every day. I have filled many journals with words God has said to me, either immediately or mediately. I have discovered the joy of hearing God. In this chapter I share with you some of the things my ears have acquired along the way.

How to Hear the Voice of God

Often people ask me the question, "How do I hear the voice of God?" A related question is, "How do I know this is God speaking to me, and not just myself, or some other voice?" In brief, here's my response.

1. Abide in Christ. Dwell with God. Spend much time with God. There is simply no substitute for this. Forget about "Mc-hearing" God. God refuses to be fast-fooded. Hearing the voice of God is largely an acquired thing, over time. Analogically, I spend a lot of time talking with Linda, and listening to her. The result is that I know her heart, and her heart's desires, very well.

2. Saturate yourself in Scripture. The greater one's familiarity with Scripture is, the greater one will know when it's God speaking, and not something else. Begin by saturating yourself in Matthew, Mark, Luke, and John. Try reading these over and over, slowly and meditatively, for a year. I did this for two years and found it very helpful. Read the four Gospels as if you've never read them before. When God speaks to you as you read, write down what he says in your journal.

3. Hang around people who do one and two. Meet with other Jesus-followers who actually pray. Talk together about what God has been saying to you. It won't do much good talking with people who don't spend time alone with God. They won't have a clue regarding what it means to hear God's voice. Meeting together with praying people provides corporate discernment. One learns a lot about hearing God in such an environment.

Don't multi-task the God-relationship. Spend time with God, alone and focused. Just you and God. Face to face. Heart to heart. If you are unfamiliar with this, my recommendation is: just start doing it. In the process you'll learn what this is about, because God wants you to know him, experientially and relationally.

How Do We Know It Is God?

Prayer is talking with God about what we are doing together. OK. But is it possible to hear God speak to us? How can we discern whether what we are hearing is really God, or not?

J.P. Moreland suggests two things.[2]

1. *First*, one can learn to discern God's voice like one learns anyone else's voice—through practice, trial and error; and in the case of God, with Scripture as one's guide and as one's primary way of familiarizing oneself not only with correct propositional boundaries, but also with the tone and texture of God's speech.
2. *Second*, I think we should take heart from the fact that, often, God speaks to us and we are unaware that it is happening because God will at times speak to us in our thoughts, feelings, and bodily sensations in a way that "sounds" like our own.

J.P. concludes that "We should take great comfort in the fact that, if we make ourselves available to Him, God will speak to and through us in many ways of which we are not aware."

Hearing God Emerges from Living in Relationship to God

Dallas Willard writes that spiritual formation into Christlikeness, meaning a true change of character, comes from living in relationship to God.[3]

These are not a string of non-referential words. The truth of Willard's statement is not mere theory. I *know* these words, in experience.

---

[2] Moreland, "On Hearing From God: Two Perspectives." http://www.jpmoreland.com/2011/08/05/on-hearing-from-god-two-perspectives/
[3] Dallas Willard, *Hearing God*, 29.

Experiential truth is more powerful than theoretical truth." This is truth that happens, ongoingly.

I know this from my vantage point as a pastor and teacher. I have seen it, in many people. A significant number of former seminary students tell me of their ongoing, experiential, conversational relationship with God, in Christ, by the Spirit.

Willard quotes 19th-century theologian Wilhelm Hermann: "We hold a man to be really a Christian when we believe we have ample evidence that God has revealed himself to him in Jesus Christ, and that now the man's inner life is taking on a new character through his communion with the God who is thus manifest." (p. 29)

I know many Jesus-followers who claim to know God as a result of a revelation of his presence. Arguing about this possibility is useless to those who have never been confronted with God's presence. But to those who have, it is more than enough.[4]

Live consistently in God's presence, and become familiar with the sound of his voice.

Recognizing God's Voice Comes by Experience

I know the sound of Linda's voice. Immediately. This is to be expected after forty-three years of marriage, plus a year of courtship. But, had she called before we met, I would have asked, "Who is this?"

I know my wife's voice by experience. Countless hours of communicating have attuned my heart to hers. I can distinguish her voice from the many other voices I hear throughout the day. This is how voice recognition happens. This is how we come to recognize the voice of God. As Dallas Willard says, "The only answer to the question "How do we know whether this is from God?" is: *By experience.*"[5]

Sheep, and other domesticated animals and pets, recognize, without fail, their master's voice. When they first heard that voice, they did not know who was speaking. But they learn quickly. Jesus said:

---

[4] See Ib.
[5] Willard, *Hearing God*, 217.

> The shepherd of the sheep… calls his own sheep by name and leads them out. He goes ahead of them, and the sheep follow him because they know his voice… I am the good shepherd. I know my own and my own know me… My sheep hear my voice. I know them, and they follow me.[6]

The more I spend time with Linda, the more I not only recognize the sound of her voice, I become familiar with the heart behind it. This comes by personal experience, and much of it. There is no substitute for this. You cannot get this out of a book. Second-hand experience will not do. The testimony of someone else won't replace first hand, personal knowledge.

Someone who does not have time to pray should not expect to recognize the voice of God, any more than spouses who have drifted apart would be familiar with each other's hearts. Only familiarity breeds discernment.

Familiarity in the sense of recognition and understanding is directly proportionate to the amount of time spent together, and spent in a certain way. That's how it is with people. It is the same with God. We come to recognize God's voice by personal experience.

On Not Having Ears to Hear

After I finished the funeral service, I was thankful when the family told me they appreciated the words I had to say. A few even asked where our church was located, and said they might drop in and check us out.

As I was standing in the funeral home after the service, an elderly man came and shook my hand. "Very good job," he said, sporting a large, genuine smile.

Thank you.

"Of course," he added, "I forgot to put in my hearing aid, and didn't hear a word you said."

---

[6] John 10:2-4, 14, 27.

He was still smiling as he told me this. I smiled back, thanking him for the compliment.

I Am a Nobody to Whom God Speaks

God speaks to me. In this regard I'm nobody special. Stanford sociologist T.R. Luhrman, in her essay, "If you hear God speak audibly, you (usually) aren't crazy,"[7] writes:

> For the last 10 years, I have been doing anthropological and psychological research among experientially oriented evangelicals, the sort of people who seek a personal relationship with God and who expect that God will talk back. For most of them, most of the time, God talks back in a quiet voice they hear inside their minds, or through images that come to mind during prayer. But many of them also reported sensory experiences of God. They say God touched their shoulder, or that he spoke up from the back seat and said, in a way they heard with their ears, that he loved them. Indeed, in 1999, Gallup reported that 23% of all Americans had heard a voice or seen a vision in response to prayer.[8]

I have had such experiences - many of them. My spiritual journals are a record of the voice and activity of God in my life.[9] I am a nobody to whom God speaks.

In my doctoral work at Northwestern, I did neurophysiological studies on language processing, especially as it relates to religious language. I am familiar with the neural happenings of linguistic experience.[10] *Of course* something neural is happening when I hear God speak to me.

---

[7] http://religion.blogs.cnn.com/2012/12/29/my-take-if-you-hear-god-speak-audibly-you-usually-arent-crazy/?hpt=hp_c1

[8] Ib.

[9] Not all my journal entries record instances of hearing God, but many do.

[10] My dissertation includes the study of how metaphor is neurally processed. It's different, e.g., from simile and the other tropes.

But it's not my physical brain that is making this up, as I understand this, via inference to the best explanation.[11]

Hearing God speak is important. If a preacher does not hear from God, then I am not interested. Hearing God should be a common experience of ordinary people, which includes your pastor.

Hearing God speak is good. Luhrman reports that one-third of the people she interviewed in her research on prayer "reported an unusual sensory experience they associated with God. While they found these experiences startling, they also found them deeply reassuring."[12]

Engage with God. Listen. Be assured.

Hearing God: Focus On the God-Relationship First

I went to my doctor for a routine physical. The blood tests showed an abnormality with my kidneys. I'm going to follow my doctor's counsel, and I am also seeking God for guidance and healing.

Many people speak to God for guidance, wanting to hear his voice direct their path. This is one element of hearing God, but it is far from the only one. Hearing God is richer, more textured, than that. Hearing God is itself part of a deeper, more comprehensive Jesus-life.

To hear God, don't focus on hearing God. Focus on cultivating relationship with him, out of which hearing emerges, as a byproduct and a skill. For example, in marriage the ongoing, sustained, relationship provides the environment for Linda and I to hear and understand one another. When it comes to hearing and understanding God, the same relational rules apply.

We must get beyond the question of hearing God, and into the life that is greater than our own; viz., that of the kingdom of God. Our concern to hear God's voice must be overwhelmed by our worship, adoration, and fellowship with him.

---

[11] I am a mind-body dualist. That is, I believe "mind" or "spirit" is independent of the physical body. See, for example, J.P. Moreland's *The Soul*, or the recent work of neuroscientist Mario Beauregard.

[12] Luhrman, op. cit.

To learn to hear God, focus on the more primordial and foundational thing, which is the abiding relationship in Christ. Engage in the God-relationship. Discover the continuing conversation, which is not like going occasionally to a fortune teller for advice.

Meditation on Scripture & Hearing God

"As fundamental a step as we can take . . . is learning to meditate - learning first to hear God's word, and let it inform and take root in us. This may be extremely difficult, for the churches have no courses on meditation, despite the fact that it is an art that must be learned from those who have mastered it, and despite the fact that the supreme task of the church is to listen to the Word of God."[13]

- Elizabeth O'Connor

Is the supreme task of the church to listen to the Word of God? I think a case can be made for this.

Remember that, by "church," we mean: a people movement called out by God to proclaim the good news of God's rule and reign, in Christ and by the Spirit. Every movement has a commander. A leader. In the Jesus Movement, God is our leader. The Lord is our shepherd.

If the Lord is our shepherd, then we are the "sheep of his pasture." Jesus said, "My sheep hear my voice, and I know them, and they follow me."[14]

We are Jesus-followers. The game of life we play is, "Follow the Leader." This is called "obedience." If we don't hear the voice of our Leader and sense his promptings, "following" won't make sense. Thus, listening and hearing from God is supremely important. Hearing God brings us into the Great Conversation.

---

[13] Cited in Richard Foster, *Sanctuary of the Soul: Journey Into Meditative Prayer*, Kindle Locations 72-72.
[14] John 10:27

If you desire to pray, as conversing with God, meditate on Scripture. Good places to begin are Psalm 23, John chapters 14, 15, and 16, and Matthew chapters 5, 6, and 7. Marinate in these verses. Slow-cook in them. Chew on them. To meditate is to chew, slowly. The more you chew, the more the words become assimilable to your spirit. God's truths get into you. They become you. When this happens, a lot of God-hearing takes place.

Meditate, ruminate, on one thing; e.g., on one verse, or part of a verse. Such as "Believe in me."[15] Or "The Lord is my shepherd."[16] Get redundant about things like this, and God will escort them from your mind into your heart.

In my praying times, I meditate on portions of Scripture. It is common, in the middle of these meditations, to hear God speak to me. And, by the way, God has much to say to us, today. He desires our presence, longs to hear from us, and yearns to communicate with us.

Hearing God: Not All of Reality Involves Space

Sometimes, God speaks to us through physical events. When this happens, his voice, to us, is *mediated* through physical reality. This is *mediated experience of God*. For example, my journal contains examples of God speaking to me through his creation. Many of these experiences have been powerful and relevant to my spiritual growth and life.

At other times, God speaks to us directly. These experiences of hearing God's voice are *unmediated* experiences. While God can speak in mediated ways, his communication to us is not restricted to this.

The plausibility of this depends on one's worldview. For an atheistic philosophical materialist (= physical facts explain all of reality) then, *ipso facto*, unmediated God-encounters are impossible.[17] Indeed, on philosophical materialism-as-atheism, "God" as an immaterial spiritual Person is impossible.

---

[15] Jesus, in John 14:1
[16] Psalm 23:1
[17] Most intellectual atheists are physicalists.

Christian theists reject physicalism, and affirm the reality of non-physical beings. Such as, e.g., God himself. God is not restricted to speaking to us through physical intermediaries. This means conversational praying is not hindered by space and distance. "When you speak to God, it is like speaking to someone next to you."[18]

Because God is non-spatial, and therefore unembodied[19], he does not require a "place" from which to communicate to us. I don't have to travel to some far away church or conference to meet with God, conversationally. Here and now, where I am, works for him.

This is why, when I pray, I often begin by slowing down in my heart and saying, "Lord, here I am, next to you. If you have anything to say to me, I am listening."

Hearing God: Deus Interruptus

Henri Nouwen once said he was bothered by life's many interruptions, until he realized that the interruptions were his life.[20] I must pay attention to interruptions, and discern whether or not they are from God. I need to have an interruptible heart.

An interruptible heart is one that hears, and follows. Without the following part, God's interruptions diminish. Why would God continue to say, "John, I know you have plans for today, but I want you to do this instead," if I would not "do this instead?"

I have friends who struggle to hear the voice of God. This is not because they are any more unwilling to follow him than I am. But some do not hear God's voice, since they wouldn't follow if he called them to do something that interrupted their own plans, or was outside their comfort zone.

Maybe many Christians like this. It would not surprise me if it was so. Some who call themselves followers of Jesus will only follow if it jives with their plans.

The Real Jesus Life is a series of interruptions.

---

[18] Willard, *Hearing God*, 96.

[19] Every body needs a space.

[20] See Nouwen, *Out of Solitude*. Notre Dame: Ave Maria Press: 2004.

Deus Interruptus.
God, interrupt us.

Praying and Interrupt-ability

Life is a series of interruptions and choices. I get interrupted, then choose whether to entertain the interruption or not.

Some interruptions are God-opportunities. I think most God-opportunities come by way of an interruption. It goes like this.

1. I have my day "mapped out."
2. The phone rings.
3. So much for my map.

When this happens, don't resent it. Instead, weigh it. Is it from God, or not? If not, dismiss it. If it is, follow it. That is, follow the Spirit's leading.

I'm thinking of something that happened on a Sunday morning at Redeemer. We have a circle of prayer in the back of the sanctuary before the God-event begins. Starting time is officially 10:30. God, however, is not bound by the clock. The Spirit of God hovers over our sanctuary hours before the first person arrives to open the building. God is already moving as the worship team is doing its sound check.

I stood with our prayer leaders, and shared that God told me, on this particular morning, that I was to preach first, and we would worship afterwards. I was not clear on what the worship would look like after the preaching. Thankfully, in our context, this kind of confession does not freak people out, since they are expecting God to break in to the service.

10:30 came. I was on the worship team, playing guitar. People stood, and began to sing. And dance. Some were shouting praises. My plan was that we'd do this song, and then I'd preach. Instead, I looked at our worship leader and said, "keep playing." Worship began before it was supposed to! It was explosive, dynamic, moving. God interrupted my plans. He had his way. This is *always* good.

Interruptibility is a mark of a Jesus-follower. It's like being in an army. My commander comes just as I am about to fall asleep, and says, "Time to move - now!" And I move. If I can't have my plans interrupted, then I am not fit to serve in the kingdom of God.

Henri Nouwen said he used to complain about his life being interrupted, until he realized that the interruptions *were* his life. This is not only an adventurous way to live, it is the only way, since interruptions are the norm.

"In his heart a man plans his course, but the LORD determines his steps."[21]

"Many are the plans in a man's heart, but it is the LORD's purpose that prevails."[22]

I am praying to be interrupt-able.

Experiencing Wordless Hearing

In 1 Corinthians 3:9 Paul claims that Jesus' followers are co-workers in God's service. Therefore, I am working, co-laboring, with Christ.

Co-working with is intimate. Christ and I are working together. This is why prayer is talking and thinking about what God and I are doing together. God is not some CEO sitting in heaven's office-suite, detached from his people. The closer I allow myself to get to him, the more I develop an intimate life partnership with him.

Such closeness and intimacy breeds familiarity. Many times I simply know what God desires of me, and I do it. I experience a wordless hearing that emerges out of our intimate relationship.

We are invited to become so close to God that we don't have to wait for his words. "We don't have to be asked but are engaged in free-hearted collaboration with Jesus and his friends in the kingdom..."[23]

Like a close friend, we just know. Sometimes words don't have to be spoken.

---

[21] Proverbs 16:9
[22] Proverbs 19:21
[23] Willard, *Hearing God*, 72.

Hearing God: Longing for What Only God Can Do

Several years ago my church changed its Mission Statement to read:

The Mission of Redeemer Fellowship Church is:
To heal the sick
To deliver the oppressed
To raise the dead
To proclaim the good news of the Kingdom of God
and that Jesus is Lord and King

I will never forget the Sunday morning I shared this with our people. Many stood up and cheered. In retrospect, I am glad we did this. Today, our Mission still stands.

I think this is the mission of every Jesus-follower. This was the mission of Jesus while he was on earth. As this mission becomes reality, it will be clear that God is doing it, and not ourselves. I am on a mission with God that I cannot accomplish by my own severely limited powers.

I am less and less captivated by what humanity can do on its own strength, by relying on its own brainpower. Of course, many of these things are good. But if Christianity and Church are only about what people can do without God, then I stand uninterested.

God produces results that go beyond the natural, and could never come from us left to ourselves. What is most needed in our world, and through God's Church, are accomplishments that could never be reduced to mere humanity. To have God accomplish his plans and purposes through us requires that we focus on attending to his directives as we hear his guiding voice while dwelling in his presence.

This is why, in my preaching, I refuse to bring God down to the level of my experience. Rather, I pray for God to raise the level of my experience to the realities of his Word. I long to be part of the kind of things that only God can do.

Laying Personal Eminence Aside

The apostle Paul was an unimpressive sight. He would never have succeeded in today's media-driven churches. He was short, bald, and according to Tertullian, had a large nose and a unibrow.[24] Paul was "a small man sitting, his head a monument for hugeness, eyebrows thick and dark and joined in the middle; his nose both narrow and hooked; his eyes red-rimmed in that tremendous skull; a swift mouth, moist red lips; an orange rim of a scar at the hairline."[25]

Paul was, by his own admission, a lousy speaker.[26] In spite of this, God used him to revolutionize Asia Minor, the effects of which are still felt today.[27] I find this encouraging. God can capture and wield a willing heart, with external appearance and intrinsic ability having little to do with it.

While it is true that, as Richard Lovelace said, a "Spirit-baptized intellect" is powerful, none of our relatively ignorant intellects are up to the God-sized tasks every Jesus-follower is called to do.[28] One example of this was D.L. Moody.

> Moody was a constant source of wonder precisely because the effects of his ministry were so totally incommensurable, even incongruent, with his obvious personal qualities. He was a man of very ordinary appearance, unordained by any ecclesiastical group and quite uncultured and uneducated—even uncouth and crude to many.[29]

---

[24] See "Bert" of "Sesame Street.

[25] Walter Wangerin, *Paul: A Novel*, 18. Grand Rapids: Zondervan.

[26] 1 Corinthians 2:1.

[27] I am now thinking of Italian atheist philosopher Marcello Pera whose recent work is a call for Europe to return to its Christian roots. See Pera, *Why We Should Call Ourselves Christians: The Religious Roots of Free Societies*. New York: Encounter, 2008.

[28] See Richard Lovelace, *Dynamics of Spiritual Life: An Evangelical Theology of Renewal*. Paternoster Press, 1979.

[29] Willard, Hearing God, 65-66.

When a pastor named R.W. Dale saw Moody in Birmingham, he wanted to know how such an unimpressive person could do such impressive things. What was Moody's secret to this success? Dale concluded that it must be the work of God, since "he could see no relation between Moody personally and what he was accomplishing."[30] Moody's response was to laugh, and say he would be sorry if things were otherwise.

Both Paul and D.L. Moody viewed their personal unimpressiveness as evidence that it must be God who was working through them. They were able to lay aside their own egos for the sake of glorifying God.

No wonder Paul, and D.L. Moody, heard from God.

The Precondition of Humility

A humble heart is a necessary precondition for hearing God. Humility opens the heart's door, and invites God in.

To be humble is to be teachable. God teaches the teachable. Humble people "have ears to hear." Psalm 29:5 says that God guides the humble in what is right, and teaches them his way.

Humility is the foundational attitude for spiritual formation and transformation. Humility is needed to pray, since conversational prayer requires listening, and to really listen we must be humble.

Our English word "humility" comes from the Latin *humus*, which means "earth" or "soil." Eugene Peterson writes:

> The Latin words *humus*, soil/earth, and *homo*, human being, have a common derivation, from which we also get our word 'humble.' This is the Genesis origin of who we are: dust – dust that the Lord God used to make us a human being. If we cultivate a lively sense of our origin and nurture a sense of continuity with it, who knows, we may also acquire humility.[31]

---

[30] Ib.

[31] Eugene Peterson, *Christ Plays in Ten Thousand Places: A Conversation in Spiritual Theology*. Grand Rapids: Eerdmans, 2008.

Our hearts must be good soil to receive the things God wants to plant in us. Pride, on the other hand, is hardness. Hardness of the heart is the great barrier to hearing God and spiritual change. Francis Frangipane once referred to pride as "the armor of darkness."[32] C.S. Lewis called pride "the complete anti-God state of mind."[33] If our hearts are proud we won't hear from God.

This is heavy stuff, stronger than saying, "God is upset," or "My pride just put God in a bad mood." Pride is a worm burrowed in the hearts of religious people. It is most destructive when it masks as humility. "When a proud man thinks he is humble, his case is hopeless... He is capable of destroying religion and making the name of God odious to men."[34]

Pride is a spiritual disease. It causes inner dis-ease. A proud person is uneasy in themselves. They are unsettled and insecure. Dis-eased insecurity constructs the mask of pride.

Are you humble, or proud? One indicator is how you handle criticism. A humble person doesn't mind being critiqued, even welcomes constructive criticism if it brings more truth. A proud person doesn't need advice. Pride's counterpart, shame, fears advice, receiving it as criticism.

James 4:6 states that God is opposed to the proud, but gives grace to the humble. This is one of those great biblical either-or ideas, stating that it's not simply a bad thing to have a proud heart, but an anti-God thing. If you are proud, God is against you. Wherever some area of the heart is hard towards God, God stands in opposition to that area.

How important is humility when it comes to the desire to hear from God? The answer is: without it, you won't. God does not guide a proud person, since they are, by logical extension, unguidable. They have deaf ears.

Pray, "Lord, teach me humility, that I might hear from you."

---

[32] Francis Frangipane, *The Three Battlegrounds*. Cedar Rapids, Iowa: Arrow, 1989.

[33] C.S. Lewis, *Mere Christianity*. New York: HarperCollins, 1980.

[34] Merton, *New Seeds of Contemplation*.

Prayer, Solitude, and Silence

It's easier to hear when I am alone and quiet. Solitude and silence make it easier to focus on God. These twin disciplines are found in the lives of every praying person who hears from God.

Success in conversing with God involves spending much alone time with him, attending to him. This is similar to a successful marriage, where husband and wife spend much alone time with one another, listening and speaking and, therefore, understanding.

What is solitude? It is getting alone and "doing nothing" for extended periods of time. This is needed to "break the grip of a God-alienated world over us at the level of our constant habits and preoccupations."[35]

This kind of "doing nothing" is actually "doing something." This is counterintuitive in our hyper-texting, multi-tasking, distracted world. Our culture lacks the focus solitude can bring. Instead of pure-heartedness, many things vie for our attention. These many things create fragmented, poly-*psuchos* (many-hearted) souls.

In the voice of James, addressing us from the first century, we encounter the "double-minded person." Today, we have multi-minded people. Cursed are the multi-minded, for they will not hear God. But there is hope. Solitude pulls the self together, and makes it whole again.

What is silence? Silence is the eradication of noise, externally, and within our own heart. Our world is wordy and pause-less. The melody of culture fills its measures with notes without rests. The world-system provides no rest for the soul. One must, therefore, get intentional and choose silence. Since the kingdom of God is not really about talk anyway, silence can be a gateway to power.

Solitude and silence "allow God to reoccupy the places in our lives where only he belongs... Once established in our mind, soul, body, and social involvements, they go with us wherever we are and need to be renewed only periodically by special times of practice."[36]

---

[35] Dallas Willard, *Hearing God*.
[36] Ib.

These disciplines morph our souls, minds, and bodies into the mind and body of Christ. We become peaceful rather than irritable, expectant rather than angry persons whose expectations are unmet, and relational rather than lonely.

In the solitary place, where it is quiet, we begin to hear from God.

In Silence, Calm and Quiet Yourself

When he opened the seventh seal,
there was silence in heaven for about half an hour.
Revelation 8:1

To find a moment of true silence in life is to find an existential pause. Like a rest in a piece of music, a much needed beat of silence, gives meaning to the sounding notes.

The heavenly, deconstructive, silence in the book of Revelation, is dramatic and anticipatory.[37] Something is about to happen. First the incense. Then, seven announcing trumpets. Silence provides the necessary background to the coming of God.

In praying, it is good to have a silent heart. A silent heart is an uncluttered heart. A quiet heart is poised and expectant. In the noiseless unclutter, one more clearly hears the voice of God.

When it comes to hearing and understanding, silence is good, noise is bad.

But I have calmed and quieted myself...
- Psalm 131:2

Silence Is Needed to Live Well

I read an article in the *New York Times* that championed the virtues of silence by citing the devastating psychological and physiological

---

[37] "Deconstruction" is about "absence" and "exclusion." See http://www.johnpiippo.com/2011/02/dialectic-between-words-of-men-and.html.

effects of constant sound.[38] For example, what happens to people who live adjacent to an airport? A 2009 study looked at the effect of airport noise on sleeping subjects. The findings showed that, even when people were asleep, the noise of planes taking off and landing caused blood pressure to spike, elevated pulse rates, vasoconstriction, and the release of stress hormones. These harmful responses continued to affect individuals for hours after they had awakened and gone on with their days.

Audible assaults affect us psychologically. A recent World Health Organization report, on the burden of disease from environmental noise, conservatively estimates that Western Europeans lose more than one million healthy life years annually as a consequence of noise-related disability and disease. Among environmental hazards, only air pollution causes more damage.[39]

An incessantly noisy soul is a diseased soul. Constant noise hinders sustained thinking. For this reason the makers of our Constitution had the street outside Independence Hall covered with earth, so that their deliberations might not be disturbed by passing traffic.[40]

Silence is needed to think well, and to be able to hear ourselves think. This is why libraries are silent. Silence helps us focus.

> *The quiet words of the wise are more to be heeded*
> *than the shouts of a ruler of fools.*
> *- Ecclesiastes 9:17*

Noise wars against hearing. Listening requires the soul to pause. Silence, therefore, is needed to pray well.

---

[38] "I'm Thinking, Please Be Quiet." http://www.nytimes.com/2013/08/25/opinion/sunday/im-thinking-please-be-quiet.html?pagewanted=all&_r=1&
[39] See Ib.
[40] See Ib.

Paul Tournier On the Importance of Silence

In the mid-1970s, while a student at Northern Baptist Theological Seminary, I was introduced to the writings of Swiss physician Paul Tournier. I picked up a volume that contained four of his books.[41] I was impressed, and began reading Tournier for inspiration as well as knowledge.

Linda and I would give, as gifts to wedding couples, Tournier's slim, profound book *To Understand Each Other*. Tournier wrote from a depth few possess. What was the source of his wisdom?

He explained this in an interview.[42] It was solitary meditation, as an ongoing spiritual discipline, for over fifty years. When asked why, he responded:

> Modern people lack silence. They no longer lead their own lives; they are dragged along by events. It is a race against the clock. I think that what so many people come to see me for is to find a quiet, peaceful person who knows how to listen and who isn't thinking all the time about what he has to do next. If your life is full already, there won't be room for anything else. Even God can't get anything else in. So it becomes essential to cut something out. I'm putting it as simply as I can.

Tournier called silence a waiting for God to stimulate his thoughts, renew him, and make him creative, instead of being a mere Pauline "clanging cymbal." "Silence,' he confessed, is "the cornerstone of my life. It is an attempt at seeing people and their problems from God's point of view, insofar as that is possible."[43]

---

[41] *The Best of Paul Tournier: Guilt and Grace, The Meaning of Persons, The Person Reborn, To Understand Each Other.* Iverson-Norman, 1977.

[42] Paul Tournier, "A Listening Ear: Reflections on Christian Caring," in Richard Foster and Emilie Griffin, *Spiritual Classics: Selected Readings on the Twelve Spiritual Disciplines*, 160 ff. San Francisco: HarperCollins, 2000.

[43] Ib.

Rather than solitude and silence being "doing nothing," they minister as restorative agents that combat world-weariness. I have discovered this after many years of disciplined, scheduled times of quiet. I get alone, and still, and wait for the Lord, listening in expectancy for his now-familiar voice.

Let Your Words Come Out of Your Silence

Where there are many words, transgression is unavoidable.
But he who restrains his lips is wise.
Proverbs 10:19

Ralph Cramden, of the ancient television series "The Honeymooners," had an unfiltered mouth. He could not keep the irritation in his mind from launching like grenades out of his troubled soul. He opened wide, and said many words he would later regret. Afterwards, in a fit of Cramdenian repentance, Ralph would again open wide and confess, "Me and my biiiiiig mouth!"

I've done the same, hopefully not as much and definitely not as loudly as Ralph. One time I opened my big mouth in a sermon, and said a sentence that I wish I could take back. Just one sentence, in a 40-minute message. It dropped on the carpet like a bomb. Next Sunday morning, I asked my church family to forgive me for saying what I did. They did.

I've done this with people I love, and confessed it with sadness. I was twenty years old, playing golf with my family's insurance agent. On the ride home, I began talking about my cat. I was especially proud of my cat's name.

"What's the name?" he asked.

"'El Gato,'" I answered, radiating great pleasure. "I didn't want to give my cat some ordinary name, like 'Mittens'."

"Do you have a cat?" I asked.

"Yes."

"What's the name?"

"Mittens."

He and I never played golf again. In fact, those were the last words we ever spoke to each other.

Ruth Haley Barton writes: "Sometimes I can literally feel—deep in my bones—that if I do not shut my mouth for a while I will get myself in trouble, because my words will be completely disconnected from the reality of God in my life."[44]

The psalmist writes:

> *When you are disturbed, do not sin;*
> *ponder it on your beds,*
> *and be silent.*
> Psalm 4:4

There is a time to speak, and a time to shut up. Which to do is a matter of discernment and prayer.

Praying with a Quiet Mind

In my doctoral program it was my privilege to take an independent study on Meister Eckhart with medieval scholar Richard Kieckhefer. I was interested in Eckhart's description of encountering God, in experience. Eckhart wrote of the need to have a quiet mind and heart. Inner quietude is undisturbed by outer noise. Eckhart believed that prayer is greater, more powerful, and deeper, when the mind is quieter.[45]

What does this mean?

The less cluttered my mind is, the more I am able to attend. The more I attend, the more likely it is that I will hear when God speaks. An uncluttered, detoxified mind is *purer*. The pure are blessed, for they shall see God. And experience God. And hear God.

How can I acquire a quiet mind? I think: 1) By spending much time, as a lifestyle, in solitary praying; and 2) by learning burden-casting,

---

[44] Barton, *Strengthening the Soul of Your Leadership*, 125. Downers Grove: Intervarsity, 2008.

[45] See, e.g., David O'Neal, ed. *Meister Eckhart: From Whom God Hid Nothing*, Shambala: London.

via 1 Peter 5:7. When my mind wanders while praying, it wanders to something like a burden. I take these burdens captive, and escort them into the presence of God. Constant burden-casting increases inner silence.

Then, when my mind is quiet, still, and receptive, it is up to God. God knows how to communicate with those who truly seek him, especially when we turn down the volume of the cultural noise around us.

Jesus Prayed in the Lonely, Hushed Wilderness

"Jesus often withdrew to lonely places and prayed."[46] He did this "often." A lot. Jesus wanted to do this. He needed to do this. "As often as possible Jesus withdrew to out-of-the-way places for prayer."[47]

Jesus checked out of crowded places and lodged in the Lonely Place Motel. Because in a lonely place, a person hears better. It's easier to hear The Voice in solitary silence. For Jesus, the Judean wilderness was a prayer outpost, where voice competition shrank to zero.

"Jesus often withdrew to the wilderness for prayer."[48] I must do the same. I must follow Jesus into the wilderness and pray. And talk with God. Listen. It's easier to hear in the wilderness. In the desert, the odds of hearing just one voice increase.

In solitude and silence, before God, the atmosphere is electric. Thick. Weighty. Get ready to listen.

Praying in the Place of Least Distraction

When I pray, I go away from my home, office, or car. Instead of praying in these familiar places, I find the Place of Least Distraction. Yes, I can and should pray at home, and in my office. But these places call for my attention. They define me, to some extent. They praise and blame. They cover over who I really am, and who God intends me to be.

---

[46] Luke 5:16, NIV
[47] Luke 5:16, *The Message.*
[48] Luke 5:16, NLT

Praying in a familiar place is not solitary enough. It's different praying alone with God in the Place of Least Distraction. Solitude is the arena of our conversion. "In solitude we stop believing our own press. We discover that we are not as good as we thought but we are also more than we thought."[49]

Today I will pray in the Place of Least Distraction. This is the place of change, the place of conversion, the locale of breaking and re-making.

Silence Is Essential for Praying

It is snowing, softly and silently. Does a snowflake make a sound when it crash lands on the ground? How much silence is needed to hear snow fall? Today's silent snow produces silence in me. My heart is quiet before it. This is good. Because...

Without silence there is no hearing. Life without silence would be constant noise, without rest.

Silence is essential to music. Silence *is* music. There is a sound that silence has. At the end of Handel's "Messiah" we have that famous pregnant pause, a rest filled with anticipated glory. How long will the conductor hold us in that quiet place? The pause signals that something beautiful is about to be born. The pause turns the volume button of silence to a "10."

Silence is hope and expectation. Silence is longing for fulfillment. Silence is filled with meaning. Timely silence speaks for itself. Swiss philosopher Max Picard wrote that "silence contains everything within itself. It is not waiting for anything; it is always wholly present within itself and it completely fills out the space in which it appears."[50]

Silence speaks where words fail. Without silence there are no words. Heaven's half hour of absolute silence makes me want to speak something, or cry, or beg. Silence in heaven. You can't hear yourself breathing, you can't hear your heartbeat, there's no sound of bodies shifting, no tinnitus, the perfect recording studio where all sound is contained and packed away for the *kairos* time.

---

[49] Barton, *Strengthening the Soul of Your Leadership*, 51.
[50] Max Picard, *The World of Silence*, 18. Eighth Day, 2002.

...a time to be silent, and a time to speak...
Ecclesiastes 3:7

The Handels of our world live in the dialectic of presence and absence. The God of this world speaks a single word - "Shabat!"[51] The discerning shut their mouths.

He was oppressed and afflicted, yet he did not open his mouth;
he was led like a lamb to the slaughter,
and as a sheep before its shearers is silent,
so he did not open his mouth.
Isaiah 53:7

Jesus remained silent and gave no answer.
Mark 14:61

Silence is a healer. In silence, he heals us.

Praying in the Stillness

For years Linda wakes in the morning, goes downstairs to our living room, sits in a chair, and gets "still." This is her time of just being with God, agendaless.

Linda is an extrovert who loves being with people. She also loves being with the Person. Some amazing things have happened during these still times. She hears from God, and has even seen remarkable, relevant visions.

Stillness with God is valuable to Linda. But not to everyone. Our culture gets a failing grade on stillness. "The words, "Be still, and know that I am God," mean next to nothing to the self-confident, bustling worshipper in this middle period of the twentieth century."[52]

---

[51] Cease!
[52] A. W. Tozer, *The Knowledge of the Holy*, Kindle Locations 25-26. New York: HarperCollins, 1961.

Stillness is a condition of the mind and heart; i.e., a condition of one's inner being. Stillness allows us to attend to one voice, in this case, the voice of God.

"Be still"[53] means, literally, "cease struggling," or "stop striving." Take off your wrestling outfit. This concerns the mind and the heart. The cluttered, linking, tweeting mind wrestles with many things at once. Multiple thoughts vie for attention. The struggling mind is a "many-thinged" thing, double, and even multi, minded.

In the praying life it's either stillness or striving. The meeting place with God resides in the former. This is why I recommend taking longer prayer times. Take an hour of praying, if not regularly, at least on occasion. It takes time to detox and slip from agitation to quietude.

Our culture places little value on this. I have to intentionally carve out these still-spaces for myself.

Effective praying happens in stillness.

Praying "In the Spirit"

In Ephesians 6:18-20 we read about "praying in the Spirit." Note the little word "in." This is one of the apostle Paul's favorite words. In his letters, he uses "in Christ," and variations of "in Christ," around 180 times.[54]

The word 'in' is a container metaphor, indicating the metaphorically spatial location of the redeemed human heart. Just as I am now "in" my office sitting before my computer, so my spiritual location is that I am "in" Christ. This is about my status, and the new environment I am situated in.

To pray in the Spirit is to pray connected with the Spirit, because Jesus-followers are new creations in Christ. This is our ontological condition, rather than some method or technique of praying. It relates to what Jesus said in John fourteen and fifteen about abiding "in" him.

This is prayer as a conversation. This is prayer-as-relationship.

---

[53] In Psalm 46:10.
[54] Variations include "with" and "through."

These Pauline "in"-phrases refer to dwelling in the presence of the Holy Spirit, a presence characterized by the Godlike qualities of power, love, joy, truth, holiness, righteousness, and peace. To pray "in the Holy Spirit" is to pray with the conscious awareness of God's presence surrounding us, sanctifying both us and our prayers.[55]

You Are the Answer to Someone Else's Prayer

Often, while praying, my mind wanders to a person. God places this person on my heart, as a burden. I am the one God is going to use as his answer to that person's prayer.

A few weeks ago, X left his work space, and found a place where he could be alone, in his office building, and pray. X's spouse had a sexual affair with another man. She filed for divorce. X wanted to get help for their marriage. She refused.

That morning X received a phone call from his father. "Your mother has cancer. She's not expected to live much longer." X felt his knees buckle, his breathing difficult, the weight too much to bear. X had to get alone with the only One who could make a way where there seemed to be no way. X prayed, "God, help me..."

I was alone, in my backyard by the river, sitting in my prayer chair when, unknown to me, X made his appeal to God. I already knew about X's evil-assaulted marriage. As I was praying the thought came to me, "Call X now." I did. I believed this thought was coming from God, to me.

I have learned, over years of praying, listening, and risking, that God can come interruptively into my wandering mind. What could I lose from calling X to check in? This was a no-lose situation.

I called X. He answered, "I can't believe you called me right now! I couldn't stay in my work space and had to get alone with God. I was asking God for help. And then you called."

We agreed this was no coincidence. It was the orchestrating work of the Holy Spirit. I was God's answer for X, at the time.

---

[55] See especially Wayne Grudem, *Systematic Theology*, 381-382. Downers Grove: Intervarsity, 1994.

When you pray, listen for the voice of God. When an interruptive thought comes, check it out. You begin to discover that such things are often from God. This increases faith and expectation. You will be used by God to help others in their prayer-cries for mercy.

This is God saying, "I hear X's cry. I am going to answer X's prayer by placing the thought of X in John's mind."

A Self-Imposed Half Day of Silence

Wyatt T. Walker, who was Martin Luther King's Chief of Staff, says the heart and soul of King lay in his self-imposed "Day of Silence." On those days, King refrained from watching television, using the telephone, and listening to the radio. Instead, he spent the time praying, meditating, and hearing from God.[56]

We need times away from our activism to nurture an inner pacifism, from which creative juices and ideas flow. As Eugene Peterson has written, "All speech that moves men was minted when some man's mind was poised and still."[57]

For forty years I've had a self-imposed half-day of silence, on Tuesday afternoons, for three to six hours. This is a "work day," not my "day off." My work, the work of a pastor, the work of a Jesus-follower, is to discern what's up with God, and meet with God to discover what I am to do. Authentic Jesus-following means one's doing or busyness comes out of one's times of listening to God, in silence.

Just me and God. You and God.

If we believed such meetings and encounters were possible, we would cast everything aside, and run to that quiet place where God awaits us.

---

[56] In Lewis Baldwin, *Never to Leave Us Alone: The Prayer Life of Martin Luther King, Jr.,* vii.
[57] Peterson, *The Contemplative Pastor*, 30.

Praying: From Absurdity to Obedience

Many Christians are deaf to the voice of God. Reasons for God-deafness include:

- Unbelief that God still speaks to his people today
- Unawareness that God speaks to his followers
- Uninvolvement with God; no time for God

The Latin word *surdus* means "deaf." Our English word "absurd" comes from this. Many Jesus-followers live such cluttered lives that they have become deaf to the voice of God, "unable to hear when God calls us and unable to understand in which direction God calls us. Thus our lives have become absurd."[58]

When we learn to listen to God our lives transform from absurdity to obedience. The word "obedient" comes from the Latin word *audere*, which means "listening" (think "audio"). By engaging in the spiritual disciplines, God's Spirit transforms us from inattentiveness to attention. We become more like Jesus, whose life was, at root, obedient to the Father. Jesus was "all ears," consistently attentive to the Father's voice, alert for his directions.

True prayer is being all ears for God. This happens as we customarily retreat to lonely places to talk with God. In the God-relationship we learn to listen, and move from lives of absurdity to lives of obedience.

---

[58] Henri Nouwen, *The Only Necessary Thing: Living a Prayerful Life*, 82.

6

PRAYING AND DISCERNMENT

A disciple of Jesus follows after him. Jesus says, "Come." We respond by coming. This requires discern-ability.

Linda and I traveled from Monroe to somewhere near Columbus, Ohio, to attend a funeral. We had never been in that part of Ohio before. Our son Josh asked if we'd like to borrow his GPS. I had never used one before. My mantra was: Real Men Don't Need Direction.

I said, "OK, I'll try it." I typed in the destination and we took off. Every time the British female voice commanded me to "Turn right in 400 yards," I obeyed. The GPS took us straight to our destination. I wondered if it would even tell us where to park in the funeral home lot! I considered getting one myself and becoming a disciple.

Our trip back to Michigan was a different experience. I like to take new roads and see places I've never seen. Linda does, too. I pressed "alternate route," and off we went.

Now we were driving in a foreign land, being led by our all-seeing Global Positioning System. At one point the omni-visionary voice said, "In 400 yards, turn right."

I was familiar with this command. Yet, somehow, it did not feel right to me.

Full stop here. How could I know? I had never been in this place before. I chose to ignore the smart-sounding British voice, and went my own way.

The GPS tried to reorient me, saying, "Turn around in one mile." Then, "Turn around." Then, "Turn around, you fool!" (Not really...)

I turned the thing off. We got lost. Finally, with encouragement from Linda, I turned on The Voice with the Global Perspective, submitted to its wisdom, and we made our way back home.

Not many of you were wise by human standards; not many were influential; not many were of noble birth.[1] That describes me. Even if we are "wise by human standards," we still see very little. To navigate the way of life we must be able to discern the guiding voice of God.

There is a God Positioning System available to every sheep in the fold of Jesus. His eyes roam to and fro, over all the earth. If I trust in the divine GPS, and not in my myopic understanding, God will make straight my path.[2]

In this chapter I share some things I have learned about discernment, and how prayer plays a role in the process.

What Is Discernment?

As we are morphed into greater Christlikeness we grow in discernability. In Romans 12:1-2 the apostle Paul says we are to be transformed, by the renewing of our minds, so that we can discern what the will of God is; viz., that which is good, acceptable, and perfect. This is not only for solitary individuals, but also for community.

Three biblical Greek words are translated as "discern": *anakrino*, *diakrino*, and *dokimazo*. *Anakrino* can mean to examine, judge, estimate, determine, or scrutinize. The verb *krino* in *anakrino* and *diakrino* means to cut, or divide.

Diakrino means to distinguish, or to judge. A discerning person rightly divides the matter at hand, and sees which alternative is true; like, e.g., "Is this word from God, or not from God?" As Paul writes in Philippians 1:9-10, "this is my prayer: that your love may abound more and more in knowledge and depth of insight, so that you may be able

[1] 1 Corinthians 1:26
[2] Proverbs 3:5-6

101

to discern what is best and may be pure and blameless for the day of Christ."

Dokimazo is also translated "to discern," and can mean to test, to examine, to prove, to see whether or not something (like a metal) is genuine or not. Such as: "Is this the genuine voice of God, or not?"

Putting these three words together we arrive at a definition: "Discernment, in a most general sense, is the capacity to recognize and respond to the presence and the activity of God—both in the ordinary moments and in the larger decisions of our lives."[3]

Discernment is a fruit of an abiding prayer life. Those who slow-cook in the abiding, dwelling, Christ-relationship are the ones who discern God's voice. This is because the more familiar or intimate we are with someone, the more we are able to recognize their heart.

The more time spent in close dialogue, the more we recognize the voice. The less familiarity, the less discernment. *Spiritual discernment is an inner capacity to hear God that is in direct proportion to our intimacy with God.*

Discernment Increases as Intimacy Increases

Praying is, as Martin Luther King, Jr. said, a "conversation with God."[4] A conversation involves speaking and listening. As I listen for the voice of God, how do I know whether what I hear is from God or not? The answer to this is: *as intimacy with God increases, discernment increases.*

This principle applies to many things. For example, when Linda and I saw a movie recently, there was a scene that produced tears in her eyes. We have been married for many years, and I had an idea about where these tears were coming from. I'm not always right about this, but this time I was. My ability to understand Linda's heart is greater than

---

[3] Ruth Haley Barton, *Pursuing God's Will Together*, Kindle Locations 186-189. Downers Grove: Intervarsity, 2012.

[4] Lewis Baldwin's *Never to Leave Us Alone: The Prayer Life of Martin Luther King, Jr.* is all about King's ongoing prayer conversation with God.

when I first met her. Discernment grows as a consequence of long-term relational intimacy. *As familiarity increases, discernment increases.*

Conversely, when intimacy is low, discernment is low. The person who does not have an abiding Christ-life lacks recognition. The growing ability to know what God is saying in the prayer relationship comes from much conversational time with God. We gradually acquire an attentiveness to God's voice as we commit to spending time with him.

Spiritual discernment is in direct proportion to familiarity.

Discern Before Deciding

Old Testament scholar Ellen F. Davis shares how a deep praying life undergirds her academic work.[5] She writes of being guided by God in "a regimen of meditative prayer and spiritual counsel... I found myself simply trusting that process and following through in obedience. It was my first conscious experience of participating in such a process of shared, prayerful discernment."[6] Engagement in a discernment process convinced Davis that Western culture hyper-emphasizes the value of individual decision making. On our own, without God, we work to identify goals, evaluate options, weigh pros and cons, and then decide for ourselves. But there is another option; viz., to surrender to being guided by the Spirit, in prayer. This often requires finding someone who prays, and coming under their spiritual direction.

Submission to the movements of God's Spirit, and being guided by God and not the self, is crucial for staying on the path of life God intends. Human abilities are not enough. Discernment "always involved factors I could not possibly have foreseen and considered in my own decision-making process."[7]

---

[5] Ellen F. Davis, in John Byron and Joel Lohr, eds. *I (Still) Believe: Leading Bible Scholars Share Their Stories of Faith and Scholarship.* Grand Rapids: Zondervan, 2015.
[6] Op. cit., 44
[7] Ib., 45

The first order of business in the life of a Jesus-follower is to place oneself in God's presence. This must become habitual. This is where the God-process happens, and discernment comes.

Discerning should always come before deciding.

Dynamics of Spiritual Discernment as Consolation and Desolation

How do we discern that the voice we hear is God's and not merely our own, or that of our culture? I think it is a learned ability. We abandon ourselves to the movement of God's Spirit. It's like floating in a tube down a river, allowing the current to transport us wherever it will. Sometimes we hold tight as we shoot the rapids. Sometime we float, moved by the gentle flow. Both floating and rapid-shooting require submission. We do not control the speed or the direction. We trust that the river is taking us where it wants, at its pace.[8]

Discern-ability involves what the Bible calls "discernment of spirits."[9] 1 John 4:1 instructs us to "test the spirits to see if they are from God." St Ignatius believed the dynamics of spiritual discernment involve "consolation" and "desolation." Consolation is the sense that this is good, this is right, and God is present in this. Desolation is the loss of sense of God's presence, that something is not right about this. A sense of consolation can be an indicator that this is from God; a sense of desolation can indicate that this is not from God.[10]

This is so helpful to me! I have found that these senses regularly accompany times of discernment. When I sense a "peace that passes understanding,"[11] it can be a sign that God is leading me. When I feel barren or empty I judge this as not from God.

---

[8] This analogy is from Ruth Haley Barton, *Pursuing God's Will Together*.

[9] 1 Corinthians 12:10

[10] I owe this insight to Barton, Ib.

[11] Philippians 4:7

Recognizing God's Voice Comes by Experience

I know the sound of Linda's voice, immediately. This is to be expected after 43 years of marriage, plus an additional year of courtship. But had she called me 44 years ago, when I did not know her, I would ask, "Who is this?"

I know my wife's voice by experience. Countless hours of communicating have attuned my heart to hers. I can distinguish her voice from the many other voices I hear throughout the day. This is how voice recognition happens, and how we come to hear the voice of God; viz., by experience, and lots of it.

Sheep, and other domesticated animals and pets, recognize, without fail, their master's voice. When they first heard that voice they did not know who was speaking. But they learn quickly. Jesus said:

> The shepherd of the sheep . . . calls his own sheep by name and leads them out. He goes ahead of them, and the sheep follow him because they know his voice. ... I am the good shepherd. I know my own and my own know me... My sheep hear my voice. I know them, and they follow me.[12]

The more time I spend with someone, the more I recognize the sound of their voice. I also become familiar with the heart behind the sound of the voice. This comes by personal experience, and much of it. You cannot get this out of a book. Second-hand experience will not do. The testimony of someone else cannot take the place of first hand, personal, experiential knowledge.

Someone who does not have time to pray should not expect to recognize the voice of God, any more than spouses who have drifted apart could be familiar with each other's hearts. *Only familiarity breeds discernment.*

Familiarity, in the sense of recognition and understanding, is directly proportionate to the amount of time spent together, and spent

---

[12] John 10:2-4; 14; 17

in a certain way. That's how it is with people. It is the same with God. We come to recognize God's voice by personal experience.

Three Steps to Discernment

If I want to know what Linda is thinking I have to spend time with her, and spend it in a certain way. We have to communicate with each other. We have to share what is on our minds, and we have to listen. Without this there will be no mutual understanding; hence, no discernment.

The same applies to the God-relationship. "To want to know God's plan and purpose without regular prayer and engagement with scripture and God's people is like trying to bake a cake without assembling the various ingredients. Discernment grows out of the life of faith rooted in community."[13]

What does God want to say to us? To know this:

1. Pray regularly.
2. Saturate in Scripture.
3. Engage in community with people who do 1 and 2.

Three Factors for Discerning the Voice of God

I hear my beloved's voice, and she hears mine. We have "ears to hear" each other. We have spent countless hours together, over four decades of pre-marriage and marriage. While only God knows my heart perfectly, Linda comes in second place.

To "hear" someone is more than being within audible range of their voice. Jesus said that those who have ears, hear. He distinguished between mere physical hearing and true listening accompanied by understanding.

Today I expect to hear God speak to me. Hearing God is normal for a Jesus-follower. I am one of Jesus' "sheep," therefore I hear his voice.

---

[13] Nouwen, *Discernment: Reading the Signs of Daily Life*, Kindle Location 15%. New York: HarperOne, 2013.

But how? How do we come to discern the living voice of God? The answer is: by much time spent in God's presence.

When it comes to hearing God there is no substitute for this. Be in relationship with God. Become acquainted with him. Then you will discover that certain factors signal the voice of God, just as one human voice can be distinguished from another." They are:[14]

1. *The quality of the voice of God*

This is about the impact or weight a thought makes on us. This is a "sounds like God to me" experience, based on much time spent in God's presence. Spending time with God, day after day, month after month, year after year, brings an increase in the ability to discern the quality of God's voice. There is a sense of authority, a weightiness, in the voice of God, that is qualitatively different from human voices.

For this reason (and others), I send my seminary students out to pray, an hour a day, day after day. As they do this, the voice of God becomes more recognizable to them.

2. *The spirit of the voice of God*

This spirit brings peace, confidence, and joy. It is wise and reasonable. It is good. It is, briefly, the same spirit that accompanied Jesus.

God's voice has a James 3:17 spirit: "the wisdom that comes from heaven is first of all pure; then peace-loving, considerate, submissive, full of mercy and good fruit, impartial and sincere."

God's voice is experienced as consolation, affirmation (love), and helpfulness. It edifies, rather than tears down.

3. *The content of the voice of God*

God's voice syncs with the biblical picture of his nature and kingdom. God will never lead contrary to what he has said or done in the past. Therefore, I must understand the activity and voice of God in

---

[14] From Dallas Willard, cited in Foster, op. cit. Kindle locations 554 ff.

the past to be able to better hear it in the present. This means keeping Scripture ever before me, reading and meditating on it during my alone times with God in prayer.

Praying as Being Led and Traveling Without a Map

Jesus never wore a "WWID" bracelet ("What Would I Do?"). As he hung dying on a cross, he didn't look to a little yellow band around his wrist, reminding him to love and forgive his enemies because that's what he would do.

When Jesus said, "Father, forgive them, for they don't know what they do," it came from his heart, from his very being. That is *who he was. Who* a person really is emerges, without striving, from within themselves, like a tree inexorably produces leaves. Jesus' heart was forgiveness shaped. His doing came from his being.

Jesus' enemies did not know what they were doing.[15] By extension, this includes me. I, who now follow Jesus and have been reconciled to God through the death of his Son, was once his enemy. Jesus, on the cross, defines "enemy" as: one who does not know what they are doing. I am the one who needs the "WWJD" bracelet, not Jesus. *But not forever.*

As one of the Reconciled and Redeemed, I am being morphed into Christlikeness.[16] As the transformation happens, I begin leaving the WWJD bracelet at home. Gaining the heart and mind of Christ means I need less reminding. I don't need to be re-minded, because I am acquiring a new mind. In Christ, I am being minded.

At this point we are traveling without a map. That same Spirit that raised Christ from the dead resides in us. The inner "GPS" ("God Positioning System") is within, and God's heart and mind become more my own.

---

[15] See Luke 23:34
[16] Galatians 4:19

7

PRAYING FOR MYSELF

I have met Jesus-followers who shy away from praying for their own selves. Perhaps they see it as too self-centered. Maybe they think their personal requests are trivial in light of the greater suffering they see around them. My counsel to them is: Go to Home Depot, buy a ladder, and get over it. Please pray for your own self!

In praying, I bring personal needs, hopes, and desires, to God. God is a giving God, one who loves to give good things to people whose lives are situated within his kingdom and filled with his Spirit.

I'm not imposing on God by asking. God is a Big Being who is not put off when his kids interrupt him. As Paul wrote to the Philippians, we are to "rejoice in the Lord always... Do not be anxious about anything, but in everything, by prayer and petition with thanksgiving, *present your requests to God.*[1]

Asking isn't just for kids. It's not some low, beggarly form of praying. "The mature spiritual person never outgrows the need to bring requests to God."[2] The more we mature, the more we ask.

My journals are filled with personal prayer requests. The Psalms are, too. As the Psalms make up the longest book in the Bible chapter-wise (150 chapters), this chapter is the longest in my book. This is because I need so much changing.

[1] Philippians 4:4-6
[2] Stanley Grenz, *Prayer: The Cry for the Kingdom*, 25

Some students in the Film Department at the University of Michigan interviewed me as part of a movie they were making on Southeast Michigan. They came to my office, and set up their equipment. They asked me one question: "As a pastor in this area, what is the one thing you see that most needs changing?"

My answer was: "Me."

I am simultaneously most aware and most unaware of my own self, and my own self needs more transformation. This is crucial, since if I don't keeping changing my marriage and family will not be what it could be, my church will not be as healthy and influential as God desires it to be, and my community will fall short of God's healing aspirations for it.

My change is important, because it is not just for me. Many others are involved.

This chapter is my personal Book of Psalms, containing how I have prayed for my own spiritual and physical being, and some conclusions I have drawn.

Praying for Change

I regularly address God for the sake of me. I need constant help and perpetual change. I have not yet made Christlikeness my own. One way I press on towards this upward calling is by petitioning God.

"Pressing on" mode begins with praying. The act of praying declares "Game on!"

I pray through this list.

Transform me into greater Christlikeness.
Assist me in the doing of your will.
Change my heart, O God.
Reduce the "me" in me.
Have your way in me.
Be gracious unto me.
Do not forsake me.
Be glorified, in me.
Orchestrate me.

Increase in me.
Decrease me.
Empower me.
Create in me.
Sanctify me.
Move in me.
Restore me.
Sustain me.
Deliver me.
Renew me.
Guide me.
Direct me.
Fill me.

In Praying, I Get Changed

When the first church prayed in the upper room in Jerusalem, "the place where they were meeting was shaken. And they were all filled with the Holy Spirit and spoke the word of God boldly."[3] One result of their praying is that God changed them. "Petitioning God on our own behalf can bring about psychological change. Fear can be changed to boldness."[4] In praying, I get changed. We see this in Ps. 118:5: "When hard pressed, I cried to the LORD; he brought me into a spacious place."

In the next verse, the praying psalmsinger experiences a new boldness that comes in response to his prayer:

> The LORD is with me; I will not be afraid.
> What can mere mortals do to me?
> The LORD is with me; he is my helper.

---

[3] Acts 4:31

[4] Stanley Grenz, *Prayer: The Cry for the Kingdom*. Note: The best book on the psychology of praying is Bernard Spilka and Kevin Ladd, *The Psychology of Prayer: A Scientific Approach*.

In praying, God changes fear into boldness, and anxiety into peace. We see this in Philippians 4:6-7:

> Do not be anxious about anything, but in every situation, by prayer and petition, with thanksgiving, present your requests to God. And the peace of God, which transcends all understanding, will guard your hearts and your minds in Christ Jesus.

God's power accompanies my praying, and I get shaped. My fearful heart gains faith. My anxious heart is calmed. The hopeless heart is strengthened. The path is made straight, the promised future is beheld, the weary head is lifted, blind eyes see again.

Praying and Being Examined by the Great Cardiologist

While I was sitting on that rusty tractor years ago, my Bible was open to Psalm 139. On that day I read - as if for the first time – verses 23-24: "Search me, O God, and know my heart; test me and know my thoughts. See if there is any wicked way in me, and lead me in the way everlasting." I remember saying, "OK, God. Do it. *Examine me.*"

I meant it. I wanted to be searched-out by God. God told me, "John, I would like to do this. You're going to need to learn heart-stillness." Every patient undergoing surgery needs to be still.

This began a several-month period of being searched-out by God. I underwent a spiritual EKG, conducted by the Great Cardiologist. It was hard and good, death and life. It was never condemning, and often exhilarating. My diseased heart was being healed, and given new life.

In praying I am searched-out by God, as I allow him access to my soul. "Without apology and without defense we ask to see what is truly in us. It is for our own sake that we ask these things. It is for our good, for our healing, for our happiness."[5]

---

[5] Richard Foster, *Prayer: Finding the Heart's True Home, 10th Anniversary Edition*, 29. New York: HarperCollins, 2009.

Praying for My Ego to Be Defeated

While reviewing notes for my spiritual formation classes I found this prayer from A.W. Tozer I had copied years ago. It still expresses a desire of my heart. Tozer wrote:

> O Christ, make me strong to overcome the desire to be wise and to be reputed wise by others as ignorant as myself. I turn from my wisdom as well as from my folly and flee to You, the wisdom of God and the power of God.
> Amen.[6]

I wrote this prayer on a card, and carried it with me, praying for my ego to be defeated, and God's reign to win me over.

Realize Your Own Faults

I had only been at Redeemer for six months when a man came to me after our Sunday morning gathering. He was crying as he wrapped his arms around me. Through his tears he told me, "I don't care what others are saying about you. I think you are a great pastor." I embraced him, with eyes wide open. Not feeling comforted, I said "Thank you."

The truth was, I had faults that needed addressing. I thought of Charles Spurgeon, who advised finding a friend who will speak straight to you and tell you your faults. Such a friend would be a blessing to a wise person.[7]

There is a time and a place for fault recognition. It may come directly from God, mediated through the Scriptures by the Spirit. It might come from a friend who knows and loves you. It might come from an enemy. Sooner or later, God will address your faults. You have them. The question is: Are you correctable?

---

[6] A. W. Tozer, *The Knowledge of the Holy*, New York: HarperOne.

[7] See *Sermons of the Reverend C.H. Spurgeon, Volume 3*, New York: Sheldon, Blake & Co., 1858. Page 16.

God uses people who come to grips with their own faults. God will not continue to use people who do not have periodic "Search me, O God," moments. When we are searched-out we should say, "Thank you, God, for revealing this to me."

Twenty years ago the great South African leader Justus DuPlessis spoke at our church. I found him to be a combination of gentleness and power. I attribute what God was able to do through Justus to his humility and teachability. He was 70 years old at the time, and stayed at our house.

Justus was the representative from the World Pentecostal Church to the Roman Catholic Church. He had met with the Pope several times. We were finishing dinner when I asked him, "What is it like to meet with the Pope?" He pulled a picture out of his wallet. There was Justus, standing beside the Pope. I thought of returning the favor by showing Justus some pictures of me on vacation. I don't think so!

Justus said, "I want to meet personally with you and show you something." The next day we were in my office. Justus pulled out a 300-page doctoral dissertation, written by a South African Christian leader. It was on the gift of tongues, and other biblical, charismatic phenomena. Justus had just spoken at Kenneth Copeland's church, and Copeland had extra copies made so Justus could give me one. "I want you to review this and tell me what you think. I believe God could greatly use this work to help pastors. Please let me know what you think about this tomorrow."

I took the dissertation home, and began to read. It was good work, but I knew that pastors would never understand it. It was technical and academic, filled with dessertationisms. I had to tell Justus what I really thought. How would he receive it?

The next day we met again in my office. I told him, "Pastors will not be helped by this book in its present form."

I will never forget what happened next. He said, "Let's go into the sanctuary and pray." Once in the sanctuary, standing by the communion table, he said, "John, let's kneel." Then Justus prayed.

I did not know what to expect. He prayed, "O God, thank you for sending me to a man like John, who would tell me the truth, and point out my error." Justus asked God for forgiveness, thanked God for his great mercy and grace, and thanked God for me.

As for me and my soul, I felt overwhelmed by the presence of God. I was not thinking about how great I was in doing this. My heart was captured by the man kneeling next to me, someone far wiser and more experienced than I.

I conclude:

Be teachable.

Realize your faults.

Confess them before God.

Thank God for the rescue.

Pray, "Search me, O God, and know my heart; test me and know my anxious thoughts. See if there is any offensive way in me, and lead me in the way everlasting."[8]

Praying to Be Released from Perpetual Ingratitude

It's hard to be thankful when you are wanting, unless you are in constant want. Poor people can be amazingly grateful. But in middle class America we are constantly alerted to how little we have, even though we have. Marketing serves to create need in us, and need indicates barrenness, since what you don't need you don't lack. This is why Linda and I mute commercials when watching TV. There is nothing in them that we need.

Thankfulness concerns something you have, not something you lack and therefore need. Deprivation mutes gratitude. Columbia University professor of religion and culture Mark Taylor writes: "We have been conned... by an economic system that creates endless desire where there is no need."[9] This is the prison house of perpetual ingratitude.

The vast, rolling, verdant pasture of gratefulness is the land of "I shall not be in want." I cultivate this by intentional abiding in Christ,

---

[8] Psalm 139:23-24

[9] Mark Taylor, "Speed Kills." The Chronicle of Higher Education. October 20, 2014. http://chronicle.com/article/Speed-Kills/149401/?cid=cr&utm_source=cr&utm_medium=en

and harvest the many fruits of a thankful heart. I find myself perpetually saying, "Thank you again, God!"

Praying Can Bring Psychological Change

When praying, I ask God to come in love and power, upon me. This has resulted in a number of changes in my psyche (soul).

In the act of praying, I have sensed fear changing to confidence and boldness. Do I, at times, feel afraid? Of course! The person who never feels fear is brain dead. "The psalmist reported experiencing this kind of psychological or emotional transformation."[10] For example:

> "In my anguish I cried to the LORD, and
> he answered by setting me free."[11]

The psalmist then expresses a new boldness that came in response to prayer:

> "The LORD is with me; I will not be afraid.
> What can man do to me?"[12]

In praying, anxiety transforms into peace. We are promised this in Philippians 4:6-7:

> Do not be anxious about anything, but in everything, by prayer and petition, with thanksgiving, present your requests to God. And the peace of God, which transcends all understanding, will guard your hearts and your minds in Christ Jesus.

---

[10] Stanley Grenz, *Prayer: The Cry for the Kingdom*, Kindle Locations 468-470. See also Psalm 138:3.

[11] Psalm 118:5

[12] Psalm 118:6

When I go alone to pray, I commonly come away less fearful, less anxious, more confident, and peace-filled. I have experienced this so often that I have come to expect it.

Henri Nouwen discovered the same, in his proof that prayer works.[13] Nouwen said that when he didn't pray, or got "too busy to pray," he found himself more fearful and more agitated. His proof was that praying calms the agitated soul. The power of the threatening situation dissipates, and I experience peace.

Meditative Praying Converts My Entire Self to God

When I was a youth pastor in the 1970s, at First Baptist Church of Joliet, Illinois, we had a big kid named Dan who boasted, "I can put an entire Big Mac in my mouth and swallow it whole." We said "No way!!!" So we drove to McDonald's, and bought a Big Mac for Dan.

Was this an idle boast because he wanted a free meal? Dan - who was a football player at Joliet Central High School - inserted the Big Mac into his mouth. That was the last we saw of it. I am certain Dan saw more of it later than he wanted. He was proof that, if you don't take small bites and chew your food well, it will not get assimilated to your physical body.

The Psalmist wrote, "Lord I love your law. I meditate on it day and night."[14] Meditation is a slow-cooker, not a microwave. It is a cow chewing its cud, not a teen inhaling a burger. Meditation on God-thoughts allows the Spirit to assimilate them to your spirit, and even to your physical body.[15]

Meditative praying converts our entire self to God, spirit and body, just as meditative eating converts food to energy. Meditative praying simmers the human spirit in the sauces and spices of the mind of Christ.

---

[13] Found in Nouwen's *Gracias! A Latin American Journal*.

[14] Psalm 119:97

[15] On the biblical nature of embodied spirituality see, e.g., Dallas Willard, *The Spirit of the Disciplines*, especially the chapters "Spiritual Life: The Body's Fulfillment," and "St. Paul's Psychology of Redemption – The Example."

Choose this day the object of your mediation, for such shall be your heart's conversion.

Praying "Save Me from Myself"

A friend asked me, "When you pray, do you pray "Save me from my circumstances?" or "Save me from myself?"" My answer was: both. But the greater percentage of my prayers are, "Save me from myself." For two reasons.

1. To be rescued from myself means many of my negative circumstances will change, since I am often the cause of my circumstances. A messed-up self creates messed-up circumstances. And note: one's changing circumstances, be they good or bad, will not change any unhealed parts of my heart.

2. God's rescue of me includes the fruit of the Spirit - things like love, peace, patience, kindness, goodness, and self-control. And faith, and hope. These things are non-circumstantial. I am promised, e.g., a peace that is non-circumstantial, thereby surpassing all human understanding. When I get Spirit-rescued this way, I live uncontrolled by life's circumstances.

I pray about circumstances. I mostly pray for God to rescue me from my own self, so that I will flourish in my circumstances.

Praying & Love

My number one prayer request for several years has been: God, produce your love in me. I want to love as Jesus loves. This will be good for others. It will also help me. As I learn to love like Christ, I will be free from what others think of me or do to me, and I will be released from fear and anxiety.

Freedom! Only a free person can do what Jesus did. There he is, dying on a cross, tortured physically, emotionally, and spiritually. Yet he loves his persecutors. He is dying *for them*! Jesus has a 0% victimization attitude. Only a free person can do this.

Fear. 1 John tells us that "perfect love casts out fear; there is no fear in love."[16] The more fear, the less love; the more love, the less fear. Fear and love do not go together. The more Christ's love becomes my heart, the less fearful and anxious I am.

I have a strategy. It reasons as follows.

1. I cannot will myself into this perfect love.[17]
2. God is able to produce such love in me.
3. So, I will submit to God, as my Shepherd.

Allow yourself to be shepherded by God and you will, more and more, "fear no evil." Why? Because, "you are with me." Here I have a choice, and a responsibility. I can choose this day whom I will follow and serve. I choose God's presence, as it is my only hope for deep change.

God brings me back, again and again, to the centrality of love. "What matters is to love, to be in one place in silence, if necessary in suffering, sickness, tribulation, and not try to be anybody outwardly. Not try to have a public identity."[18]

I am asking God for a greater heart of love. I am abandoning myself to him, who is my only hope.

Praying for Love for My Enemies

My prayer today is that God would form a Christlike love in my heart that loves my enemies. I ask, because I do not have. Jesus had it. I want what he had. I want his heart to be formed in me.[19] In praying this, I am asking for *the greatest thing.*

---

[16] 1 John 4:18

[17] No "will worship," as Richard Foster would say.

[18] Thomas Merton, *Learning to Love: Exploring Solitude and Freedom (The Journals of Thomas Merton)*, 15. New York: HarperCollins, 2010.

[19] Galatians 4:19

If it happens, it will be supernatural. I'm good with this, because I believe in supernatural healings. I have seen them. God can heal my heart and form his love in me.

Transformation of a loveless spirit into "no greater love" is superior to physical healing. Love will endure for eternity. Love is heaven's *modus operandi,* its *raison d-etre.* As wonderful as healings are, they are a subset of a greater, all-encompassing reality that is the love of God. I need a love healing. Love always comes first. It is possible to heal a person without loving them; it is not possible to love them and not desire their soul and body to be well. I can desire my enemies to be healed and flourish in life. This means praying for my enemies requires forgiving them. True love forgives. Loving forgiveness cancels indebtedness. Inability to forgive indicates the absence of love.

I'm thinking of Jerry Sittser's excruciating and hopeful *A Grace Disguised.*[20] Sittser's car containing himself, his mother-in-law, his wife and daughter, was hit by a drunk driver. Only Sittser survived. The drunk driver was acquitted by a clever lawyer. Sittser writes of the agony of this injustice piled on the loss of his loved ones.

> During the months that followed the trial I thought often about the driver of the other car. I fantasized reading reports in the newspaper that he had died hideously or that he had committed a crime that put him behind bars for life. I wanted to see him suffer and pay for the wrong I believed he had done...
>
> It eventually occurred to me that this preoccupation was poisoning me. It signaled that I wanted more than justice. I wanted *revenge.* I was beginning to harbor hatred in my heart. I was edging toward becoming an unforgiving person and using what appeared to be the failure of the judicial system to justify my unforgiveness. I wanted to punish the wrongdoer and get even. The

---

[20] The best book on going through grief ever written?

very thought of forgiveness seemed abhorrent to me. I realized at that moment that I have to forgive. If not, I would be consumed by my own unforgiveness.[21]

The options are: 1) I will either be consumed by the love of God that forgives; or, 2) I will languish in the poison of my unforgiveness. The first is freedom, the second is imprisonment.

God, produce in me the love you have for all people, even those who hate me, speak against me, and work for my undoing![22]

Praying for God-love to Totalize Me

Jesus tells me to love my enemies. I understand this. My problem is that my heart has not caught up with my mind. I'm asking God to fully bring the beautiful "love your enemies" command into my entire being. How important is this?

In God's kingdom, everything rises and falls on love. The mark of the Christian,[23] and the sign that God reigns in their life, is that they love one another, love their enemies and die for them, and do good to those who don't love them.

I am to love all people. No exceptions allowed. God's love does not discriminate between friends and enemies. Greg Boyd explains this.

> Notice that there are no exception clauses found anywhere in the New Testament's teaching about loving and doing good to enemies. Indeed, Jesus' emphasis on the indiscriminate nature of love rules out any possible exceptions. The sun doesn't decide on whom it will and

---

[21] Jerry Sitttser, *A Grace Disguised*, 135. Grand Rapids: Zondervan, 2009.

[22] How much do you want this? How radical does this get? Amy Laura Hall and Kara Slade present love for one's enemies as the answer to the question: "What would you do if someone was raping your wife?" The Jesus-answer is: you would love them, just as you love your wife. That's how wide and deep and high and long the love of Christ is. (In *A Faith Not Worth Fighting For: Addressing Commonly Asked Questions About Christian Nonviolence*. Ch. 3. Eugene, Oregon: Cascade, 2012.)

[23] I remember reading Francis Schaeffer's *The Mark of the Christian* in the 1970s.

will not shine. The rain doesn't decide on whom it will and will not fall. So too, Kingdom people are forbidden to decide who will and will not receive the love and good deeds we're commanded to give.[24]

God is love. Jesus had compassion on people, seeing them as sheep without a shepherd. Jesus died for his enemies, including *moi*. I am praying for this love to totalize me.

Praying and the Weakness That Is Still Unliberated

More and more, I see the depth of Christ's love, and my need for a greater baptism of it. Jesus loved his oppressors. He didn't need reminders to love, because his heart was love-shaped.

I am a rookie when it comes to praying for enemies. God has given me a simple strategy to learn enemy-love. I have decided to immediately pray for them whenever they come to mind. I pray to see any part I have in their animosity, because on some occasions "I" am the problem. And, if they were true Jesus-followers, they would love me, in spite of me. This sounds so idealistic! I rarely meet such love, both in others and in me.

Recently I was praying for some "enemy" when God told me, "John, I love them as much as I love you." This stuns me. I know, theologically, this is true. I know it in my head. I want to experience it in my heart.

My obligation is to hate no one, to condemn no one, to reject no one. I owe it to people to love them. I am not to be impatient with the faults of others. Nor to rage at people and condemn them to hell. "How true that the impatience that fumes at others and damns them (especially whole classes, races, nations) is a sign of the weakness that is still unliberated, still not tracked by the Blood of Christ, and is still a stranger to the Cross."[25]

It takes a liberated person to love like Jesus loved. The freer I am, the wider, deeper, higher, and longer is my love. If it has flesh and blood it

---

[24] Greg Boyd, *The Myth of a Christian Religion*, 99-100. Grand Rapids: Zondervan, 2009.
[25] Thomas Merton, *A Year with Thomas Merton*, Kindle Locations 3870-3873.

is not my enemy. The real battle lies elsewhere. God's love extends over all humanity. This is crazy love, right?

Because there is now no condemnation for those who are in Christ Jesus, I am not to condemn another Jesus-follower. In condemning them I become an instrument of unrighteousness, wielded by the fingers of darkness. This is, understatedly, serious.

I am to hate sin and love people. Like Jesus did, who most completely exemplified this when he died for me while I was his enemy. Note: I was his enemy, not he, mine.

Recently, while teaching at Payne Seminary, my students and I spent four days meditating on Psalm 23. Verse 5 reads: "You prepare a table before me in the presence of my enemies. You anoint my head with oil. My cup overflows." One of my students received a God-insight I never thought of before. God told him that, not only is the "prepared table" visible to my enemies, but so is being anointed with oil and the overflowing cup. I took this thought and related it to my cry for a greater love. Through me, the chalice filled with God's unending love overflows onto my enemies.

I am praying, "God, let your love so shape and fill my heart that it overflows even to my enemies." I desire release from the chains of hatred. For any weakness in me to be liberated.

Praying for God's Perfect Love to Be Manifested

I am in a calm so great
that I fear nothing.
What could I fear?
I am with Him.
- Brother Lawrence[26]

One of my favorite relationship verses in Scripture is 1 John 4:18: "There is no fear in love. But perfect love drives out fear, because fear has to do with punishment. The one who fears is not made perfect in

---

[26] Brother Lawrence, *The Practice of the Presence of God*. New Kensington, PA: Whitaker House, 1982.

love." The logic goes like this. The more fear, the less love; the less fear, the more love. Psalm 23 is about this. We read: "I will fear no evil, for you are with me." As I know God is with me, fear flees. My fear is in inverse proportion to my knowledge of God's presence.

Brother Lawrence reasons this way:

1. God is perfect love.
2. Where God's love is, there is no fear.
3. God is with me, and I am with God.
4. Therefore, "I am in a calm so great that I fear nothing."

This is not theory, but experience. Because I have embraced Christ, I am "in Christ." I experience his presence, and the reality of his resources. I access this by praying, "God, let these truths become my experience, now." Let these truths descend from my mind into my heart.

I am praying for the perfect love of God that indwells me to be manifested in me.

Praying for Love to Fill the Hidden Harbors of My Heart

John Ortberg, in his memorial tribute to Dallas Willard,[27] shares that Willard struggled with love. Ortberg writes: "I remember hearing him talk once about his struggle with harboring contempt for people. If he did, it was in a very deep harbor. But God alone knows the human heart."

I feel better. If Dallas struggled with love, I am in good company. He was praying for Jesus-love to overwhelm his contempt. I am, too. How important is this? It is God's greatest hope for us. "God's deepest desire is not that we would help the poor; God's deepest desire is that we would love the poor; for if we love them, we will surely help them."[28]

---

[27] http://www.christianitytoday.com/ct/2013/may-web-only/man-from-another-time-zone.html?start=1

[28] Richard Stearns, *Unfinished: Filling the Hole In Our Gospel*, 76. Nashville: Thomas Nelson, 2013.

See what love does? Or, see *that* love does. Love produces actions. God so loved the world, that he acted. Jesus loved people. Out of his love, he did things. "Everything Jesus did was an expression of his love for the Father and his love for people. He embodied love as no one else ever has."[29]

True love *does*. If I love, I will act. I am praying for this kind of love to fill the hidden harbors of my heart.

Praying for a Love that Is Not Jealous

One of the best books I have read on Jesus-like love is Lewis Smedes' extended meditation on 1 Corinthians 13:4-7.[30] In it Smedes says that love, among other things, is not jealous. Wow. I get jealous. Which means, if Smedes is right as well as the apostle Paul, then I am not loving.

This makes total sense to me. It goes like this, using *modus tollens*:[31]

1. If love, then not jealousy.
2. Jealousy, in me.
3. Thus, not love.

The reason *agape*[32] is not jealous is because "it is the power to move us toward another person with no expectation of reward - not even the reward of exclusive loving. That is why agape is not jealous."[33]

Jealousy is not the same as envy. Envy is the wish that I had something that belongs to someone else. Envy does not have pain associated with it. "The people we envy are not a threat to us; they only

---

[29] Ib.

[30] Lewis Smedes, *Love Within Limits: Realizing Selfless Love In a Selfish World*. Grand Rapids: Eerdmans, 1989.

[31] *Modus Tollens* is the name for one of the rules of inference in logic. It means, to deny the consequent of a conditional statement. *If p, then q. Not-q. Therefore, not-p.*

[32] *Agape* – the biblical Greek word for 'love' used in 1 Corinthians 13.

[33] Smedes, op. cit., 23.

happen to have what we would like to have." But jealousy "is aimed at someone who threatens us, threatens to take away someone we love."[34]

It's not just persons I can be jealous of. I can be jealous of things. I have met wives whose husbands spend more time fishing, than with them. These wives become jealous of fish, who at least get to be held by their husbands as they die.

This is why pornography ruins marriages. The wife wants her husband's eyes looking at her, not at other women. And, of course, the shoe can be on the other foot. A husband can be jealous of his wife's friends, or her family, or her job, or even their children if she spends more time with them than with him.

Jealousy and envy are different feelings. The first brings pain, the second does not. "Jealousy is the pain we feel when our role, our position, is threatened by someone close to us. Envy can stimulate us to try harder. Jealousy stimulates us only to resentment of the person who does better."[35]

I remember a time at Linda's home, before we were married. I was falling in love with her. We were with her family when someone knocked on the door. It was one of Linda's old boyfriends! She stepped outside and talked with him. Jealousy seeped into the crooked spaces of my soul. I looked on a table next to me and saw a little booklet entitled, "How to Win Over Jealousy." God has a sense of humor, right? Following in the steps of St. Augustine, I picked it up and read.[36]

When her old boyfriend left, I asked Linda, "What did he want?"

"I told him you and I were dating. He said 'OK,' but asked me to go out anyway."

When I heard that, I lit up! A fire, not to be mistaken for the fire of God, burned in my spirit. I couldn't believe he would ask her out, knowing she and I were in a relationship! Didn't I trust Linda? This event showed me I still had a lot of garbage inside that needed healing.

---

[34] Ib., 24

[35] Ib., 25

[36] God said, *"Tolle lege."*

"Agape love transcends jealousy without destroying it."[37] This means the more possessive and controlling I am, the more a normal, protective jealousy will turn cancerous. *I must pray for release from controlling others.*

> If we have nothing else in the world to live for but our lover, we are vulnerable to the worst fits of jealousy. The person who tells someone "I *can't* live without you" is threatened at his deepest selfhood when the one with whom he cannot live has to be shared in the *smallest* way. Such a person always suspects the worst, and this very suspicion prods him to cruel reactions... Agape does not let us give our souls to idols, even to the idol of the ideal husband or wife or friend... So agape will not let us be so deeply threatened that our very existence seems at stake.[38]

Linda and I have always told others that, if you marry, marry someone that can live without you, and you without them. The only one we cannot live without is Christ. Agape love is the power to admit that you cannot meet all the needs of your loved one, or friend, and are thankful that someone else can add what you lack.

Jealousy is painful, but with God it can be transcended. Agape love can block jealousy from erecting walls of self-protection against the sharing of love with others, even your most loved ones.

Agape love is, among other things, the power of sharing. Only the non-jealous can share. I am praying for a heart filled to overflowing with a Jesus-like love that is not jealous.

Praying for Courage to Love

What our diseased world needs now is love. I am praying for love to capture my imprisoned heart. Thomas Merton writes: "Now I see more

---

[37] Ib.

[38] Ib., 28-29

and more that there is only one realistic answer: Love. I have got to dare to love, and to bear the anxiety of self-questioning that love arouses in me, until "perfect love casts out fear.""[39]

How do I "dare to love?" I think it means abiding in Christ and, in the intimacy of this, trusting God to produce his love in me. As this happens, I will acquire love's attributes. I will…

- become patient
- become kind
- not envy
- not boast
- not be prideful
- not dishonor others
- not be self-seeking
- not be easily angered
- keep no record of wrongs
- not delight in evil
- rejoice with the truth
- always protect
- always trust
- always hope
- always persevere
- never fail

I will sacrifice for others. Jesus said, "anyone who loves their life will lose it."[40] And, "Greater love has no one than this: to lay down one's life for one's friends."[41]

My love domain will expand. Jesus said, "Love your enemies and pray for those who persecute you."[42] In this way love is power. With

---

[39] Merton, *Learning to Love: Exploring Solitude and Freedom* (The Journals of Thomas Merton), New York: Harper Collins, Kindle Locations 857-858, April 25, 1966.
[40] John 12:25
[41] John 15:13
[42] Matthew 5:44

love things come together; with war things fall apart. Christ's love, in me, will be reconciling and restoring.

This world needs love. I need love. The only answer is God. Love's primal, aboriginal, simultaneously source and subject, is God. Jesus said, "'Love the Lord your God with all your heart and with all your soul and with all your strength and with all your mind'; and, 'Love your neighbor as yourself.'"[43] Love is defined by the being of God. God *is* love, in essence.

The world fails to find love without God. Love makes no rational sense without God. Without God, and if there is no God, love does not exist. Atheist physicist Stephen Weinberg acknowledged this.[44] Weinberg's scientism causes him to conclude that...

> ...the worldview of science is rather chilling... the emotions that we most treasure, our love for our wives and husbands and children, are made possible by chemical processes in our brains that are what they are as a result of natural selection acting on chance mutations over millions of years.

Weinberg is correct. If there is no God there is no "love," since all our emotions, to include "love," are but chemical processes in our physical brains. Weinberg is incorrect. There is a God. This God is love. God's love looks like Jesus. It is the only answer.

I once heard that the actor John Wayne defined "courage" as being afraid, but saddling up anyway. It is a fearful thing to grow in love, because it requires deep change. Say the word "change," and chords of trepidation ring. Courage is needed. I am praying for the courage to love.

---

[43] Matthew 22:37-39
[44] Stephen Weinberg, "Without God." *The New York Review of Books*, September 25, 2008.

Praying to Deepen My Conviction that God's Love for Me is Enough

I have struggled with self-hatred. The way out has been a life of prayerful dwelling in God's presence. I continually thank God for leading me out of the wilderness of painful self-obsession.

The apostle Paul knew about our pre-Jesus condition when he wrote, "I find this law at work: Although I want to do good, evil is right there with me."[45] When we become Jesus-followers, this is defeated in us. We discover that God's love now rules our hearts. In spite of this, the powers of darkness come to accuse us, even "day and night."[46]

This should not surprise us. As we determine to live out the calling God has for us, attacks of the enemy will increase. We hear voices telling us we are worthless, unloved, even despised. The cure is constant immersion in this truth: God loves me.

This loving voice is heard, repeatedly, in the abiding relationship in Christ. To hear the inner voice of love requires much intentional time spent in God's presence. When I assign my seminary students to do this, and I read their spiritual journals, it is common to see the words, "Today, God told me that he loves me." This is God, freeing my students from self-hatred.

Do not expect to follow after Jesus and escape voices of hatred. But the fire from these darts will be extinguished as the knowledge of God's love deepens.

I know in my mind that God's love is enough for me. I am praying for this truth to take up residence in my heart.

Praying to Be Released from the Punishing
Prison-House of Self-Hatred

The whole problem of our time is the problem of love.
Thomas Merton[47]

---

[45] Romans 7:21
[46] Revelation 12:10
[47] Merton, *The Living Bread*, Farrar, Straus and Giroux: 2010, xii.

This Sunday at Redeemer I'm preaching on crossing over from hatred to love, on moving from hating others to loving them. In the process, I'll say something about the punishing, imprisoning, darkness of self-hatred.

I have personal experience in hating the self. And, I have hated others. Hatred towards others grows from the soil of self-hatred. I can't peace at peace with others until I am at peace with God, and then at peace with myself. My fear of others is rooted in the fear of self. It is all a cycling and recycling of hate and fear, mistrust and alienation. Such is the human condition without Christ.

There is a solution. It is: Be at peace with God, and you will be at peace with self. Be at peace with self, and you will be at peace with others. Accept, as 1 John tells us, that you are a deeply loved child of God. His seed is in you, and the DNA of his seed is love: for self, for others, for God.

Love God, and you grow in self-acceptance. This leads to a transforming experience where, instead of beating yourself for faults and failures, you rejoice in the greater purposes of God manifested in them. God knows how to draw glory even from your faults. Not to be self-hating after committing a fault is one of the marks of true sanctity, which is rooted in God's parental love for you.

A life of radical freedom issues from a deep life of dwelling in the presence of God. We come to accept our true identity, and live out of it. We see how it is possible to love, not hate, because God loves us.

Many are locked in dungeons of self-hatred. I keep praying for their release, and for mine as well.

Bringing My Weakness to God in Prayer

I woke early this morning and was drawn into praying. I have fears that keep poking their heads through the thin skin of my resistance. I will address them. How?

I will be alone and silent before God. I will not fight the fears, but allow them to identify themselves. I name them. I write them in my journal. My journal is a fear-filled place. Now they are in the light, where God and I do business together. In my journal, fears brought to light evaporate.

I sit before God in solitude and silence. This is my strategy. There are many things I cannot do, no matter how hard I strive. Eliminating fear is one of them.[48] But God can do this. I come before God, in my identified weakness, and trust him.

Just naming my fears is a victory, for I sometimes have a fear of addressing my fears. This is a doubly fearful condition. It works to shut me down spiritually. So, this morning, I do what I have done for many years, and find that God is with me and working within me.

To leave weaknesses and fears unaddressed is bad for me, and punishing for the people I love and lead. I only end up communicating my unhealed issues to others. I fail in leading people out of the desert if I have not been delivered myself. "Only those who have faced their own dark side can be trusted to lead others toward the Light. *This is* where true spiritual leadership begins. Everything that comes before is something *else*."[49]

Praying to See *Sub Specie Aeternitatis*

When Jesus calmed the storm on the Lake of Galilee, he was calm. He was calm because he saw the storm in a non-earthly way.[50] Medieval theologians would say Jesus saw the earthly storm *sub specie aeternitatis*; i.e., from the perspective of eternity. Jesus viewed the wind and waves through heaven's eyes.[51]

The Quaker theologian Thomas Kelly wrote, in his exquisitely beautiful book *A Testament of Devotion*, this prayer: God, let me "see earth, through heaven."[52] Viewing the things of earth through the

---

[48] Of course I can eliminate a fear of the roof leaking by patching it. But deep, existential fear is not so easy. The more one tries to will-power there way out of it, the more

[49] Barton, *Strengthening the Soul of Your Leadership*, 13.

[50] Arguably Jesus saw the storm as demonic, for he "rebuked" it.

[51] Lit. "under (*sub*) the aspect of (*specie*) eternity (*aeternitatis*).

[52] Thomas Kelly, *A Testament of Devotion*, New York: HarperOne. I have read Kelly's book at least three times. I underlined so much that a friend suggested I simply spray paint it.

lens of God's heaven results in the dissolution of fear and doubt. One sees, in the circumstances, God working all things together for good. Dietrich Bonhoeffer wrote:

> From all this it now follows that the content of ethical problems can never be discussed in a Christian light; the possibility of erecting generally valid principles simply does not exist, because each moment, lived in God's sight, can bring an unexpected decision. Thus only one thing can be repeated again and again, also in our time: in ethical decisions a man must consider his action *sub specie aeternitatis* and then, no matter how it proceeds, it will proceed rightly.[53]

God, give me the grace to view things as you view them. I desire to hear what you hear, feel what you feel, touch what you touch, smell what you smell, and behold what you behold.

Praying to See the Bigger Picture

For years Linda rises early and has "be still" times with God. In the receptive, uncluttered heart-condition of stillness she meets and "knows God."
The Lord says,

> *"Be still, and know that I am God;*
> *I will be exalted among the nations,*
> *I will be exalted in the earth."*
> *The LORD Almighty is with us;*
> *the God of Jacob is our fortress.*[54]

Heart-knowledge, gained in stillness before God, is an experiential reality, even while outer chaos and forces work to dislodge me.

---

[53] Dietrich Bonhoeffer Works, Volume 10, 368. Minneapolis: Fortress, 2008.
[54] Psalm 46:10-11

Therefore we will not fear, though the earth give way
and the mountains fall into the heart of the sea,
though its waters roar and foam
and the mountains quake with their surging.[55]

In stillness I gain experiential knowledge of God-with-me, no matter the circumstances. My heart and mind is brought into The Bigger Picture.

Praying to See Unseen Realities

Faith is the substance of things hoped for, the assurance of things unseen.

Hebrews 11:1

I received my hard copy of the spiritual classic *The Sacrament of the Present Moment*, by Jean-Pierre de Caussade. In the first chapter, de Caussade writes about Mary, Joseph, and Elizabeth. Here we see three ordinary people living hard, mundane lives. But God has given them promises. These promises plant seeds of hope in their hearts, shining a light on the dark circumstances surrounding them. De Caussade writes:

> What do they discern beneath the seemingly everyday events which occupy them? What is seen is similar to what happens to the rest of us. But what is unseen, that which faith discovers and unravels, is nothing less than God fulfilling his mighty purpose.[56]

Faith, hope, and love, are realities that transcend empirical reality. When I live by faith, I see the ongoing activity of God and his kingdom that is "unseen" by physical senses, and thus are not contingent on physical circumstances. For example, where someone sees a failing

---

[55] Psalm 46:2

[56] Jean-Pierre de Caussade, *The Sacrament of the Present Moment*, 3. New York: Harper & Row, 1982.

marriage, I see a restored marriage, and point people in that direction. In this way, faith has substance now.

By faith, I make purchases today that are grounded in my real, unseen hope in Christ. I pray to see the unseen realities of God, so that I might please God in living by faith.

Praying to Become Nothing

In his second letter to the Corinthian church, Paul defends his credentials as an apostle, a messenger sent from God. The new Corinthian Jesus-followers look at Paul and find it hard to believe he is who he says he is. They thought, writes N.T. Wright, that...

> ...an apostle needs to be a showy leader, a flowery and entertaining speaker, with personal charm and flattery, like the kind they were used to in their culture. What Paul ultimately wants to say to them is that all these things are nothing... compared with the lifestyle which embodies the gospel of Jesus.[57]

Paul confesses to "have made a fool of myself, but you drove me to it. I ought to have been commended by you, for I am not in the least inferior to the "super-apostles," even though I am nothing."[58]

How can someone who is a "nothing" *not* be inferior to everyone? "Nothing" is the bottom of the barrel. Nothing plus nothing adds up to... nothing.[59] The answer is that Paul's "nothingness" is a holy nothingness, a sacred insufficiency. Such nothingness is the necessary precondition for divine everythingness. This is a reverse *kenosis*, whereby a person self-empties, so as to see Christ's righteousness as something to be grasped.

---

[57] N.T. Wright, *Paul for Everyone: 2 Corinthians*, 32-33. Downers Grove: Intervarsity, 2010.

[58] 2 Corinthians 12:11

[59] For an interesting philosophical/scientific discussion of this see *Nothing: A Very Short Introduction*, by physicist Frank Close. New York: Oxford.

Paul views himself as unqualified, in himself and in his abilities, to minister in Jesus' name. But Christ, in Paul, *is* sufficient. He writes: "Not that we are competent in ourselves to claim anything for ourselves, but our competence comes from God. Christ," Paul discovers, "has made us competent as ministers of a new covenant."[60]

The reality of the "new covenant" is that God has placed his desires, not on tablets of stone (the old covenant), but in the hearts of all who embrace Christ. Now, amazingly, I "partake of the divine nature."[61] As Paul says in 2 Cor. 5:17, "if anyone is in Christ, he is a new creation. The old has passed away; behold, the new has come."

All this is in fulfillment of God's promise of a new covenant, as expressed in Ezekiel 36:26: "I will give you a new heart and put a new spirit in you; I will remove from you your heart of stone and give you a heart of flesh." God's Holy Spirit, put within me, is the reason I have confidence and am "sufficient."

In Paul I see the following pattern:

1. I am nothing.
2. The everything of Christ fills my nothingness.
3. I can do all things in Christ, who dwells in me and strengthens me.

Praying to Be Quiet and Small

Years ago Linda, Dan, and Josh accompanied me to Singapore, where I taught at a Chinese seminary for 20 days. Good friends connected us with David and Sue Pickard, of Overseas Missionary Fellowship. David was the director of OMF, formerly China Inland Mission, which was founded by Hudson Taylor. David and Sue had us over for dinner. It was Josh's birthday, and they prepared a birthday cake.

David showed us Hudson Taylor's Bible. That was an awesome moment. God took Taylor out of his comfort zone and greatly used him. How was this possible? Taylor himself said: "God chose me because I was weak enough. God does not do his work by large committees. He

---

[60] 2 Corinthians 3:6
[61] 2 Peter 1:4

trains somebody to be quiet enough, and little enough, and then uses him."[62]

I love how Oswald Chambers expresses this Pauline truth:

> God can achieve his purpose either through the absence of human power and resources, or the abandonment of reliance on them. All through history God has chosen and used nobodies, because their unusual dependence on him made possible the unique display of his power and grace. He chose and used somebodies only when they renounced dependence on their natural abilities and resources.[63]

I am praying to become nothing so that Christ can become Something, in me.

Praying to Be a Servant

There's an old worship song we used to sing called, "Change My Heart, O God." Sometimes when I sang it, I would extend my arms in front of me, lifting my palms up in an act of receiving. I prayer-worshiped before God, petitioning him to change the shape of my heart into greater Christlikeness. Morph me, O God.

Inner morphing is not for the self alone. As one's heart takes more and more the shape of Christ's heart, the person becomes a servant. Now they live to serve others, not to be self-served. "Our transformation is never for ourselves alone. It is always for the sake of others."[64]

What is good for me is good of others. What is done for me is done unto others. Personal transformation is for the benefit of many. God is into community, otherness, and paying it forward.

---

[62] In R. Kent Hughes, *2 Corinthians: Power on Weakness*, 71. Wheaton: Crossway.
[63] Oswald Chambers, *My Utmost for His Highest*. Grand Rapids: Discovery House, 1992.
[64] Barton, *Strengthening the Soul of Your Leadership*, 74.

When Jesus humbled himself, he took on the form of a servant. Transformation begets servanthood. As I pray for change, I am asking to be a servant, like Jesus.

Praying to Be Flexible

Linda and I had plans for the evening. An hour before we were to go out, things changed. Our plans got shelved, because God had another idea. God directed. We adjusted.

Praying people flex with the movement of the Spirit. Praying people are responsive, so as to be response-able. We become less interested in our own plans and purposes, and invested in how God wants our lives to go.

God is accomplishing his Kingdom Mission, and I am in his army. God directs. He shepherds. His sheep move. This is *obedience*. There is no such thing as a praying, obedient person who does not flex with the Spirit.

This is why some don't pray. They will have to relinquish their own agendas for the sake of the Lord's leadings, and are unwilling to do this.

How will I grow in flexibility, in moving with the Spirit?

1. Have a deep prayer life.
2. Listen.
3. Respond in obedience.

I must live the interruptible life. I am praying to be flexible.

Praying Against Self-Delusion

Solitary alone-time with God is an antidote to our culture's shallowness and illusions. Spending time alone with God clears away the false self I so easily construct and wear before others. In solitude, it's just me and God. Before God there's no faking it, no posing, posturing, and preening. There is no hiding. In solitude before God I discover that my real life is not as awesome as it appears to be on Facebook.

Solitary praying includes "search me, O God" time. Yes, God can, and does, search me out in community. But true community is a function of alone-time spent with God. I am better in community as a result of soloing with God.[65]

In praying-solitude, God defeats self-obsessiveness. Only then do I experience renewal and transformation. This is why Henri Nouwen has called solitude "the furnace of spiritual transformation."

If solitude is a "furnace," what gets burned away? The answer is: the negative aspects of "self." Unless I daily practice self-denial, self-centered ideas rise up against the desires of God.

I have discovered several negative aspects of the self. One is self-love. This thing runs deep. Self-love, writes Thomas Merton, "is the source of all boredom and all restlessness and all unquiet and all misery and all unhappiness - ultimately, it is hell."[66]

How much easier is it to love my self before loving others. This is like the British politician's actions that were described as, "Greater love hath no man than this, that a man lay down his friends for his life."[67]

I have discovered in my heart a deep-rooted propensity to love "me" as my first priority. This needs to be burned away in the solitary furnace of transformation.

As a young Christian I was counseled to keep my priorities as follows:

Love God first.

Love others second.

Love self.

---

[65] I understand that the Bible is overwhelmingly a community text. But I'm advocating for a communitarianism that explains and plays off the relationship between the individual and the community. In my spiritual formation writings and seminary classes I structure the learning environment as a dialectic between individual and community, and back and forth between the two, each one informing the other.

[66] Thomas Merton, *The Waters of Siloe*. New York: Harvest/HBJ, 1977.

[67] Eddie Askew, No Strange Land, 20. Leprosy Mission International, 1987.

When I live in this way, the love I have for myself is healthy and godly. I often ask God to burn away prideful self-love, and free me from self-grandiosity and delusion.

Praying to Be Free from the Need for Things to Go My Way

In one of Thomas Merton's journals he writes about life in the monastery of Gethsemane.[68] He struggled with the CEO of the place (the "Abbot"), Dom James. Dom James had big problems, as Merton saw it. Merton knew he had to accept this, and wrote: "I do not criticize Dom James – his nature is what it is, and he must see things as he does. And he is the Abbot God has willed for me."[69]

Then he has this God-given insight: "I know I will never have things exactly as I wish they ought to be – and as I would take pride in them."[70]

Take note! In that singular sentence we see a free person. God desires to free us of the terrible burden of always having to have things go our own way.

Is that really a terrible burden? Wouldn't it be ideal to have everything go our way? As interesting as these questions are, they are irrelevant. Because everything in life will *not* go your way. Indeed, everything in life *should* not go your own way, unless you are a god who knows the best way for the world to go. You can sing "I Did It My Way" as many times as you want. It won't happen.

The person who needs things to be as they desire will be forever weighed down by the fact of such a non-happening. They will be everlastingly miserable as expectation after expectation remains unmet. But the one who learns how to *be,* in and through whatever comes their way, is the free person, living transcendent to life's circumstances.[71]

---

[68] The Abbey of Gethsemane in Kentucky, a Trappist monastery where Merton came as a novice.

[69] Merton, *Learning to Love: exploring Solitude and Freedom* (The Journals of Thomas Merton), 27.

[70] Ib.

[71] Also called "living by faith."

Pray to be free of the need to have things always go your way.

Praying to Be Inwardly Healed

As a pastor I have been with many people who have suffered. Some were in excruciating physical pain, which is horrific. Some were in mental anguish. I have talked with people who suffered inner pain and said they would rather have physical pain than mental torment.

Just as we all experience physical pain, so we all have inner pain. I've experienced both. I have asked for prayer for both. Some of my inner pain is from this less-than-heavenly fallen world I live in. The creation in its fallen aspects has impinged on me. Things like death and loss have robbed my heart of peace. I have officiated the funerals of my parents, and Linda's as well. I had a baby son that died. If you are blessed to live long enough, you will know. Is long life a blessing? No and yes. My grandmother lived to the age of ninety-seven. She attended the funerals of her husband and all her children, except for my father. When the broken world cracks and falls on your soul like a shattered tree limb it leaves a wound.

Other people have wounded me. God has used me to help some people, only to have them crucify me. I have discovered that, even if you give your life for someone, they may turn against you. I can show you the scars on my heart left from the fiery darts shot by people, some of them Christians.

Some of my inner pain has been self-caused. Some has been willful, some has been out of ignorance. I have made bad choices that kept me awake at night. I have failed and made mistakes that hurt others. In my life I have hurt people. This does not set right in my soul.

When I hurt someone I act as an unhealed wound-giver. Inwardly I hurt; therefore, I hurt others, irretrievably. I cannot stop myself from hurting. But if the bleeding within gets stopped, I can be transformed into a wounded healer.

I have prayed with countless people for physical and inner healing. I also am praying for my own inner heart-healing, for my soul to be set right so that, in my woundedness, I would not wound, but love.

In Praying I Consent to Be Searched-Out by God

God Is all-knowing. Therefore, God knows me. C.S. Lewis said we are completely known to God - known like earthworms, cabbages, and nebulae, as objects of divine knowledge. Lewis wrote that "This is our destiny whether we like it or not. But though this knowledge never varies, the quality of our being known can."[72]

That is, we may not consent to be known by God. We might stay veiled, refusing to offer ourselves to view. When this happens praying gets weird.

I knew a man who was so embarrassed to be seen by me that, in conversation with him, he wore sunglasses so I could not look into his eyes. I knew him well. I knew the source of his shame. But I did not lift the glasses off his face.

If I choose hiddenness God will not forcefully unveil me. Like the psalmist who prayed, "Search me, O God, and know my heart," I must consent to be searched-out by God. Without this, my praying will be a one-way street, with God being disinvited to the conference.

In praying I sign a consent form stating, "Search me, O God, and know my heart." I assent with all my will to be known by him.

Thanks, I Needed That

One of my students has continued to pray thirty to sixty minutes every day. They told me of a time when God confronted them with unrighteous behavior they were engaging in. It broke their heart. I told them, "This is good. Thank God for breaking you!"[73]

I remember an old television commercial for an after shave called "Mennon Skin Bracer." It shows a man in a bathroom. He's done shaving and looks in the mirror. He takes a bottle of Skin Bracer, pours some on both palms, and baptizes his cheeks. Then a hand comes out of the mirror and slaps his born-again face. The man says, "Thanks, I

[72] C.S. Lewis, *Letters to Malcolm: Chiefly on Prayer*, 20.
[73] The best book I have read on brokenness is *Broken In the Right Place*, by Alan Nelson. Grand Rapids: Thomas Nelson.

needed that!" That's how bracing and refreshing this after shave was supposed to be. It gave the man a wake-up call.

Many times, while praying, I have had a "Thanks, I needed that!" experience. A divine wake-up call. God points out something about me that is diseased and needs renewal. When this happens I write words like, "God, you have searched out my heart, and shown me something that needs to be removed." It could be pride, a bad attitude, hatred, lust, envy, covetousness, jealousy, a controlling spirit, lack of compassion, resistance to God, or God knows what else. Revelations of my inner garbage are always accompanied by brokenness, with thanksgiving.

In over forty-six years of following Jesus God has uncovered all these things and more, in me. This is good. When it happens (and it *will* if you continue to meet one-on-one with him), it is another "Thank You God" moment. It is another RESCUE OF ME.

Some fear meeting with God because of this. They are like a person who resists going to the doctor because an illness may be found. I need to remember that to live under the illusion of health is to be on the road to spiritual disaster.

I may not like being told, "You are sick." Who wants to hear that? But I should be glad for any revelation of disease when it is there. This is always the beginning of its removal. God never reveals failure only to leave you in that miserable place. That would be like a doctor who diagnoses but does not cure.

When God shows something about me that is not of him it is not accompanied by condemnation. People do that. God does not. There is no condemnation pointed at me, for I am in Christ Jesus.[74] God comes only to rescue, to save me from myself.

I may not have thought I needed a rescue. Then, as I meet with God for another praying hour, God the Great-Physician identifies a spiritual cancer, operates, and bathes me with radiating, healing love. All of this breaks my heart. I see it as very good. I cry out, "Thank You God, I needed that!"

---

[74] Romans 8:1

Praying and Tearing Down Spiritual Strongholds

Yesterday morning at Redeemer God was moving, changing the direction of our service from the start. In the middle of worship there was a call to come forward and receive prayer for tearing down inner spiritual strongholds. Many people came forward and were released from lies of the enemy.

We find the "spiritual stronghold" idea in 2 Corinthians 10:3-5:

> For though we live in the world, we do not wage war as the world does. The weapons we fight with are not the weapons of the world. On the contrary, they have divine power to demolish strongholds. We demolish arguments and every pretension that sets itself up against the knowledge of God, and we take captive every thought to make it obedient to Christ.

A "spiritual stronghold" is an argument, a pretender that builds itself "against the knowledge of God." Spiritual strongholds are fortresses made of pretense-thoughts that need to be torn down, lest our souls become captive to their lies.

Examples of pretender-strongholds include:

- Cares of the world
- Anxiety
- Unforgiveness
- Bitterness
- Grief (lasting)
- Instability (emotions rule; the emotional rollercoaster)
- Accusations (the "accuser of the brethren")
- Condemnation
- Sin and patterns of sin

I have battled all these. One of the weapons I use to demolish strongholds is praying.[75] In praying, I take thoughts captive, such as "I am a failure in God's eyes," or "God could never love someone like me." These are pretenders to the throne. They have no place in the fortress of God. I am a temple of the Holy Spirit, and God's Spirit never speaks like this to one of his own. I ask for God's truth to defeat any lies in me. I ask God to:

- Make me be anxious for nothing
- Give me his heart of forgiveness
- Uproot any bitterness within me
- Give me a heart of thankfulness
- Heal my hurting, wounded heart
- Have his truth, not my emotions, rule my heart
- Free me from self-condemnation
- Defeat sin in me once and for all

I write these prayers down on a list and carry them with me. I pray them, repetitively. I pray the Big Truth, which is: God loves me. As the Big Truth descends from my intellect to my heart, it overwhelms the lies that threaten my status in Christ.

I pray this way *a lot*. Repetition on God's truths is good for the soul. While it's true that God can remove things once and for all, I am also in a spiritual battle, and the enemy of my soul does not let up.

Praying for the Strength of Gentleness

(The ultimate anti-Nietzsche claim is: Gentleness is power.)

After listing several bad behaviors Paul instructs Timothy to run from them, and go after "righteousness, godliness, faith, love, endurance and gentleness."[76] One of these pursuable qualities is gentleness. On this, Ben Witherington writes:

---

[75] See Ephesians 6:18
[76] 2 Timothy 6:11

"Gentleness" was a moral ideal in the Greco-Roman world, despite all its wars and brutality. It was not some weak and wimpy character defect. To a Greek, gentleness was strength. Plato wrote that all good persons have the virtue of gentleness. "Gentleness was especially said to be a virtue of leaders. It involved calmness and moderation, and a kind wielding of power towards others that promotes reconciliation. Gentleness is the opposite of brutality or raw rage.[77]

Instead of gentleness being weak, raging anger is weak. Rage is a loose cannon whose origin is the loss of self-control. Raw rage is destructive; gentleness is productive. Therefore, gentleness is power, since power produces. It is the power to win over enemies, rather than create more of them (which any fool can do).

"The fruit of the Spirit is love, joy, peace, patience, kindness, goodness, faithfulness, gentleness and self-control."[78]

"A gentle answer turns away wrath, but a harsh word stirs up anger."[79]

Gentleness deflects wrath, like a lancer parries an incoming attack. Harsh words and rage add fuel to the fires of conflict. Spirit-empowered gentleness puts fires out.

Rage is weakness. Gentleness is strength. I am pursuing gentleness by praying for God to shape its reality in me.

Praying to Be Free of the Double Imprisonment

Thomas Merton, in a moment of feeling rejected, wrote in his journal that there was no point in trying to pretend that he was superior.[80] This

---

[77] Ben Witherington, *Letters and Homilies for Hellenized Christians, Volume 1: A Socio-Rhetorical Commentary on Titus, 1-2 Timothy and 1-3 John*, 292-293. Downers Grove: Intervarsity, 2006.

[78] Galatians 5:22-23

[79] Proverbs 15:1

[80] In *A Year with Thomas Merton: Daily Meditations from His Journals*, May 11, "On Being a Stranger".

is because superiority, and its evil anti-twin inferiority, are illusions in the kingdom of God.

Delusions of superiority and inferiority find their meaning in honor-shame hierarchies. The demonic nature of these hierarchies is that they measure the worth of people on cultural scales of "least" to "greatest." When I tacitly buy into this I see my own value as, relatively, "superior," or "inferior." On the logic of honor-shame I will always be simultaneously superior and inferior, unless I am the king (having risen, like cream, to the top for a brief historical moment), or reside beneath the basement of the hierarchy (a criminal, e.g.).

In the honor-shame hierarchy "value" is relative to position. Any inner, mental striving to reposition oneself is a living hell. Merton concludes, correctly, that there is no point in doing this. I have done that, been there, experienced the hell of it, and agree. Any felt pride or shame resulting from my place on a nonexistent ladder is pointless.[81]

The good news is that the Real Jesus rejects honor-shame hierarchies. He refuses offers of earthly kingship, and dies a lowly, abased expendable. Paul expands on this by saying that, in Christ, there is neither slave nor free, Jew nor Greek, male nor female. All Jesus-followers belong to Christ and are one in him.

Have you ever imagined yourself as mentally or physically superior to someone you don't like? Have you angrily defended yourself as being above another person? I have. I have met many others who have, too. I once visited a young man in prison (his fourth incarceration) who said to me, "I have an IQ of 160." I doubted this, and looked on him as doubly imprisoned, in chains both physically and mentally. Yes, he is valuable; no, his value has nothing to do with the illusion of his comparative intelligence.

Have you, in some lonely moment, despaired because you are not as smart or rich or successful or powerful as "everyone else?" I have. I have read of others who have, as well. For example, while painting the Sistine Chapel, Michelangelo hit an emotional low point. He wrote, "I

---

[81] See Thomas Merton on the banality of hellish behavior in *New Seeds of Contemplation*.

am not in a good place. I am no painter." Even gifted people can feel they don't measure up. Have you ever felt you don't measure up? If so, the question is: to what, or to whom?

The Jesus-truth that frees me from the double imprisonment is that God doesn't measure me when it comes to love and acceptance. This is called *grace*. I must extend grace to others and value them as God sees them. I must receive God's grace for my own self and experience his valuing of me.

I am praying to accept God's grace, carved out for me, and to live free of all human hierarchies of value.

Praying to Be at Home with God

C.S. Lewis believed all humans have within them an "inconsolable longing" for "we know not what." Lewis used a German word, *Sehnsucht*, to express this longing which is, ultimately, for God. The French mathematician and philosopher Blaise Pascal famously identified a "God-shaped vacuum" in the heart of every person.[82] No created thing can fill this empty place. Only God can. This is the place where God makes his home; viz., in my heart.[83]

In Ecclesiastes 3:11 we read that God "has made everything beautiful in its time. He has also set eternity in the human heart; yet no one can fathom what God has done from beginning to end." God manifests his being without (his creation), and within (the moral law). In the latter eternity is set in our heart. The everlasting omnibenevolence of God resides like a fire that warms the living room of our soul.

God tabernacles in us. Jesus said, "Anyone who loves me will obey my teaching. My Father will love them, and we will come to them and make our home with them."[84] As a Jesus-follower I am in Christ.

---

[82] See Blaise Pascal, *Pensees*. New York: Oxford, 2008.

[83] John 14:23. The "heart" is a metaphor for the core, or essence of one's being. The "heart" is who I really am. This is what Jesus is out to rescue and redeem and restore and renew.

[84] John 14:23

"Christ in me, the hope of glory." Which means: In Christ, God fathoms me. God and I go deep-sea diving to discover me, and to know him.

Christ is the fulfillment of my deep, existential, heart-longing for "something more." As God makes his home in me, I find my reason for being in Him. Homesickness for God is a mark of the life of prayer.

In praying I cry out for more experiential knowledge of his presence. I am praying to be at home with God. To be accustomed to him and his presence, in me. Do not make the mistake of thinking that acclimatizing to the depths of the being of God and the heights of his glory are easy for people who have spent years living in the two-dimensional flatlands.[85]

Praying for Judgmentalism to Be Exchanged for Understanding

Jesus instructs me to stop judging other people.[86] Here are some thoughts I have about this.

I can, and will, make "judgments" in life. This is unavoidable, and is *not* the thing Jesus warns me against doing. Consider this judgment: *Killing people for fun is wrong.* I judge that to be true. Every day I make hundreds of judgments, ranging from moral judgments ("It is wrong to behead people"), to non-moral judgments ("This cup of coffee is too weak"). When Jesus says, "Judge not," he is referring to judgmentalism, which is different from making judgments.

A "judgmental" person weighs in on the hearts of people, and pronounces, like a trial judge, a verdict. Such as: "guilty." Or: "That person is bad." Or: "You deserve punishment." They act as judge and jury over others. A judgmental person feasts off evaluating the character and motives of others. Judgmental people lack understanding and compassion, and become bedfellows with gossip and slander.

Behaviors can, and should, be judged, but the human heart is hard to assess. If someone steals from me it is not wrong to say, "They stole

---

[85] I am thinking here of Edwin Abbott's *Flatland: A Romance of Many Dimensions.* Abbott's books is a rebuke to anyone who believes there are no realities beyond what can be perceived via the five senses.
[86] Matthew 7:1

from me; stealing is wrong; therefore, what this person has done is wrong." But *why* did they steal? What is the root of this? Here caution is advised, because I do not have access to the human heart. I can judge the behavior. I can refrain from judging the person's heart. How many times I have been surprised, either positively or negatively, when a person's true heart becomes evident, and my evaluation of them was wrong.

I have assessed the hearts of people incorrectly. When my assessment has been negative, I've built a case against them. This has bred bitterness in me. I have made mountains, not only out of mole-hills, but out of no-hills.

Consider Proverbs 20:5, which says that, "The purposes of a man's heart are deep waters." I lack epistemic access to the deep waters of another person's heart. I cannot even figure my own heart out! How can I expect to accurately read the hearts of other people?

If God shows me a negative aspect of another person's heart, it is only so I can pray for them or, with permission, help them. God doesn't entrust such privileged information to judgmental people.

In one of his confrontations with the Jewish religious leaders, Jesus asks them to "Stop judging by mere appearances, and make a right judgment."[87] They have, again, misjudged Jesus. This is because what is seen with the eyes is not equivalent to what lies in the heart. It may appear that a person has given me a nasty look. I should not conclude from this that they have a nasty heart. When Linda and I were dating, one of her friends told Linda that it appeared I did not like her (the friend) because of the look on my face. Linda assured her that I did like her, and by the way, that's how my face normally looks. You can't judge a book by the cover.

Judgmental people are fearful people. Judgmentalism erects barriers to ward off self-scrutiny. If I deflect attention away from my own sin and failure, and get people to look at the surface-appearance of sin and failure in someone else, I breathe easier. Instead of crying out, "Search

---

[87] John 7

me O God, and know my heart," the cry becomes, "Judge them, O God, for I know their hearts." Probably not.

It's hard work being judge of the world. I have spent too many hours trying to figure out what is going on in the brains of others. Now I am giving this responsibility to God. What a relief! God calls me to love others, not judge them. God is able to speak into the hearts of every person I wonder about. In the meantime, I do well to allow him to speak to my own heart, and leave the judging of others to him.

I am asking God for freedom from judging the hearts of others. I cannot make a reasonable judgment without first *understanding*. It is foolish to judge without understanding. When understanding is achieved, judgmentalism often morphs into compassion. So I am praying to understand others, and to be understood by them.

Time spent judging the hearts of other people is wasted time, because: 1) My judgments can be wrong, and are surely incomplete; 2) Judgmentalism has no redemptive value; and 3) I can't change peoples' hearts anyway, so why waste time judging them? Years ago God spoke to me, and I wrote these words in my journal: "John, why are you trying so hard to change other people when you can't even change your own self?"

Jesus said, "Judge not, that you be not judged."[88] There is something about a judgmental heart that backfires, exploding onto my own soul. If I point my big critical guns at others I will also wound myself. If God shows me some truth about another person's struggle, I am to thank God that he has entrusted me with this knowledge, and begin praying for that person.

As God morphs the heart more and more into a Christ-shape, he removes the critiquing thing. We can leave that to God, thus removing the terrible burden of having to change the hearts of others. Judging others is a heavy load. Why not let it go? Pray to be set free from a judgmental heart.

---

[88] Matthew 7:1

Thank God for the Stripping Away

One of my father's hobbies was woodworking, and refinishing old furniture. Dad built clocks and chairs and tables. We commissioned him to build a wooden music stand for Linda's sister's wedding. He had no prototype for this, so he built it from scratch. It was amazing and beautiful!

My mother joined him in the refinishing part. I can see them both in the basement of our house, stripping away layers of old paint and varnish to reveal the original wood finish. I can smell the materials they used and hear the sound of the sander.

This is called "restoration." It's about stripping away things that have covered up what was originally there. When restoration happens to people it is a beautiful thing. Some of the most heart-moving acts of God I have seen are when Christians experience restoration, return to their first love, and use their gifts and talents to minister to the people of God and beyond. Just this past weekend at Redeemer I heard two testimonies from young men who were drug addicts, but got released from their captivity and restored to God's family. One of them gave his testimony, and then was baptized.

God not only *can* restore fallen followers of Jesus to fellowship, God's job description includes *doing* this. God *desires* to restore people. God is *able* to restore people. God can strip away the false layers that have covered up the heart's real, first love.

The classic restoration story is that of David. To say David fell away from the heart of God is an understatement. David went after another man's wife (Bathsheba), and then out of fear orchestrated things so her husband (Uriah) would be killed on the battlefield. David was involved in adultery, lying, and murder. In spite of this, God eventually restored him, and wielded David to further His purposes. What a crazy, brilliant idea!

One of the precious deposits the Lutheran church left in me as a boy was the singing, liturgically and repetitively, of the Psalms. They meant little to me at the time. But when I became a Jesus-follower some of them kicked-started my spirit. Psalm 51 was inside me. The words became important to me. This is David's song of repentance and cry for restoration.

> Create in me a clean heart, O God,
> and renew a right spirit within me.
> Cast me not away from your presence
> and take not your Holy Spirit from me.
> Restore unto me the joy of your salvation
> and uphold me with your Spirit.

Before Christ found me I was an alcohol abuser, and a daily drug user. So, I like David's story. Over the years I have sung his song, a lot. Whenever I take the Lord's Supper these verses do a number on me. I sing them and love them, because *I* have needed restoration, many times. Any follower of Jesus who lets an ounce of evil contaminate their heart needs it stripped away. That includes me.

Sadly, I am aware of stories where churches cooperate with the enemy and shoot their wounded. These are the Judging, Condemning Churches; the Anti-Jesus Churches; the Covens of Banning and Shunning.

The Real Church is different. God the Redeemer heals wounded warriors, restores the fallen, and in the restoration defeats the enemy. The Real Jesus[89] does not avoid fallen people like they are the plague; he moves towards them. God's people rejoice and cry for joy when they see this happen. And, Jesus' followers join him in the great Restoration Movement.

When I am alone with God, I often thank him for the many restoration moments in my life. Amazingly, my fallen failures do not permanently disqualify me for ministry and full life in the kingdom. If that were true, I would dwell outside the city walls among the untouchables.

---

[89] By the term "Real Jesus" I mean Jesus, as found in Matthew, Mark, Luke, and John, and in contradistinction to the "Jesus" that is often preached in American media. Here is where the Church needs scholarly, Christological studies.

The most beautiful Jesus-followers I have met testify to having been lifted out of the dungeons of their failures.[90] God loves to not only restore people, but to apply an in-your-face-to-the-enemy by calling the restored person, like he did David, "a man after God's own heart."

You learn a lot about yourself and the Real Jesus in the process of being stripped away by love. Restored people are not marked as "adulterer," "liar," or "murderer," but wear the cleansing blood of Christ which declares, "I am His child forever!"

This is the heart of the Gospel. We get new names in the stripping away.

Praying to Be God-Dependent Rather Than Circumstance-Dependent

The great virtues of the Jesus-life - faith, hope, and love - are circumstance-independent. So are the "fruit of the Spirit" - love, peace, patience, joy, etc.[91]

"Peace," for example, the kind Jesus (not the world) gives, is independent of life's impinging environment. It is precisely when life's circumstances disrupt that we need some not-of-this-world peace.

When Paul was imprisoned in Ephesus, he wrote letters to various churches, like his letter to the Colossians. Paul was in chains. But this did not stop his ministry, nor did it hinder his calling as a messenger to the Gentiles. He spent much time praying for the Colossian Jesus-followers. "I have not stopped praying for you," he writes.[92] Paul's physical circumstances did not hinder or halt the calling God had on his life.

God is not bound by circumstances. Therefore, as I abide in Christ, neither am I. I am praying to understand and live this. Otherwise my sense of God's calling will be a function of the ups-and-downs of my environment. I must remember that I am engaged in a spiritual

---

[90] One of the best books I read a few years ago was *Save Me From Myself*, the testimony of Korn guitarist Brian Welch and his redemption and restoration to Christ. I was crying as I read part of it. New York: HarperOne, 2008.

[91] Galatians 5:22-23

[92] Colossians 1:9

battle. There will be ups and downs, victories and defeats, healings and casualties. Still, God's plans and purposes for me remain, and will ultimately win the day.

I must keep my eyes on the calling of God and off the stormy waters of the seas around me.

I am praying to be more God-dependent, which will result in living circumstance-independently.

Praying for a De-buttoning

I'm counseling a marital couple, helping them learn healthy ways to communicate in the middle of conflict. Their anger towards each other keeps escalating. He protests, "She keeps pushing my buttons!"

I respond: "But they're *your* buttons. She didn't sew them onto your soul."

If this young man didn't have "buttons," like the "need to always be in control" button, or the "need to always have things go my own way" button, or the "need to not be interrupted when I am busy" button, or the "denial button," then no one could push them, because there would be none to push.

Jesus didn't have "hot buttons." People kept trying to agitate him, but to no avail. Hanging on the cross, he refused to react and express frustration by saying (as I believe I would have), "That's it - when you mocked me right there you pushed my buttons!!!" Instead, Buttonless Jesus responded with, "Father, forgive them, for they know not what they do."

Every "hot button" has a sign which announces, "I am a victim. Push me." Hot-buttoned people are adorned with the spirit of victimization. Things are always "being done to me." Every time I think, "My buttons got pushed by you!", it indicates a refusal to take responsibility for my own behavior. I wear a badge saying, "I am emotionally and spiritually imprisoned."

The testimony of a hot-buttoned person is: "I am controlled by your behaviors toward me. You push; like a machine, I react." That's not good. As Paul wrote: "It is for freedom that Christ has set us free.

Stand firm, then, and do not let yourselves be set off again by a button of slavery."[93]

How do I get de-buttoned, and enter the arena of freedom? The only answer I have found is: I must dwell in Christ. Live the connected life. Be a branch, connected to Jesus the Vine, and his nature shall flow into me. He will give me his peace. Jesus said, "Peace I leave with you; my peace I give you. I do not give to you as the world gives. Do not let your hearts be troubled and do not be afraid."

As Christ is formed in me[94] and people try to push me to my limits, they bump into a love, compassion, mercy, and grace that knows no limits. This changes things. I wear different clothing, and if this clothing has any buttons at all they are labeled "love," "joy," "peace," "patience," "kindness," "gentleness," and "self-control."[95]

Remove my hot buttons, Lord. Take away my reactiveness and free me to respond, as you did. The only button I want to wear says "Jesus."

Praying for Faithfulness in Small Things

Today, like most days, will be a day of small things. My prayer is to be faithful in them. I am a small person facing small tasks, interacting with small people.

God can turn a small thing into a big thing, should he desire. It's up to him. But my focus is not to be on faithfulness in "big things." If I am not faithful in small things I cannot be trusted with big things. I don't even believe God evaluates things by "small" and "big." Be faithful to God's calling. That's all I need to do.

Faithfulness is qualitative, not quantitative. If I fail to love those in my own environment, I cannot be trusted to love others. I am not interested in "swimming with the big fish." Rather, I am a little fish, called to swim with whomever God brings into my life.

---

[93] Galatians 5:1; Piippo translation.
[94] Galatians 4:19
[95] Galatians 5:22-23

Jesus said that "he who is faithful in a little" is the one who will be rewarded much.[96] C.S. Lewis put it this way. "This then is the great secret. Good and evil both grow at compound interest. That is why the SMALL things you do each day are of such infinite importance. It is the small things that will turn you into either a heavenly or hellish creature."[97]

Who dares despise the day of small things...[98]

Worry Is a Crooked Path Leading Back to Itself

I come from a long line of worriers that stretches back to Adam. My mother, wonderful person that she was, suffered from excessive worrying. I think my father worried, but it was hard to tell since he was, generally, non-expressive. Our roots are in Finland, and Finnish men tend not to show emotion.

"Worry" is part of our fallen, subhuman condition. "Worry" is endemic to humanity, in general. I come from a long, wide path of worriers trailing back to Old Testament times. Fallen humanity broods, negatively.

Worry is not helpful. Brooding on darkness brings on more darkness. Worry says, "Something bad is happening. You cannot stop it. Do worry, be unhappy."

Worry is passive, like waiting for the tornado that never comes. This adds nothing of value to life. Jesus said, "Who of you by worrying can add a single hour to his life?"[99]

Worry is non-additive. Worry is not neutral. Worry subtracts, knocking minutes off life.

Worry is absurd. This is because worry's concerns are things that cannot be controlled. Like people. I can't control others. I can love and serve them, but love and service will not inexorably come back to me.

---

[96] Luke 16:10
[97] C. S. Lewis, *Mere Christianity.*
[98] Zechariah 4:10
[99] Matthew 6:27

Sometimes it does, sometimes it doesn't. When it comes to others, worry is a non-player.

I control none of this. Most of what happens to me in life is not in my control. This being the case, one thing that will not comfort me is worry. To ruminate on negative possibilities is absurd because it effects nothing. Except to subtract from me. Worry is a thief. Worry steals joy, peace, and hope from my heart.

Worry is a bad thinker. Worry needs to take a logic course. Anyone who has responsibilities exhibits care. Caring is good. Worry is caring gone berserk, which is bad for my soul. At this point caring mutates into worry. Caring packs its bag of burdens and hauls it south to the land of anxiety.

The antidote to worry is trust. The more I trust, the less I worry. The question then becomes: In whom, or in what, shall I place my trust? Trust must be rightly placed. Trusting in just anything will not do the job.

Proverbs 3:5-6 says, famously: "Trust in the Lord with all your heart. Do not rely on your own understanding. In all your ways acknowledge Him, and He will make your paths straight."

Worry is a crooked path that leads back to itself. But as I trust in God, my convoluted mental highways are made straight.

Praying for the Level of My Experience to Be Raised

I wrote a worship song called "Reveal Yourself." It has the line, "Come and show us what You've got; things that are, things that are not." I want to see what God has, not what I, or the world, has. Back in the 1980s, I read how God spoke to John Wimber and told him, "John, I have seen what your ministry can do. Now I want to show you *my* ministry."[100] When I saw that, I thought, "God, show me *your* ministry!"

Walter Wink writes: "People with an attenuated sense of what is possible will bring that conviction to the Bible and diminish it by the poverty of their own experience."[101] My praying-desire is that God

---

[100] John Wimber, *Power Evangelism*. Grand Rapids: Baker, 1986.
[101] Walter Wink, quoted in Craig Keener, *Miracles: The Credibility of the New Testament Accounts*, 85. Grand Rapids: Baker, 2011.

would raise my level of experience to that of the Bible, rather than interpreting the Bible through the level of my impoverished experience. If this happens, what might God do in and through me?

Praying for Humility

On New Year's Eve I challenged people in our church family to a game of chess. I wanted to play 10-20 people at a time. To my slight disappointment, only two took my challenge. Perhaps, I thought, they feared me?

They were two kids. I was confident. I thought I was doing well when suddenly, out of nowhere, one of them spotted my king trapped in the corner of the board, with no place to move. They advanced their queen from d1 to d8 and... yikes! I was checkmated.

And humbled. (And afraid?)

Everyone gets humbled, multiple times in life. But *being humbled* is not the same thing as *being humble*. Everyone gets humbled; not everyone acquires humility as a heart-condition.

This is so important that James 4:6 tells us that God is opposed to the proud, but gives grace to the humble. This is the foundational attitude in the spiritual, praying life, without which progress in holiness will not happen, and one will not hear.

God has struggled mightily with me about this over the years. I'm not there yet. So, I continuously pray for God to remove pride, and replace it with a humble heart.

Praying for the "No" of Christ to Be Formed in Me

> "The making of a man is making your body
> do what it doesn't want to do."
> Robert Bly[102]

One sign of spiritual maturity is the ability to wield the word "No." The Jesus-idea is that, as I connect to him as a branch to a vine, I bear

---

[102] Robert Bly, *Iron John, A Book About Men*. Boston: Da Capo Press, 1990. Please put Bly's possible Platonism aside.

"fruit." Part of which is awe-inspiring "self-control."[103] People drop their jaws and stare in wonder when one revolutionary person stands within the blind masses and says "No" to self-gratification.

If I am Spirit-led and self-controlled, I am a free person. I mature in my ability to say "No" to eating the wrong things, spending money I don't have, and engaging in behavior that objectifies other persons. M. Scott Peck described this revolutionary "No!" as "gratification delay."[104]

"No" is the ultimate boundary word. "No" is where the road narrows. The ability to wield it will not come from postering will-power slogans like, "Just say 'No'." Authentic, boundary-setting, No-ability must become my heart, my inner being. This happens as Christ is formed in me.

Think of Jesus, after he fed the 5,000. The people rushed to make him an earthly king. Jesus exercised innate self-control and refused. His "No" was not only for him, but for the sake of others; indeed, for the whole world. This is a narrow road, said Jesus, and few take it. It is the road to freedom.

"No" might be the ultimate other-centered word. "No" is for the sake of the world. I am praying for the "No" of Christ to be formed in me.

Praying for God to Lead Me

"I am tired of being my own Providence"[105]
Thomas Merton

I am tired of making all decisions by myself. I'm weary of self-seeking and self-wanting, depleted of energy spent on trying to control people and outcomes. In my leadership, I am asking God to lead me, and take control of me.

---

[103] Galatians 5:23
[104] See M. Scott Peck, *The Road Less Traveled*. New York: Touchstone, 1978.
[105] *A Year with Thomas Merton*, June 23.

In praying God will reveal the depth of our addiction to control, and the need to be released from the illusion that we are in control.[106] I have experienced this. I've been addicted to control, and am in what I hope are the later stages of being set free.

This is about getting free from our need to control people and situations. Remember what Jesus said to Peter: "I'm telling you the very truth now: When you were young you dressed yourself and went wherever you wished, but when you get old you'll have to stretch out your hands while someone else dresses you and takes you where you don't want to go."[107]

...And takes you where you don't want to go. This is hard for the control freak in me who, in my own mind, is my own Providence.

Trusting in God means letting go of control. It is root-level radical to pray, "God, lead me. Take me where you want me to go." Really? Do you mean it?

Praying to Make My Life Add Up

I'm in Urbana, Ohio, this morning. I went for an early morning prayer walk, using Psalm 23 to meditate on. What a beautiful fall day it is!

When I pay attention to God, I see things. Ahead is a billboard that reads, "Make Every Day Count." These words seem important for me. I begin repeating, while walking, "I will make every day count. I will make every day count." This is not "mindless repetition." Repetition on truths are profoundly mindful.

I will make my life "count" - for what?

I will make every day "add up" to something. When I die perhaps someone will "sum up" my life. I hope it "amounts" to something more than "He liked watching sports while eating pizza and Cadbury eggs."

---

[106] Similar to Jacques Ellul's "illusion of technique." See Ellul, *The Technological Society*. New York: Vintage, 1964.
[107] John 21:18

There is something called "the sum total of my life." There is an "amount" to my life. My life can amount to something. My life can have eternal results.

I prayed, "God, pour everything into this present day. Into this present moment. Now. Make my "now" count, for you."

Praying to Be Free from Comparison

Wasting time comparing ourselves with other people produces the bitter twin fruits of self-obsession, which are: shame, and pride. Shame is the feeling that I am no good, of no value. Pride is the feeling that I am more valuable than other people. Shame says, "I am nothing," pride says, "I am something."

There is a "healthy pride." C.S. Lewis talks about it in his chapter "The Great Sin," in *Mere Christianity*. But self-obsessive pride and shame punish the soul. Here are some things about this, sort of a phenomenology of *comparison*.

Comparison rank-orders people on an honor-shame hierarchy, with its various manifestations (like: good-bad; beautiful-ugly; worthy-worthless; useful-useless). In this world there are many kinds of honor-shame hierarchies. Compared to other people, you and I are either: 1) better than they are; 2) worse than they are; or 3) the same as they are. This is in relation to some specific attribute, quality, or talent. You are not as beautiful as some; you are more beautiful than others. A whole lot of people are smarter than you; you are a whole lot smarter than a lot of people. If you can read this, you are ahead of the world's twenty percent of adults who cannot read. If you scored 50% on the ACT, then half of our nation's teens are smarter than you.

Compared to others, you are either up or down. If you measure up, you look down; if you measure down, you are looking up.

The honor-shame hierarchy creates "haves" and "have nots," relative to a person's position on whatever social ladder we are considering. Pride looks down on others; shame looks up at others. Most are "pride-shame" people who are both looking down and looking up. For them, life is a ride on a never-ending roller coaster of emotions that simultaneously please and punish.

Hierarchization was a kingdom-of-darkness idea. For example, while I was in India I beheld the brutal, hierarchizing, caste system. Upper-casters are perceived as better people, having been better in their previous life, and thus promoted upwards on the honor-shame hierarchy in their current life. I was in several low caste villages. One village leader in central India told me that "The government does not think of us." Their low social status was reflected in their impoverished social conditions. Not only were they economically poor, they were socially scorned. This is the double whammy of hierarchizing honor-shame cultures. If this sounds primitive, note that this kind of thing is alive and well today in America (and everywhere).

We see it in the Bible, in the story of the man sitting outside the Temple, as Jesus and his disciples walk by. The man is blind. Jesus' disciples reason that either he, or his parents, sinned. The man's blindness must be caused by someone's failure. Now here's the double whammy. First, the man is blind and cannot work, but only beg. Second, the man is morally and religiously unclean. He's a sinner who deserves to be blind. These twin miseries place him low, very low, on the totem pole. He is at the bottom of the pecking order, and therefore a deserving recipient of scorn. Then Jesus, in yet another jaw-dropping, a-cultural moment, tells his disciples that neither this man nor his parents are responsible for his condition. Imagine the blind man hearing Jesus say this. Can it be true? The comparative rank-ordering world of pride and shame is dissolving before his ears, and the eyes of his disciples.

I went to a village located on the Deccan Plateau in central India. There were 300-400 people in the village. There was no electricity, no running water, and tiny mud-brick houses. The entire village greeted me as I arrived in an all-terrain vehicle. They placed garlands of flowers around my neck, two men held umbrellas over my head to shade me from the sun, and I heard the sound of drums coming toward me. Three men slinging drums on their hips came, and the parade began, with me as the center of attention. We processed to a small building that housed meetings of the local church. The small room was packed, with people overflowing out the door and peeking through the windows. I was introduced, then spoke to them. Here was I, the rich white man from America, an "upper caste" person in the midst of a forgotten bunch of lower caste, no-name, nothing-people.[108]

I opened my Bible and read Galatians 3:28: "There is neither Jew nor Greek, slave nor free, male nor female, for you are all one in Christ Jesus." I told them Jesus came to remove the human-made caste system. Now, they are free from being rank-ordered according to honor-shame valuations. God doesn't compare them with other people. Instead, God came down and rescued them from the hierarchizing world that enchains their hearts. Now, they are free to look only to God, who loves them, and has come to make his home in them.

In comparison with God, who is all-knowing, all-powerful, and all-loving, our knowledge, power, and love are nothing. In that regard we are all the same. Comparison with one another in light of the being of God is logical nonsense. It is like hierarchizing acorns while surrounded by a forest of giant sequoias.

That God loves you and I should cause us to wonder and worship, rather than compete and compare. The honor-shame hierarchy *does not even apply* in the kingdom of God. We are released from striving to measure up to others. This has been, and remains, good news for me.

Look to God.

You are sons and daughters of God.

You are loved because of this relationship, not because of any intrinsic abilities you have, which are nothing in comparison to God.

Be free from spending time comparing yourself to other people.

Set your eyes on Jesus, the author and perfecter of your faith.

Pray to be free from the punishing spirit of comparison.

Praying to Be Searched Out by God

One of the most influential teachers of preaching in the late 20th century was Haddon Robinson. Many of us were schooled through his

---

[108] At least from the POV of India's "upper caste." As one villager told me, "They do not care for us."

wise writings. Robinson began his sermons with this brief confession: "God, if people knew about me what you know about me, they wouldn't listen to a word I said."[109] Here was a thoroughly searched-out person. Pay attention when such people preach.

In Psalm 139 we read, "Search me, O God. See if there is any offensive way in me." Philip Yancey writes that "In order to overcome self-deception, I need God's all-knowing help in rooting out hidden offenses like selfishness, pride, deceit, lack of compassion."[110]

How much I need a constant searching-out, by God! Thank God that his eyes are healing, loving, and non-condemning. If you only knew...

I am praying for self-clarity today.

Praying and Self-Control

Being self-controlled is part of a flourishing, fruitful life. In 1 Thessalonians 5:6-8 Paul writes:

> So then, let us not be like others, who are asleep, but let us be alert and self-controlled. For those who sleep, sleep at night, and those who get drunk, get drunk at night.... But since we belong to the day, let us be self-controlled...

"Drunk" is bad, because it is "of the night/darkness," and leads to out-of-control-ness. Paul informs me in Galatians 5:22-23 that I am, when under the influence of the Holy Spirit, self-controlled. This is part of the fruit of the Holy Spirit. When I am attached to the Spirit, self-control grows like grapes on a vine.

This is a great gift in today's addiction culture. Addicts are "attached" to things that control them.[111] The addict is a controlee to sexual urges,

---

[109] In Philip Yancey, *Prayer*, Kindle Location 540.

[110] Ib.

[111] The French word for 'addiction' is *attache*, as Gerald May has told us in *Addiction and Grace*.

drugs, food, even control itself. The addict cannot say "Yes" to the good, or "No" to the bad.

Self-control is as valuable today as it has ever been. *Self-control is freedom.* I am praying for this fruit to grow in me today.

Freedom from Unfulfilled Longing

An "If…, then…" statement is a conditional statement. For example: *If it rains, then the ground gets wet.* On the condition of rain, the ground gets wet. A conditional statement is also called a hypothetical statement. It's a hypothesis. It's hypothetical, not actual. It describes a possible state of affairs, not an actual one.

Human longing is about unfulfilled desire. *If only I could be/have/ achieve _____, then I would be happy/content.* The antecedent of the conditional statement expresses the longing, the consequent its fulfillment.

Conditional thinking operates in a world of perpetual discontent. Fulfillment of our many longings rarely brings lasting satisfaction. Shortly after we acquire, we hear the knock of desire. The single person longs to be married; the married couple longs for children; the parents long for grandchildren; the grandparents long to see their grandchildren get married. In this life there is perpetual incompleteness.

Not all longing is bad. Many good longings this side of eternity remain unfulfilled. This reality could leave us in unremitting devastation if we become enslaved to conditional thinking. The way to freedom in a world of unfulfilled dreams is to be released from the inner "If… then…" This is called *contentment.*

Contentment is non-circumstance dependent. One no longer thinks, *If these circumstances happen, then I will be content.* As Paul wrote:

> I don't have a sense of needing anything personally. I've learned by now to be quite content whatever my circumstances. I'm just as happy with little as with much, with much as with little. I've found the recipe

for being happy whether full or hungry, hands full or hands empty.[112]

Conditional thinking demands circumstances to change for there to be contentment. Unless one is healed of this, discontentment reigns. The Jesus-solution is to eliminate perpetual discontent by revealing the heart's true resting place. "Whatever I have, wherever I am, I can make it through anything in the One who makes me who I am."[113]

Years ago one of my baby sons, David, died. *If only David were alive, then I would be satisfied.* The longing expressed here, in the antecedent clause, is pure. But the consequent is false. It is false, because things run deeper than life's circumstances, fulfilled or unfulfilled. The idea that I will be forever satisfied in this life if only one of my circumstances would change is an illusion.

To realize this is to focus my heart and mind on something else. My soul finds rest in God alone. When I direct and order my life to rest in the One who makes me what I am, tears of unfulfilled longings are not polluted by unmet desires.

To pray is to rest in the Lord. Soul-rest is the locus of contentment.

Praying to Live as God's Beloved

I preached this morning on 1 John 2:7-11. The first word in verse 7 is John's address to his audience: "Beloved." The NIV says, "Dear friends." The Greek word is *agapetoi*, which means "Beloved," or "Loved ones."

As I prepared for this sermon I thought much about *agapetoi*. It contains *agape*, the unique word used to especially describe the love of God. Sometimes this is called "unconditional love."

God's love is unconditional. Conditional love is "if..., then..." love, which says things like, "If you do well, then I will love you," or "Because you have sinned, I am withholding my love from you." Conditional love is "love" in the kingdom of darkness. It is not the love of God. Conditional love is punishing because it is performance-based.

---

[112] Philippians 4:10-12, *The Message.*
[113] Philippians 4:13, *The Message*

I am loved by God. Dearly and unconditionally. This is intimate, tender language. As I reflected on this word I thought of many things. Linda and I used to lead ministry to children, and taught them a song that began, "Beloved, let us love one another." I think I'll teach that to our Redeemer kids in a few weeks. I want that truth to get into them!

I thought of my friend, Pastor John Grove, who always addresses his church family with the word "Beloved." I remembered the brilliant theologian Karl Barth, who wrote millions of words in books like his massive *Church Dogmatics* (containing footnotes as long as 60 pages!). On a visit to America, Barth summarized his writings by saying, "Jesus loves me this I know, for the Bible tells me so."

I think of a pastor in one of my seminary prayer classes. As a class assignment I sent him out to pray for one hour, and he didn't return to class. I was concerned that he didn't like me. The next day I asked him what happened. He replied that God spoke to him, saying "I love you," and he could not leave that place. He just stayed there, praying, basking, in belovedness.

I think of my conversion to Christ. I was 21. I'd heard the words "God loves you" countless times. But one day a campus minister at Northern Illinois University told me, "I don't know the answers to all your questions, but I do believe there is a God, and that God loves you." These words exploded in my heart. I knew, experientially and existentially, in a whole-being way, that I was beloved, by God. *This was the turning point of my life.*

"Could it be that beneath all the lures to greed, lust, and success rests a great fear of never being enough or not being lovable?"[114] Indeed. I'm in a spiritual battle. Contrarian voices whisper, "You're no good. You deserve to be rejected and abandoned." These accusing voices are my greatest enemy, because they violate and contradict the Great Truth, which is: I am God's beloved.

This is the core truth of my existence. My continual prayer is that this truth would move from mere intellectual acknowledgment to heart knowledge.

---

[114] Henri Nouwen, *Discernment*, 26.

8

PRAYING FOR OTHERS

I pray for people. I pray for those in my church family. At a Sunday morning worship service, I told my people that I would pray for them during the week if they write a request on a 3X5 card and give it to me. Several people came to me with their prayer cards. I took them home and typed them up. I gave a copy to Linda. We both prayed these requests throughout the week. They totaled twenty typed pages!

Praying for people is a holy burden. That week I interceded for many, before God. In the process I was touched, moved, saddened, sympathetic, hopeful, and faith-filled. What a privilege to be entrusted with these prayer requests!

Over the years I have prayed for countless others. In this chapter I present some things I have thought and learned from this.

Praying with a God-Burdened Heart

The word "intercession" means: "to come between." To pray, in the sense of interceding for someone, means to come between that person and God, on that person's behalf. In intercessory praying I stand in for someone else.

Lloyd Ogilvie defined intercessory praying this way: Intercession is not so much placing our burdens on God's heart, but God putting his burdens on our hearts.[1] How does this happen? The God-burdened heart arises from a God-presenced heart. As I consistently and deeply abide in the presence of the Almighty, I encounter people-burdens that lie on the heart of God.

There are many people to be praying for today. As God places his concerns for people on my heart *this* will be my praying life.

Intercessors Pray Like This

Intercessory praying brings changes in the lives of other persons. "Intercession can alter the spiritual situation of those for whom we pray."[2] Do I believe this? Of course. I would not pray for others if I did not believe this.

Paul assumed his prayers for people had causal efficacy. Praying strengthens the people you pray for. Where praying focuses, power falls. In Paul we have a model of how to pray for others. For example:

> I pray that, according to the riches of his glory, he may grant that you may be strengthened in your inner being with power through his Spirit, and that Christ may dwell in your hearts through faith, as you are being rooted and grounded in love. I pray that you may have the power to comprehend, with all the saints, what is the breadth and length and height and depth, and to know the love of Christ that surpasses knowledge, so that you may be filled with all the fullness of God.[3]

Using this prayer, we construct a template for intercessory praying that looks like this.

---

[1] In Sam Storms, *The Hope of Glory: 100 Daily Meditations on Colossians*, Kindle Locations 575-577. Wheaton: Crossway, 2007.
[2] Stanley Grenz, *Prayer: The Cry for the Kingdom*, 33
[3] Ephesians 3:16-19

God, I pray that _____ would be strengthened in their inner being through Your Spirit.

I pray that You, Jesus, might make _____'s heart Your home.

I pray that _____ might have the power to understand and know Your great love that transcends mere human knowledge.

I pray that _____ would be filled with all Your fullness.

In another place Paul prayed for others this way:

Now may our Lord Jesus Christ himself and God our Father, who loved us and through grace gave us eternal comfort and good hope, comfort their hearts and strengthen them in every good work and word.[4]

Intercessors, therefore, can pray like this:

God, I pray that You bring Your comfort and hope to _____'s heart and strengthen _____ in every good thing they do and say.

Intercessory Praying is Burdened Care-Praying

Praise be to the God and Father of our Lord Jesus Christ, the Father of compassion and the God of all comfort, who comforts us in all our troubles, so that we can comfort those in any trouble with the comfort we ourselves receive from God... If we are distressed, it is for your comfort and salvation; if we are comforted, it is for your comfort...
2 Corinthians 1:3-4; 6

---

[4] 2 Thessalonians 2:16-17

This afternoon I go to my solitary praying place, apart from home and office. Some of my praying will be intercessory. I will pray for people who have sent me prayer requests. I will stand in the gap for them, bringing their burdens before the throne of God's mercy, grace, love, and power.

To intercede for people is to shoulder a bag of hopes, fears, possibilities, and cares to the mountain of God. As I pray for them I often feel burdened. I'm not burdened by the act of praying. In praying I *bear one another's burdens, and so fulfill the law of Christ.*[5] In intercessory praying, burden-bearing happens.

I take on my brother's and sister's heaviness. I *feel* it, as compassion. Then, in the act of praying, I unload the burdens on Christ. I *cast my burdens upon him, for he cares for me.*[6] I lift the worry and anxiety of friends and enemies, carry their heavy loads to Christ, and lay them upon him.

Intercessory praying is not dispassionate, neutral, care-free praying. Intercessory praying is burdened care-praying. Heart, mind, and soul are all engaged in such troubled-waters praying. Praying for others involves compassionate weight-bearing and unloading.

Intercessory praying *feels*. Intercessory praying takes on weightiness. Intercession ignites when the burden is felt.

I'll be asking God for his thoughts and feelings about the requests of my brothers and sisters. How grateful I am for the many people who have shouldered *my* troubled soul into the presence of God!

Praying and Poverty

I embarrassed myself when I was in Kenya. I was the speaker at a Pastor's Conference in Eldoret, with sixty wonderful men and women from Kenya and Uganda. They were part of a network of 150 churches. Part of the event was sharing three meals a day, together. We ate authentic Kenyan food – vegetables, cooked raw bananas, rice, maize... I loved it!

---

[5] Galatians 6:2
[6] 1 Peter 5:7

At one meal I noticed that some of the pastors were filling their plates to overflowing. I made a joke, saying, "Kenyans and Ugandans eat a lot but still are slim and run so fast!" (Some of the world's greatest long-distance runners train in Eldoret.[7]) Later my host, Cliff, gently informed me that the reason these men and women put lots of food on their plates is because, for the most part, they only eat two meals a day. When they have a chance to eat, they eat a lot.

My heart sank. Who am I, what have I become, that I am so out of touch? The prayers of many Kenyans and Ugandans is that they would have food to eat *today*. I, on the other hand, fight overeating. My problem is not securing the next meal. It's that so much food is available, and I'm praying to be rescued from overeating.

Now I am back home in the land of over-plenty and over-eating. I am being processed by God. I don't know how it's going to turn out for me. Here are some things I am able to identify.

1. I am not to see someone who has no food and thank God that I have food. I *am* to thank God for food, for a roof over my head, for clothing. But this thanksgiving is *not* to come at the expense of someone else's lack. God has showed me that there is something evil about this. It uses another person's bondage as an occasion for rejoicing. Jesus never looked on hungry people and said, "Thank God that I am God and am not like these hungry people." Instead, he had compassion on them. He *became one of them*, the Son of Man who had no roof over his head. I must be praying for God's mercy, rather than giving thanks that I am not among the mercy-deprived. I am not to be like the Pharisee who prayed, "I thank you, God, that I am not like other people."

2. If the thought comes to me, "Thank God that I have more than these poor people," I must assume this is God calling me to help. Why would God show me a person poorer than I as a means of making me feel thankful? I must understand that authentic thankfulness results in overflowing, sacrificial giving. To those who have much and thank God

---

[7] Eldoret is a city in west Kenya. The famous long-distance runner Kip Keino has his high altitude training camp there. See http://www.runnersworld.co.uk/training/kenya-training-diary-day-two/8278.html

for it, much is expected. Thankfulness is hypocritical and meaningless if it does not overflow to others. Pure Pharisaic "thankfulness" thanks God that I am not poor; true thankfulness to God impacts the poor. Self-centered gratefulness is faux-gratitude.

3. At one of our Redeemer worship services God addressed me about these things. It was a beautiful time of praise and intentional thanksgiving to God for how he has blessed us as a church family. God told me this: "John, when you see someone who has nothing and give thanks for what you have that they don't have, that is the spirit of poverty on you." A spirit of poverty, a spirit of "lack," whispers to me, "You do not have enough." This heart of not-enough-ness, when it sees someone worse off than me, feels thankful.

This is the spirit of poverty's solution to my dilemma; viz., to keep me perpetually enslaved to a poverty mentality by comparing me with others. Some people drive a new car and I feel deprived; some people have no car and I feel thankful. A spirit of poverty is never satiated, and in this way it continuously punishes. Feeling gratitude in seeing someone who has no food happens because I feel I don't have enough myself. I think, "Whew, I'm not so bad off after all!" One only says those words if one feels, after all, "bad off." Real thanksgiving has nothing to do with any of this. I confess I've been living under a spirit of poverty, and now revolt against it.

I'm praying for a true heart of thanksgiving, because it is clear that I do not yet have it.

Praying and Healing

I pray for other people to be healed. Why not? After all, Jesus did it, and told us that if we abide in him we will do the things he has been doing.[8]

I was Associate Pastor at First Baptist Church of Joliet, Illinois, from 1974-1981. We had many wonderful friends there. One was a beautiful,

---

[8] See John 14.

Jesus-filled, elderly lady named Elsie. She was so kind to Linda and I. I can hear the sound of her voice and see her smile now.

Elsie had become physically frail. One day I got word that she was sick. I visited her and prayed for God to make her well. I always pray this way for sick people. To be honest, I did not expect much to happen. Yet it felt good to lovingly pray for her, and she seemed to appreciate it. When I left her that day, the thought came to me that I would soon be doing her funeral.

That evening Elsie called. Her voice was alive and vibrant. "I am feeling so much better. Thank you, John, for coming and praying for me. God has healed me!" Really? I was happy, and stunned. We all loved Elsie so much. The illness that had a grip on her physical body was gone! To my surprise, Elsie was alive, and would be for several more years.

As significant as that experience was for Elsie, I wonder if it was not more important for me. I gained confidence in praying for people. I had a greater expectation that praying is a powerful thing to do. I found that God's healing love was not corrupted by my mini-sized faith.

This is biblical, right? If you believe Genesis 1:1, then you can believe that God is able to heal people. If you believe God is love, then you can believe God hates sickness and desires to see his children well. And if you believe the words of James 5:14-15, then you will comply:

> Is anyone among you sick? Let them call the elders of the church to pray over them and anoint them with oil in the name of the Lord. And the prayer offered in faith will make the sick person well; the Lord will raise them up.

The first time we see the word "pray" in the Bible is in a healing context. In Genesis 20 the king of Gerar, Abimelek, takes Abraham's wife Sarah, since Abraham said Sarah was not his wife but his sister. God appears to Abimlelek in a dream, telling him to return Sarah to Abraham. "Abraham is a prophet," God said, "and he will *pray* for you and you will live."

So Abimelek obeyed God. "Then Abraham *prayed to God*, and *God healed Abimelek*, his wife and his female slaves so they could have children again, for the Lord had kept all the women in Abimelek's household from conceiving because of Abraham's wife Sarah."[9] I find it interesting that the initial biblical window into a life of praying has to do with healing power.

God's healing of Elsie encouraged me to pray for the sick. Since then I have seen healing happen many times. While it's true that I have prayed for sick people and not seen the results I hoped for, the times when prayer brought God's healing power have given me confidence when facing the humanly impossible.

I pray because I know that *where prayer focuses, power falls*.[10] I pray for the sick. They don't refuse my prayers, and neither does God. In my journals I have recorded many answers to prayers for healing.

Praying for My Enemies

The most radical thing Jesus ever told me was that I am to love my enemies.

> Love your enemies, do good to them, and lend to them without expecting to get anything back. Then your reward will be great, and you will be sons of the Most High, because he is kind to the ungrateful and wicked.[11]

Jesus didn't just say this, he lived it. This is so off-the-charts that to ask "What Would Jesus Do?" trivializes it, as if merely answering that question will empower me to love my enemies.

---

[9] Genesis 20:17-18

[10] For the best empirical study on the power of praying, see Candy Gunther Brown, *Testing Prayer: Science and Healing*. Harvard University Press, 2012.

[11] Luke 6:35

Jesus' words drop me to my knees, for I am not him. This kind of "no greater love" seems so far from me as to be unattainable. Yes, I am a Christ-follower. Yes, I am not enough like Christ.

Try this, as an experiment. Soon, if not now, someone will hate you. Their hatred will be personal. Call that person your enemy. They will speak, maybe even physically act, against you. They will crucify you with thoughts, words, and actions. They will mobilize an internet army to attack you. They will unfriend you on Facebook. They don't like you, and are out to reify this; viz., to demonstrate that their hatred of you is not a mere abstraction.

Now think of this enemy, and love them. From your heart. As you hang on the cross, let words of compassion flow. "God, forgive them, for they don't know what they are doing." As I consider doing this I can hardly believe it could really happen.

C.S. Lewis writes:

> We must try to feel about the enemy as we feel about ourselves - to wish that he were not bad, to hope that he may, in this world or another, be cured: in fact, to wish his good. That is what is meant in the Bible by loving him: wishing his good, not feeling fond of him or saying he is nice when he is not.[12]

How radical is this? If I lived this way, the Revolution would be breaking out around me.

Meanwhile, I am in trouble. I am irritated with people who are not even my enemies. I have a heart problem. God, be merciful to me.

Praying for My Enemies, Redux

"You have heard that it was said, 'Love your neighbor and hate your enemy.' But I tell you, love your enemies and pray for those who persecute you, that you may be children of your Father in heaven.
Jesus, in Matthew 5:43-45

---

[12] Lewis, *Mere Christianity.*

When I asked God to fill my heart with his love, I was forced to look into the hearts of my enemies. This is hard. It is hard because I am hard. There are things I want to judge, but do not desire to understand.

I have enemies, and have despised them. I have done things to people that caused them to hate me. Sometimes my words and deeds have been good, from God, and yet I was crucified. God has used me to rescue people, and some eventually turned against me. Sometimes I have been unloving towards others, and been hated for it. Love is risky. You could die for it.

Some have come after me, and I have hated them. This includes Christians hating Christians which, for me, is the most painful kind of hatred. How narrow, how shallow, how short, how low, is the hypothetical love of this world.

Into this mess comes Jesus. He has the nerve to upset the rotten apple cart. The deep thing that inspires me to sing songs of hatred is interrupted by the words, *love your enemies, and pray for those who persecute you*. How shall I do this?

Here is my love experiment. I have begun to deliberately and intentionally pray for people I hate. By "hate," I include euphemisms like, "am irritated by," "dislike," "frustrated with," "upset with," and so on. When I think of someone I hate, I force myself to pray for them. I ask God to bless them, and fill them with his goodness. I ask God to be merciful and gracious to them. I ask God to help and heal them, and to prosper them.

I force myself to pray this way for my enemies because this kind of love does not yet form my heart. This is unnatural to my subhumanity. I am weak in love. So in my weakness I pray words of love, not hate, to those who, for whatever reason, hate me.

I am *disciplining* myself to do this, because I am a *disciple* of Jesus. This feels new to me, praying for people who persecute me. I am certain God is pleased with what I am choosing to do, since this is his desire. I believe God's power is in this, and that he will take my weak prayers and form in me his strong heart of love.

As I have been doing this I have experienced moments of compassion, the initial drops of a purifying rain, heading my way.

Praying Brings Awareness of God's Heartbreak

I looked at photos of atrocities in South Sudan. They are heartbreaking. I need to see them. I cannot live in a fabricated world, insulated from the suffering of others. While I cannot be expected to know the total troubledness of the world's peoples, God knows, and opens a window into this world.

When I pray at the Solitary God Conference[13] one of the main sessions is called "Global Suffering." An awareness of God's heartbreak must be mine. In real praying I come to know more of what God knows.

In praying for global sufferers I unite myself with Jesus and, through him, lift up the whole world in cries for mercy and justice, peace and healing. Compassionate praying feels with the starving, tortured, and displaced. This is good, since awareness plus true compassion can lead to action, as God directs.[14]

Praying for the distant suffering of others attunes my heart to the suffering of those around me. I am thinking that if I prayed more globally, more would be accomplished through me locally.

Praying for My Persecuted Brothers and Sisters

Over the years I've taught pastors and Christian leaders from countries where persecution of Jesus-followers is the norm. These include...

- three pastors from Egypt who collectively told me it would be safer for them to live in Saddam's Iraq than in Egypt.
- two pastors from Pakistan who told me of the horrors of anti-blasphemy laws.
- many pastors from China who told of suffering under China's atheist government.

---

[13] Just God and I, conferencing together.

[14] Praying for suffering peoples might seem impractical and useless. Yet the idea of a monastery is grounded in the belief that solitary and community praying is what is needed for there to be an authentic and effective activism.

- a pastor from Cuba who was imprisoned for years under Castro's declared atheist-communist state following the Cuban revolution.[15]
- a pastor who fled Liberia during the civil war as Muslim persecution of Christians grew.
- a Christian leader in Ethiopia who was imprisoned after her husband was killed in the Marxist coup.

Global persecution of Jesus-followers is very much alive. Some are even saying that this reality is *the* story of today. Eric Metaxas writes:

> [Today] persecution is rampant in many places in the world - in the former Communist countries, and in Southeast Asia, Africa, and the Middle East. But we hear so rarely about Christian persecution. Such stories are mostly glossed over in favor of the latest political news, or, far worse, an inane story about some celebrity. Can we doubt that God will judge us for what we allow to occupy our attention?[16]

I am praying for my persecuted sisters and brothers.[17] God, what would you have me do?

The Weight of Praying

It's Monday morning. I'm thinking of many people who have asked me to pray for them. I experience a heavy overwhelmingness because of the requests, all of which are important, some of which are matters of survival, life, and death.

---

[15] See here, e.g. - http://www.minnpost.com/christian-science-monitor/2012/03/fidel-castro-excommunicated-1962-meets-pope-benedict

[16] Eric Metaxas, Forward, in Marshall, Gilbert, and Shea, *Persecuted: The Global Assault on Christians*, VIII. Nashville: Thomas Nelson, 2013.

[17] See, for example, Rupert Shortt, *Christianophobia: A Faith Under Attack*. Grand Rapids: Eerdmans, 2013.

I am burdened. I slouch beneath the weight of others. This is good. Real praying includes a crying out to God, a fervent petitioning, on behalf of the persons I am praying for.

To pray for others is to carry their petitions, so they don't have to go it alone. In praying I come to God with a bag of heavy burdens. I deliver them, like large stones, to him.

Praying From My Nothingness

This morning I am praying. I have many requests in mind. With some of these, from others and for myself, I do not have answers. I do not know what to do.

This is normal for me. On my own in intercessory prayer, I often think of nothing and can do nothing. I have no answer for my nothingness except to stay connected to God and pray. I look to the promise of Jesus, who said, "If you remain in me and I in you, you will bear much fruit; apart from me you can do nothing."[18]

I know little, but I am connected. I dwell, via the spiritual disciplines, in the house of God, whose temple is my heart. I read John 15:7, where Jesus says, "If you remain in me and my words remain in you, ask whatever you wish, and it will be done for you."

I hear God tell me, "Why not try this, John?" So I do. Today, I am abiding in him. His words are in me. It is appropriate to ask God for help. So I do. "God, show me what to do to help these people I am praying for. Lead me and empower me. Give me your words of wisdom for others. Help me lead and minister to my church family in these days. Amen."

I am thinking this way:

1. If I abide in Christ and his words abide in me, then I will know what to ask of God.
2. I am abiding in Christ.
3. Therefore, my requests that arise in God's presence will be done.

---

[18] John 15:5

Praying and Compassion

My four-decade prayer experiment has resulted in an increase of compassion towards other people. This has developed slowly, over time. I have marinated in the teriyaki sauce of God's presence, listened for his voice, and communicated in the voice he has given me.

I also know that the compassion of Jesus does not yet fully occupy my heart. But I have a plan. My plan is this: Devote much time to praying, and my transformation will slowly happen. God will morph my unfeeling heart into one that feels for others in their weakness.

I do not yet love as Jesus loves. As I pray, I expect God to get his hands on my unfeeling heart, and shape it into a heart of compassion.

How to Pray for Other People's Change

I cannot change people. But I can pray that people would change. I can pray that that the abusive spouse would change. I can ask God to break them in the right place, thereby giving an invitation to change. But only God can change them.

It is a major step forward in the spiritual life to realize that God is the agent of change, not me. This helps me focus on changes I need. As God changes me, he can use me to influence people. The spiritual transformation that happens in my heart is not only for my benefit.

I have seen people change. Their transformations have influenced me for the good. I understand the power of influence. Influence is more powerful than control. Trying to control or guilt-manipulate others de-influences and distances them. More and more, I see that I can let that go. At this point *I* am free to change. The transformation of my heart is in inverse proportion to my controlling demands that others change.

Sometimes God allows me to see how some other person, X, desperately needs change. God gives me eyes to see so I can pray for them, not judge or critique them (which any fool can do).

Here is a way to pray for X, and their need to change.

First, pray for your own self-transformation into greater Christlikeness. Pray, "God, change *my* heart!"

Second, trust that God can use what is happening in you to influence X. Pray for God to guide you in ways to relate to X (what to do, what to say).

Third, since all change requires brokenness, pray for X to be broken in the right place.

Finally, pray for a fresh baptism of love that transcends irritation with people, such as X and yourself.

Praying and Letting Go of People

As Jesus was going into a village, ten men who had leprosy met him.[19]

Over the years many people have come and gone in my life. They arrived and departed. God gave, and took away. Several came for help. Some stayed, as friends. Some said thank you, some did not.

("The ten lepers stood at a distance and called out in a loud voice, "Jesus, Master, have pity on us!"")

I'm thinking of a man who called me for help. I spent many hours with him. According to him, God worked through me to save his marriage and family.

("When he saw them, he said, "Go, show yourselves to the priests." And as they went, they were cleansed.")

Things got stabilized in his life. And he left, not telling me why, or where, he was going. This was hard for me.

("One of them, when he saw he was healed, came back, praising God in a loud voice. He threw himself at Jesus' feet and thanked him—and he was a Samaritan. Jesus asked, "Were not all ten cleansed? Where are the other nine?"")

I cannot control the choices people make. I don't have epistemic access to the deep waters of troubled human hearts. I can, however, pray to be set free from a spirit of rejection. How? Ruth Haley Barton's question helps me. She asks, "Are there places in your life and leadership where you recognize that you are holding yourself tight rather than

[19] Luke 17:11-19

experiencing full surrender to God, where you recognize that you are not free?"[20]

When I experience rejection, it is mostly not because someone has rejected me. It's more complicated than that. Often, my perceived rejection has nothing to do with me. Yet I take it on myself, because I am holding myself and others too tightly.

I must not allow these kind of things to degenerate into morbid introspection. Instead, I must pray to give other people, and even my own self, over to God, inviting him to guide the process.

I am praying to let go of people so as to love them better.

Praying for God's Truths to Descend From My Mind into My Heart

It was my privilege to speak to 175 inmates at a large state correctional institute.[21] This prison has a full-time chaplain. I was impressed and thankful for God's presence in him, and with the work he was doing with inmates.

After I spoke, I talked with many of the men, and prayed for them. One of them, a man in his sixties, approached me. He asked, "Would you pray for me?"

Yes.

"Please pray that I could forgive myself."

I would like to do that.

Then he said, "I understand God's forgiveness up here (he pointed to his head), but I cannot forgive myself down here (pointing to his heart) for killing my parents."

I was stunned.

---

[20] Ruth Haley Barton, *Strengthening the Soul of Your Leadership: Seeking God In the Crucible of Ministry*, 57.

[21] I spoke at Mansfield Correctional Institute in Mansfield, Ohio. It is adjacent to the old correctional center, the prison where "The Shawshank Redemption" was filmed.

The forgiveness of God is the only answer for those imprisoned by their past sins.[22]

I gathered ten inmates around the man who killed his parents. We placed our hands on him, and I prayed, "God, let the truth _____ knows in his mind now become the reality of _____'s heart."

I can't get him out of my mind and heart this morning. I am praying for God's truths to descend from his mind into his heart. Would you join me in praying for him?

---

[22] For empirical corroboration see University of Wisconsin psychologist Robert Enright, *The Forgiving Life: A Pathway to Overcoming Resentment and Creating a Legacy of Love*. Washington, D.C.: American Psychological Association, 2012.

9

PRAYING AND MONO-TASKING

It's Tuesday. This afternoon I'm going to the back of our three acres and sit, beneath the tall oak and sycamore trees, on the riverbank. I'm going to pray. And meditate on Scripture.

When God speaks to me, I will write it down in my spiritual journal. I'll do this for three to four hours. Just God and I.

I've done this for decades. I'm not trying to make something happen. I do it to discern what is happening in, around, and beyond me. I'm looking forward to meeting with God today!

One byproduct of these times is that creative juices begin to flow. Clear thinking happens. Awareness and attentiveness get readjusted. God tells me I am loved. All as a result of intentional God-attending.

I'm going to be quiet and still.

There is a season for everything. This includes a time to shut up and listen.

Susan Cain, in *Quiet,* cites studies indicating that excessive stimulation impedes learning. People learn better after a slow walk through the woods than after a noisy walk down a busy city street. One study of 38,000 knowledge workers across different sectors "found that the simple act of being interrupted is one of the biggest barriers to productivity."[1]

---

[1] Susan Cain, *Quiet: The Power of Introverts In a World That Can't Stop Talking,* 85. New York: Random House, 2012.

Excessive multitasking impedes learning, since multitasking is being-interrupted. Cain writes:

> Even multitasking, that prized feat of modern-day office warriors, turns out to be a myth. Scientists now know that the brain is incapable of paying attention to two things at the same time. What looks like multitasking is really switching back and forth between multiple tasks, which reduces productivity and increases mistakes by up to 50 percent.[2]

I have learned to mono-task the God relationship. This is essential to praying. This chapter contains reflections I have about single-minded attentiveness to God.

Blessed Are the Mono-Taskers, for They Shall See God

My Payne Theological Seminary class is called Spiritual Formation. My main assignment is: set apart one hour a day, five days a week, for seven weeks. Use this time to pray and listen to God. Keep a record of the voice and activity of God in a spiritual journal.

Needed: listening skills, ability to meditate, and focus, to allow God to dive deep in your heart.[3]

I also teach three philosophy courses at Monroe County Community College: Introduction to Logic, Introduction to Western Philosophy, and Philosophy of Religion. The ability to stay on task is needed to learn philosophy, and to think philosophically. A philosopher must have a great capacity to go inward, to ponder, and ruminate.

---

[2] Ib.

[3] See Proverbs 20:5 – "The purposes of a man's heart are deep waters, but a man of understanding will draw them out."

Spiritual formation and philosophy are slow cookers, not microwaves. Both, if attended to, produce lasting fruit in a person's life. Oak trees grow from the soil of slow thinking about life's big ideas.[4]

Deep, lasting, relationships are slow-cookers, too. This includes the God-relationship. Knowing God involves more than theoretical knowledge, just as one learns to ride a bike by actually riding it, not by reading books about bike riding.

Kierkegaard told us that a pure heart, untainted by distractions, wills one thing.[5] To "will one thing" is to focus on, attend to, be captivated by, be still before, one thing. What is the benefit of that? Nothing less, said Jesus, than the *visio dei*.

Blessed are the mono-taskers, for they shall see God.[6]

Woe to the Neurally Incapable, for They Shall Miss God

An entire generation has formed that is neurally incapable of attending to one thing, for any period of time. For these people, praying will be difficult.[7]

Mono-tasking is a lost art.[8] Matt Richtel, in his essay "Growing Up Digital, Wired for Distraction,"[9] makes the case that singlemindedness is rare among today's high school students. Richtel cites, as typical, a bright 17-year-old student who confesses, "A book takes so long. I prefer the immediate gratification."

---

[4] On the distinction between slow thinking and fast thinking, See Daniel Kahneman, *Thinking, Fast and Slow*.

[5] Soren Kierkegaard, *Purity of Heart Is to Will One Thing*. Feather Trail Press, 2009.

[6] Matthew 5:8. Translation mine.

[7] To understand this, see Nicholas Carr's *The Shallows: What the Internet Is Doing To Our Brains*; and Howard Gardner's *The App Generation*, where the distinction is made between "app-dependency" (bad) and "app-enablement" (good). New York: Norton, 2010. See also Sherry Turkle's amazing study *Reclaiming Conversation: The Power of Talk In a Digital Age*.

[8] See Turkle, op. cit.

[9] http://www.nytimes.com/2010/11/21/technology/21brain.html?pagewanted=all&_r=0

Professors take note. This student *cannot* attend to you. He's not being rebellious if he's not paying attention. Neurally, he is attention-incapacitated. "Developing brains can become more easily habituated than adult brains to constantly switching tasks — and less able to sustain attention."[10]

In my spiritual formation classes, it is beyond-hard for more and more seminary students to pray, listen to God, and meditate on God-things for even a few minutes. This is because their brains are rewarded not for staying on task, but for jumping to the next thing.

Richtel cites studies showing that students now lack the attention span to read the assignments on their own. The ability to focus, to deep-think, is going... going... gone..., and with it, the God-relationship is going..., at least in terms of the wired generation.

What am I doing about this? In my philosophy classes I assign little or no reading for homework, since I assume ninety-five percent of my students won't read it anyway. I ban texting and laptops in class. In my lectures I look for dialogue and interaction, exposing students to the wonder of thinking conversationally.

I give seminarians prayer assignments (not books to read on prayer, which may or may not be read anyway), and require that spiritual journals be kept. In some cases, a student is met by God. A new-yet-ancient habit begins to form, fresh neural connections are made, the joy and value of heart-stillness and heart purity are acquired, and it's like life begins.

Praying Is Ontologically Antecedent to McPraying

Can we tweet occasional prayers to God while on the run in this crazy, busy life? The answer is: Yes. Call this "McPrayer."

Is it OK to McPray? Yes.

Is McPraying the kind of thing the Scriptures talk when it comes to praying? No.

---

[10] Ib.

No, because praying is a relationship, not something we pull out of our hip pocket in an emergency. Biblical praying is pure, which means it wills one thing. Jesus-type praying is monocular and single-minded.

The prayer relationship with God should be like a good marriage. McMarriages are shallow, disconnected, and troubled. So is multi-tasked McSpirituality.

No praying person in the Bible, or in church history, would have concluded that praying was like a microwave. Real praying is a slow cooking kettle of simmering stew. Praying is engagement in relationship with God. Real relationships require much time, space, and focus. So does real praying.

Slow-cooked praying hosts the primal soup out of which authentic occasional prayers emerge. Praying is ontologically antecedent to McPraying.

Multitasking Is the Road to Mediocrity

I teach mono-tasking. Mono-tasking is focusing on one thing for the sake of learning it to excellence. Mono-tasking is required to achieve excellence in anything. Like learning a musical instrument.

I started playing guitar when I was five. I taught in a music studio in my 20s. I practiced like a *mono*maniac! I was so focused that my parents had a hard time interrupting me to do my homework. I was uninterruptible. I had an undivided heart. To do *anything* well, this is required.

I isolated myself while working on my Ph.D. I would hunker down in a library bunker, remove all distractions, set a book before me, and *attend*. I was all eyes and ears, towards one thing. This focus was so intense I can feel it now as I write about it.

I remember taking a doctoral seminar on the phenomenologist Edmund Husserl. Our text was Husserl's *Experience and Judgment*. Each student had to teach one chapter out of the book. In preparation, I studied my face off. I deprived myself of all distractions and honed in on the text. This was hard work that could not achieved by multitasking.

Multitasking, the ability to switch from one task to another, is valuable when we need to do more than one thing at a time. We multitask when we drive a car, when we exercise on the treadmill while listening to music, and when we do the dishes while planning the day that lies before us. In such examples we're not really *attending* to multiple things simultaneously, because our brains are not capable of that.

While multitasking is needed, the chronic, neurally determined multitasker becomes, at best, average at many things. A mile wide and an inch deep. One will never really learn Philosophy, or brain surgery, or golf, or baking, this way. Nor will one succeed in relationships, to include the God-relationship.[11]

Jesus said, more than once I am sure, "Whoever has ears to hear, let them hear."[12] Multitasked distractedness subverts listening. It is the path to shallowness, mediocrity, and failure. When the heart surgeon opens up our chest, holding the scalpel in one hand, we don't want him holding his cell phone in the other hand, right?

Solitude - the Great Struggle & the Great Encounter

Solitude is the place of the great struggle, and the great encounter. One wrestles with the false self and its pretensions, and wrestles with God, who works to establish the humanity of our real self in us. God gets his way as the false, subhuman self is stripped away.

This is soul-restoration. It happens in solitude.[13] Layers of cultural veneer are stripped away to expose the original human "finish," which is: created in the image of God. Transformation happens, which is the metamorphing of the false self into a new creation. This is why Henri Nouwen refers to solitude with God as "the furnace of spiritual transformation." Things get burned away and refined.

---

[11] Linda and I still go out on weekly dates and mono-task.

[12] Mark 4:9, et. Al.

[13] Soul-restoration also happens in authentic community. It is my opinion that solitude precedes community, dialectically.

Intentionally spend much time praying alone with God, in a monotasked way, and you will be restored. God will peel the false skin off you. The agent of this is God. *He* restores your soul. By his Spirit you get changed into greater and greater Christlikeness.

You Can't Multi-task the God-Relationship

"I pray when I shop. I pray when I'm at work. I pray when I'm doing a lot of other things." I hear people say this. Is it possible? Yes. Is it the kind of prayer we see in the Christian scriptures? No.

My father could watch TV, read the newspaper, and sleep - all at the same time. If we tried to change the channel, he would preternaturally wake up, and announce, "Hey, I was watching that!" I would think, to myself, no, that's not possible.

Prayer, as talking with God about what we are thinking and doing together, is all about relationship. It's a relationship of love. When I was dating Linda, I could have spent time with her while accomplishing other things as well. I could have mowed the lawn while on a date. She could have walked next to me, and we could have talked, right?

What is wrong with this picture? What's wrong is that when personal love-relationships are multi-tasked, the tasks win, but love loses. The lawn gets mowed, the relationship gets marginalized.

Jesus didn't multi-task relationship with the Father. He spent a lot of time going off to pray, heart to heart with the Father, alone. Jesus mono-tasked his relationship with the Father. If Jesus needed to do this, who are we not to?

The multi-tasking approach to prayer is typical of our anemic Western culture's spirituality. Intimate prayer-oneness with God has been lost. In its place prayer is one of many balls being juggled, and mostly dropped.

I hear people say, "I pray everywhere I go," as if that's some badge of honor. That kind of prayer is *not* the heart of what is meant by "prayer" in the Christian scriptures. Real, authentic prayer is radically attentive, because the pray-er is in a love-relationship with their God.

Mono-task the love relationship with God, by praying.

Super-glued to God in the Act of Praying

Stanley Grenz wrote, years ago, that "prayer is the greatest challenge to the church today."[14] I believe it still is. 2 Chronicles 7:14 does not say, "If my people, called by my name, will humble themselves and get busy."

A lot of church energy and effort is placed on raising money to maintain programs and infrastructure. Prayer, on the other hand, requires no money, and is non-programmatic, since it is, essentially, a relationship with God. Poor people and poor churches can pray. Indeed, such communities *do* pray, usually more than wealthy churches. When Jesus says, "Blessed are the poor in spirit, for theirs is the kingdom of heaven," their blessedness lay in their hunger and need for connection to God.[15]

Look at the poor, program-barren, building-less, first-century church. They are a model of a praying church. Prior to Pentecost they were "devoted" to praying. The upper room fellowship was an experiment in continual praying. We read that, in obedience to the command of Jesus, "they all joined together constantly in prayer."[16]

Post-Pentecost praying proceeded forth. It wasn't like they were thinking, "Well, we prayed. The Big Event happened. Now, we can lighten up on this praying-thing since we're so busy we don't have time to pray." I imagine them thinking more like this: "Wow! Prayer is a God-relationship that *does* things." In the language of philosopher J.L. Austin, prayer is a performative speech-act having illocutionary force.[17]

We read:

> They *devoted themselves* to the apostles' teaching and to
> the fellowship, to the breaking of bread and to *prayer*...
> Every day they continued to meet together in the temple

---

[14] Stanley Grenz, *Prayer: The Cry for the Kingdom*, 1.

[15] Matthew 5:3

[16] Acts 1:14

[17] See J.L. Austin, *How to Do Things with Words*. New York: Oxford, 1962.

courts. They broke bread in their homes and ate together
with glad and sincere hearts, praising God...[18]

These first Jesus-followers were *devoted* to praying.[19] "Devoted"
(προσκαρτερέω; pros-kar-ter-eh'-o) means: to adhere; to be constant
to one; to be steadfastly attentive unto; to give unremitting care to one
thing.

Real praying adheres to one thing; viz., God. Super-glued to God,
in the act of praying.

Praying is Absolutely Unmixed Attention on God

The French philosopher Simone Weil wrote: "Absolutely unmixed
attention is prayer."[20] I would add "towards God," to read: Absolutely
unmixed attention towards God is prayer.

Praying is a challenge to we who live in the Age of Increasing
Distraction. We are linkers, tweeters, Net-surfers, skimming over the
surface of life. Fewer and fewer can focus and attend to one thing. Rare
are those who dig deep in one location.

Ours is a world of information overload. In 1600, an English writer
named Barnaby Rich complained, "One of the great diseases of this age
is the multitude of books that doth so overcharge the world that it is
not able to digest the abundance of idle matter that is every day hatched
and brought into the world."[21] Poor Barnaby Rich would not believe
the gigatons of idle matter being hatched today!

Stanford University's Clifford Nass wrote that internet multitaskers
are "suckers for irrelevancy." "Everything distracts them," and their
minds are programmed to pay attention to the garbage of life.[22]

---

[18] Acts 2:42; 46-47

[19] In Greek Acts 2:42 reads: ἦσαν δὲ <u>προσκαρτεροῦντες</u> τῇ διδαχῇ τῶν ἀποστόλων
καὶ τῇ κοινωνίᾳ, τῇ κλάσειτοῦ ἄρτου καὶ ταῖς προσευχαῖς. I've underlined the
word we translate into English as "devoted."

[20] Simone Weil, *Gravity and Grace*.

[21] In Carr, *The Shallows: What the Internet Is Doing to Our Brains*, Kindle Locations
2872-2874.

[22] Ib., Kindle Location 2424.

Perpetual distractedness is an enemy of real relationship. It is, as such, an enemy of praying, since true praying *is* relationship with God.[23]

"Unmixed attention" is heart-purity that wills one thing. This is relationship language. Love language. To pray is to love, just as the hours Linda and I spent yesterday talking and listening to one another *is* to love each other. Spending time listening, talking, and sharing with God - one-on-one - is loving God.

There is a kind of "knowing" which only comes from one-thing attentiveness. Philosopher of science Michael Polanyi called this "personal knowledge."[24] We get captured by the object of our attentiveness.

Praying is being captured by God alone, in loving relationship. When that happens, the multitasking disease is healed, and prayer as conversation with God begins.

Cast Your Distractions on Him

Distraction.

That, according to Richard Foster, is the primary spiritual problem in our day. "The Internet culture is only a surface issue. Our problem is something far more fundamental. This deeper, more basic issue can be summed up in one word: distraction."[25]

The inability to focus.

Difficulty in attending to just one thing.

The tweeting soul.

The linking brain.

This is nothing new.[26] It has always been with us. "People were distracted long before it [the Internet] came along. Blaise Pascal

---

[23] For a fuller understanding of this see Richard Foster, *Prayer: Finding the Heart's True Home.*

[24] See Michael Polanyi, *Personal Knowledge: Towards a Post-Critical Philosophy.* Chicago: University of Chicago, 1962.

[25] Foster, *Sanctuary of the Soul: Journey into Meditative Prayer*, Kindle Locations 709-710.

[26] See, e.g., Maggie Jackson and Bill McKibben, *Distracted: The Erosion of Attention and the Coming Dark Age.* New York: Prometheus, 2008.

observed, "The sole cause of man's unhappiness is that he does not know how to stay quietly in his room.""[27]

Minds are prone to wander. Today, they seem to divert more than ever, because our culture profits in the sales of mental and spiritual rabbit trails. Ours is an atmosphere of distraction, a world economy sustained by distractedness. To *un-attend* is the norm.

This is changing the nature of interpersonal relationships, in some ways for the worse. M.I.T. professor Sherry Turkle argues that digital connectedness has caused the loss of empathy, and results in increased loneliness.[28]

This affects the God-relationship, and if, and how, people pray. Single-mindedness, the ability to attend to one thing over a sustained period of time, is needed to succeed at anything, including praying.

If someone wanted to overcome this, how could it be done? Foster writes: "The first counsel I would give regarding a wandering mind is for us to be easy on ourselves. We did not develop a noisy heart overnight, and it will take time and patience for us to learn a single-hearted concentration."[29]

Don't be impatient with yourself here. That is precisely the problem: impatience.

Learn about your inner chaos. Identify it. When your mind wanders, note where it wanders to. It always wanders to something like a burden. Identify the burden, and give it over to God. As 1 Peter 5:7 says, "Cast your burdens on him, for he cares for you."

Discern if a particular distraction is from God. "If one particular matter seems to be repeatedly intruding into our meditation, we may want to ask of the Lord if the intrusion has something to teach us. That is, we befriend the intruder by making it the object of our meditation."[30]

Find ways "to crucify the spirit of distraction."[31] Fast for periods of time from electronic media (how badly do you want this?). Choose

---

[27] Foster, op. cit., Kindle Locations 710-711
[28] See Turkle, *Reclaiming Conversation*
[29] Ib., Kindle Locations 716-717
[30] Ib., Kindle Locations 725-726
[31] Ib., Kindle Location 727

to turn off the cell phone and see if you can survive without it (a new kind of reality survival show?).

Remember: people don't need you as much as you think they do. Constant textedness with people increases inner chaos. Foster writes: "I would suggest a fast from all our Internet gadgetry for one hour a day, one day a week, one week a year. See if that helps to calm the internal distraction."[32]

Find a place to meet with God. Post a sign saying, "Distraction-Free Zone." In that quiet place, take off your hard hat and pray. Dialogue with God. Listen, and speak. Learn the Relationship. Get away from the to-do list and *be* with God. Live life with your *doing* flowing from your *being* with the Almighty.

Ahhh... to calm the inner distraction... To learn simply being with Immanuel... To receive and respond to God's earth-shattering presence... To be in love with your Maker...

...that I might come to the place where other voices are silenced, my own voice is muted, and I hear the footsteps of him, and nothing else.

Undistraction Increases God-Attraction

I did a two-year degree in Music Theory. One of my requirements was to learn some basic piano skills. This, of course, required practice, in a designated practice room.

These practice rooms were empty, except for a piano, piano bench, and a chair for the teacher. Austerity ruled. Music practice rooms are the ultimate anti-sports bar environments. There were no pictures on the walls. There was nothing to divert one's eyes and attention away from the focus, which was the instrument. You cannot learn the instrument without concentration.

I once had a student who was a Coptic monk. He lived at the Monastery of St. Anthony of Egypt of the Fourth Century. He called his room a "cell." His cell contained only a bed and four walls that

---

[32] Ib., Kindle Locations 728-729

were bare, except for a cross. A music practice room is a monastic cell, containing one thing, which is the object of one's focus.

Such rooms promote purity of heart. They are places of least distraction, focused environments that are serious about purpose. Within them, the distracted mind is channeled into a river where all things flow.

Jesus told his disciples to pray in their secret room,[33] with the door closed. These rooms were barren and bare-walled, except for perhaps symbols of a fish, or a cross.[34] An uncluttered prayer chamber facilitates focus on God. Undistraction increases the possibility of God-attraction.

Jesus often withdrew to lonely places where he prayed.[35] In such places, praying is more effective.

Praying and the Wandering Mind

It often happens that the praying person's mind wanders to things other than God-ideas. When this happens, what should you do?

Some suggest you just "shut it off." My experience is that most are not able to do that. Trying to shut off the wandering mind can turn into an extended meditation on it.

I suggest that, when this happens, write in your journal. Write down where your mind wanders to. You'll find that your mind never wanders arbitrarily. It always goes to something like a burden. In this way your wandering mind is a barometer of your spiritual condition. Write the burden down. Once you get it on paper, it can feel like it's distant from you.[36]

The wandering mind could be a God-prompting. God could be leading you to pray for someone, or for something. When this happens, bring the burden to God and involve him in it.

---

[33] Matthew 6:6, *tameion.*

[34] See, e.g., James Charlesworth, *Jesus Within Judaism*, on the discovery of the house of Peter and what was found on the walls. New York: SPCK, 1989.

[35] Luke 5:16

[36] Henri Nouwen writes about this in *The Genesee Diary.* New York: Image, 1981.

The burden is either some area of disquiet in you, or about someone who is hurting or a troubling situation. In both cases, this can be a God-thing.

The more I pray and spend time with God, the less my mind wanders. If I haven't prayed for an hour in a long time (or ever), I should expect my thoughts to be all over the place. The more I pray, the less my mind wanders, because I live in a place of constant de-burdening.

True Praying and One Thing Theology

Blessed are the pure in heart, for they will see God.
Jesus, in Matthew 5:8

The act of praying brings focus to the heart. The more we pray-as-keeping-company-with-God, the more we experience a decluttering of the heart. This is the achievement of purity.

A pure heart wills one thing. Sees one thing. Hears one voice. Is centered. Is not distracted by other voices. The achievement of heart-purity brings success in relationships, and in life. This is "one thing" theology.

Jesus said, "You still lack *one thing*."[37]

The blind man who was healed replied, "*One thing* I do know."[38]

Paul wrote, "*One thing* I do."[39]

Peter counseled, "Do not forget this *one thing*."[40]

Paul said, "For I resolved *to know nothing* while I was with you *except* Jesus Christ and him crucified."[41]

"One thing" language is the discourse of the pure heart. In true prayer, we lay our Tweeter down.

---

[37] Luke 18:22

[38] John 9:25

[39] Philippians 3:13

[40] 2 Peter 3:8

[41] 1 Corinthians 2:22

By the rivers of Babylon we sat and wept
when we remembered Zion.
There on the poplars
we hung our iPhones...[42]

After years of praying and praying and praying, and getting alone with God, concentration and God-focus is easier for me. One thing God does in a praying person's life is strip away distractions. One dwells more and more in the clearing, not the clutter. God pulls us out of the noisiness and wordiness of the world, and escorts us into his fields. There, we behold him.

There is where the pure in heart towards God are blessed.

This is where the listening happens.

---

[42] Psalm 137, my translation.

10

PRAYING AND COMMUNITY

I am of Finnish descent. On both sides of my family. Finns tend to be reclusive.

This is an understatement. Finnish men would rather bale hay alone in the field than sit around the table looking at faces and sharing life together.[1]

My ethnic background mitigates against fellowship. Community has not been easy for me. Which may explain why I read Dietrich Bonhoeffer's *The Cost of Discipleship* in 1971, but picked up *Life Together* a few years ago.

In spite of this, Linda and I have been in a small fellowship group every week of every year of our Christian life together. I need community. I need the praying that happens there, plus the desserts and coffee.

The sad truth for Finnish Christians is that the Bible is essentially a communal document. It's not a book for solitary individuals. Writing about the Psalms as a prayer book, Bonhoeffer states:

> This prayer belongs, not to the individual member, but to the whole Body of Christ. Only in the whole Christ does the whole Psalter become a reality, a whole which the individual can never fully comprehend and call his

---

[1] "Finland is a famously introverted nation. Finnish joke: How can you tell if a Finn likes you? He's staring at your shoes instead of his own." Susan Cain, *Quiet: The Power of Introverts in a World That Can't Stop Talking*, Kindle Location 434

own. That is why the prayer of the psalms belongs in a peculiar way to the fellowship.[2]

"The psalms," he writes, "teach us to pray as a fellowship."[3]

My solitary times with God prepare me for community. In community I have learned much about praying. Here are some things I have discovered.

Community Is Where Humility and Glory Touch

The Real Jesus called forth a community to dwell in and work through, not a bunch of isolated, detached individuals. Call this "church." *Ekklesia.*

Ek + kaleo. The called-out-by-Christ people of God.

Effective, Jesus-indwelt community, requires individual and corporate humility. Every single person in the totality abandons themselves to the will, and ways, of God. This is Real Church. It's a Communal Movement.

I have met community-rejecting Christians who refuse to assemble with other believers. In this, they are biblical and theological apostates, no matter how bad they were treated. They have chosen pride over humility, bitterness over forgiveness, division over reconciliation, and fear over faith.

If community-despising is in you and you don't want to let it go, then I suggest you *not* get a praying life. Because if you commit to praying, God will break your heart about this. This will be the initial thing God does for you. This is crucial, because his glory refuses to descend on a proud heart. Rather, God's glory graces the humble heart.

"God opposes the proud, but gives grace to the humble."[4] God graces and blesses the humble. This is community language.

---

[2] Dietrich Bonhoeffer, *Life Together*, Kindle Locations 450-452. New York: HarperCollins, 1954.
[3] Ib., Kindle Location 479
[4] James 4:6

How very good and pleasant it is
    when kindred live together in unity!
It is like the precious oil on the head,
    running down upon the beard,
on the beard of Aaron,
    running down over the collar of his robes.
It is like the dew of Hermon,
    which falls on the mountains of Zion.
For there the LORD ordained his blessing,
    life forevermore.[5]

The humble, unified Jesus Community can expect to experience God's...

- blessing
- grace
- glory
- presence
- leading
- power
- love

Fellowship is where a lot of the action happens.[6] "Community is where humility and glory touch."[7] Be praying for your Jesus Community, and your place in it.

Solitary Praying Is a Platform for Authentic Community

One consequence of praying is that I find myself loving Linda more than ever. I feel softness and compassion towards others. Linda knows

---

[5] Psalm 133:1-3

[6] There is action in solitude. But solitude is primarily a preparation for community, and for the world.

[7] Henri Nouwen, *Bread for the Journey: A Daybook of Wisdom and Faith*, 130. New York: HarperOne, 1997.

this happens in me. For that reason alone, she is thankful that, many years ago, I got a praying life.

Solitary praying is necessary for real, authentic community. Community works well as it emerges from communion with God. The order is: intimacy with God; solidarity with people. The indwelling presence of God produces both. These two realities cannot be separated.

In praying, God expands our hearts. God pours his love into our being by his Holy Spirit. We know, experientially and viscerally, that we are deeply loved and in relationship with God. From this comes a God-heart for others. His love is wide, and covers many.

Community development is on the heart of God. His is an other-heart. God's vision is expansive, and is realized as God enlarges human hearts in their act of praying.

Out of Solitary Praying, Prayerful Community Grows

Solitude provides fertile ground from which community grows. The more alone-time I take with God, and take this time in a focused way, the less edgy I am. I am a better husband to Linda, a better father to my children, and a better pastor to my people. Solitary praying makes me better with people, period.

This is because, in my prayer meetings with God, I release stresses and burdens and fears to God and leave them with him.[8] This is not theoretical for me. I have learned it, in habitual praying.

One cannot consistently meet with God and remain judgmental of community. Consistently abide in Jesus, and your love for the Church will expand. Our spiritual formation, our being-morphed into increasing Christlikeness, is to *be* the Church, that Jesus-community which is the Christ's Bride.

He loves us.

You will too, as you meet up with God.

---

[8] See 1 Peter 5:7

From Solitary Prayer to Community, and Back Again

When I teach my Spiritual Formation classes, I intentionally structure them in a back-and-forth ("dialectical"[9]) movement from solitary prayer to small group sharing to large group sharing, then back again to solitary prayer to small group sharing to large group sharing, to solitary prayer... and so on, round and round.

I begin with solitary prayer, and end with sharing in community. It's a movement from solitude to community, then back into solitude, which leads to community, and so on.

When I teach a seminary class I begin our first session like this.

1) I instruct students to find a quiet place to go alone to pray, using Psalm 23 as their meditative focus. I say, "When God speaks to you, write it down." (Warning: do not over-direct at this point!)

2) After an hour of alone-prayer with God, return to class. We form small groups of four to five people. Each person shares what God said to them. One person takes notes of this sharing time.

3) After a half hour of doing this, return to class. Each note-taker shares with the entire group the bullet points of what God said to the individuals in their group. During this time, I begin teaching and coaching, and discerning what God is doing.

I've found this works well. The energy level of the students is high. The sharing is electric and inspiring. We're experiencing true Christian community, authentic *koinonia*.

Koinonia is the biblical Greek word for "community," or "fellowship." It comes from the root word *koine*, which means "common." True community is formed around commonality. What I and all my seminary students have in common, in spite of our many external differences, is Christ in us, the hope of glory. The experience and the sharing revolves around this, and we are captured by it. What happens in our solitary alone-times with God gets shared in community. Good things happen at that point.

---

[9] I like using words like 'dialectical' when I teach at seminary. I want students to feel they are getting their money's worth.

Henri Nouwen talks about this in *Spiritual Formation: Following the Movements of the Spirit:*

> Spiritual formation requires taking not only the inward journey to the heart, but also the outward journey from the heart to community and ministry. Christian spirituality is essentially communal. Spiritual formation is formation in community. One's personal prayer life can never be understood if it is separated from community life.[10]

Solitary praying transforms the heart into a heart for others. A heart for others compels one to engage in community. Without a heart for others, community relationships degenerate into individualism and competition. Spiritual formation always leads to formation to life, in community.

Journey inward, journey outward; journey alone, journey together. Solitary praying is the foundation for authentic community.

The Danger of Glorifying the Past

One thing that can destroy community, and infect it with guilt and condemnation, is misrepresenting the past by inflating it. Over the years I have met Christians who, rather than serving and ministering with God's love and power in the present, critique the church by pointing to the past as glory days that need to be recreated. The further one gets from those "good old days," the better they look.

But truthfully, the "good old days" had their problems too.[11] Nineteenth-century Dutch historian Johan Huizinga said, "There is not

---

[10] Henri Nouwen, *Spiritual Formation: Following the Movements of the Spirit*, Kindle Location 300.

[11] Teaching at an African American theological seminary has healed me of the delusion that the church in America needs to go back to "the good old days" of racism and oppression.

a more dangerous tendency in history than that of representing the past as if it were a rational whole and dictated by clearly defined interest."[12]

In the glorification of the past, the past gets distorted. The person who glorifies their past lives an illusory life, rooted in falsehood.

As for me, I find myself rarely wanting to go back to the past. It's true that I have good memories. I sometimes think of Linda and I, living in East Lansing, with our two little boys. We did not have a lot of money (that was hard). We did have one another (that was good). Sometimes I think of those days, but I never want to go back and do them again. My desire is not to recapitulate the past.

My heart aligns strongly with the apostle Paul's view, which is: "One thing I do: forgetting what is behind and straining toward what is ahead, I press on toward the goal to win the prize for which God has called me heavenward in Christ Jesus."[13]

Moving forward and finishing well - that's what I am praying for. Pressing forward, not compressing backward. With this viewpoint I am freed from the tyranny of an often-distorted past, and released to love God and move with His Spirit *now, today.* The Word does not say, "*Yesterday was* the day that the Lord *had* made," but...

"*This*, today, *is* the day the Lord *has* made. Let us rejoice and be glad *in it!*"

---

[12] Quoted by Thomas Merton. *A Year with Thomas Merton*, Kindle Locations 2389-2390
[13] Philippians 3:13-14

11

PRAYING AND THE KINGDOM

This morning I am praying for:

> a young adult who contacted me last night and shared
> that he is drinking to escape depression;
> parents who discovered their baby has a tumor on its
> spine and faces surgery tomorrow;
> a friend undergoing treatment for cancer;
> a homeless person who regularly comes to church on
> Sunday mornings;
> and a woman who left her young husband for another man.

All this would overwhelm me if I did not understand the heart of Jesus!

One of the most revolutionary events in my theological life was discovering that Jesus' main message was about the kingdom of God. The term "kingdom of God" means the rule, or reign, of God. God's kingdom is not a place or location, but wherever his power and love manifest themselves. Jesus' parables were about the kingdom. His miracles and exorcisms were demonstrations of the kingdom. He viewed himself as the real King. And he taught us to pray for the kingdom to come, not only in the future, but presently.

My kingdom studies resulted in viewing "the Lord's Prayer" differently. I used to see this as entirely future-oriented. Now I see it as including praying for God to do something here, on the earth. Presently. This is wonderful, for I and my people need God with us, now.

This makes praying a kingdom activity. Now-activity. I, and the people I fellowship with, desire God to be "Immanuel," with us, today. This chapter contains some of the connections I have made between praying and the kingdom of God.

The Kingdom Prayer of Jesus

Authentic praying is situated in the environment of the core message of Jesus, which was: repent, and hear the good news of the kingdom of God. When this is understood, everything about praying changes.

What we refer to as The Lord's Prayer might better be called The Kingdom Prayer of Jesus. We cry out for the in-breaking of the kingdom into the brokenness of the present.[1]

Praying is kingdom-activity. Praying is conversing and conferencing within the realm, the domain, of the King.

Ponder, and salute this, as you pray, "Let your kingdom come, let your will be done, on earth, as it is in heaven." In praying, we bring the realities of God's reign into our present circumstances.

It's not just words. To pray is to cry for the kingdom to come, now and forevermore.

Praying Aligns With God's Redemptive Kingdom Agenda

The baseball player hits a home run that wins the game. As he crosses home plate he looks up, points his finger heavenward, and thanks God. That's cool. But did God really take sides in a baseball game? While it could happen, I mostly doubt it. Yes, I am thrilled every time the Tigers beat the Yankees, but God is not.

Many petitionary prayers are not especially enlightened appeals to the Deity. The plea of a professional fighter asking God to help them render their opponent unconscious, and a shopper's cry for a parking

---

[1] See Grenz, *Prayer: The Cry for the Kingdom*, 23.

space, may be common, but are violent, trivial, and irrelevant to God's plans and purposes.

We can bring all our requests to God, but God is not obligated to deliver on them. Jesus, in John 14:13-14, said, "I will do whatever you ask in my name, so that the Father may be glorified in the Son. You may ask me for anything in my name, and I will do it."

That little phrase "in my name" means: according to Jesus' identity and purposes. For example, if someone asks for something that is "not me," I will not grant it. I will not give a heroin addict money. In the same way, requests that are "not God" are responded to with a divine "No." God is not our Big Heavenly Butler in the sky who exists to fulfill all our earthly desires.[2]

Pure requests emerge from constant connection to God. They align with God's redemptive, kingdom agenda. We come to realize that even asking for our own selves is fundamentally for the glory of God. All things are for his name's sake.

The order is:

Live attached to Jesus.

Out of this connection, request.

Prayer as Involvement in His-Story

In prayer, we converse with the king of heaven and earth. Therefore, praying is kingdom activity.

Every Jesus-follower is on a Mission of Redemption, led by God. Mixing headship metaphors, God is our shepherd, as well as our king. The New Testament's Big Idea is that our king died, was raised, and now lives to build his kingdom people on earth, as is built in heaven.

In prayer with God we learn how to build lasting things. This is a privilege, as Wayne Grudem writes:

> God wants us to pray because it allows us to be a part
> of a story that is greater than our own. It allows us to

---

[2] Compare Moralistic Therapeutic Deism, as described by sociologist Christian Smith in *Soul Searching*. New York: Oxford, 2005.

be involved in activities that have eternal significance. When we pray, God's kingdom is advanced as his will is done "on earth as it is in heaven" (Matt. 6: 10).[3]

To pray is to be involved in the final act of God's grand narrative. This happens as you and I pray today.[4]

Prayer and Contentment as Thing-Independence

This earthly kingdom has its relative treasures. On earth, we have gold and silver. These metals have no intrinsic value. Their value is that people value them. Why are diamonds valuable? Because people value diamonds. In logic, this is called "begging the question." Jesus knew this. For those who follow Jesus, the things of earth grow strangely circular in the light of the glory of his kingdom.

What we treasure shows what kingdom we belong to. In praying, we become thing-independent and God-satiated, indicating our place in God's economy. Philip Yancey writes:

> I remembered reading the account of a spiritual seeker who interrupted a busy life to spend a few days in a monastery. "I hope your stay is a blessed one," said the monk who showed the visitor to his cell. "If you need anything, let us know and we'll teach you how to live without it."[5]

That is, we'll teach you the secret of being content in all circumstances. The biblical experience of contentment is circumstance-independent. As are peace, joy, love, and so on. These realities of the "fruit of the Spirit" are circumstance-independent. Were this not so, things such as inner

---

[3] Wayne Grudem, *Christian Beliefs: Twenty Basics Every Christian Should Know*, Kindle Locations 600-602. Grand Rapids: Zondervan, 2005.

[4] This is similar to N.T. Wright's idea of the Bible as a 5-act play, with Act 5 being "The Church and the People of God" as an ongoing final act to the great drama of the Christian story, in which we have a part.

[5] Philip Yancey, *Prayer*, Kindle Locations 1012-1015.

peace would be conditional, and that would be bad news for all of us. Our hopes would then be expressed as, "IF I have _____, THEN I will have inner peace."

Real contentment is thing-independent and circumstance-independent. As the apostle Paul writes:

> I am not saying this because I am in need, for I have learned to be content whatever the circumstances. I know what it is to be in need, and I know what it is to have plenty. I have learned the secret of being content in any and every situation, whether well fed or hungry, whether living in plenty or in want.[6]

Pray that these verses would move from your mind into your heart. Pray, "God, teach me how to live without things."

In Prayer, Get a Grip Off This Life

For many years, we at Redeemer have spent New Year's Eve worshiping with our church family. I love doing this! And often, in the worship, God speaks to me. This happened on New Year's Eve 2011.

It began when I saw X come into the sanctuary. "Yay," I thought. "X is here! " Good. X needs to be here. X needs God, and needs to get close to God. Then I prayed, "God, I hope X stays for the entire worship experience. I hope they enjoy the whole evening and don't get bored. I'll be disappointed if they leave."

I was burdened, and concerned. God spoke to me, saying, "John, don't hold on to people. Wear them loosely."

God would *not* tell me this were I *not* holding on to people too tightly. I picked up my journal and wrote: "This is a good word for me. Deepen this in me, Lord. Then I will be free to love people with no strings attached."

Attachment to God produces non-attachment to people. We then become free to love them. This is called "trust."

---

[6] Philippians 4:11-12

I cannot control the hearts and minds of others. Therefore, I must hold on to people lightly. Hold on to things lightly. Keep a loose grip on people, things, and plans. This will allow me to be non-manipulative and non-controlling of others.

It's easy to hold lightly to people, things, and plans, if they mean little to me. If some people were gone, it would mean nothing to me. There are certain things that, should they be missing, I would not care at all. Indeed, I am certain there *are now* things I am missing that I don't know of, which shows they don't mean much to me!

It's the people *I* love, and the things *I* cherish, and the plans *I* hope work out - these are hard to part with. It is this clinging that skews my life, stunts my spiritual growth, and hinders my appreciation and love for people.

Hold lightly to your own plans and your own agenda. In praying, get a grip off life, so as to take firm hold of God's Kingdom plans and purposes.[7]

Praying Is Bigger Than I Can Think and Wider Than the World

In praying, I encounter and experience God. In praying, I know God and am known, reciprocally. Praying is a core way of abiding in Christ.

The biblical claim is that God has come to make his home in me.[8] God and I converse in the living room of my heart. When this is actualized, the listening part of praying takes center stage. This is real praying, and has little or no relation to reading books about prayer, or saying "I believe in prayer but can't find time for it."

In praying, I am introduced to a world of moral and spiritual vastness. I communicate with the Maker of Heaven and Earth! Because praying originates from the very character and being of God, who cannot be contained, praying cannot be contained. "Prayer is wider

---

[7] Henri Nouwen's "ministry of presence" and "ministry of absence" is helpful here. There is a time to be with people and time to be apart from people. Which to do is a matter of discernment. What's required is: trust.

[8] John 14:23

than the world, deeper than the heart, and older than the origin of humanity… Its possibilities are infinite and so our explorations in prayer can be vast."⁹

When I was studying Old Testament theology in seminary, one of the scholars I became familiar with was Walter Eichrodt. Here, Eichrodt illustrates the scope and sensitivity of a praying life.

> The man who knows God hears his step in the tramp of daily events, discerns him near at hand to help, and hears his answer to the appeal of prayer in a hundred happenings outwardly small and insignificant, where another man can talk only of remarkable coincidence, amazing accident, or peculiar turns of events. That is why periods when the life of faith is strong, and men have enthusiastically surrendered themselves to God, have also been times rich in miracles.¹⁰

To pray is to explore and venture into the vast, limitless regions of God's beautiful kingdom. Praying is bigger than I can think, and wider than the earthbound world.

Praying as Overcoming the World

A consistent, ongoing, praying life brings an overcoming of our fear-driven, anxiety-producing world. For me it looks like this:

1. I abide in Christ, in the act of praying.
2. Christ has overcome the world (John 16:33).
3. Therefore, I overcome the world. (Christ in me, the hope of glory - right?)

---

⁹ Houston, *The Transforming Power of Prayer: Deepening Your Friendship With God*, 75.

¹⁰ Walter Eichrodt, *Theology of the Old Testament*, Westminster Press: Philadelphia, 164.

My status as a Jesus-follower is that I am "in Christ." Praying reifies my in-Christ status. As Christ is formed in me,[11] he gives me his peace and joy.[12]

Transformation into Jesus-likeness brings world-overcoming. God's voice grows stronger and stronger in us. The world's solicitations diminish into increasing dimness. And there is peace.

God's kingdom is peaceable. In solitary praying I come to know this peace, and thus overcome agitation. I am made whole, by Christ, and grow beyond the chaos and fragmentation around me. Praying results in overcoming.

Pray, Not for the Self to Come, But for the Kingdom to Come

Seek Christ for the sake of Christ, and not essentially for the sake of self. To do the latter is to *use* Jesus, as if that could be done. "As long as your own personality is what you are bothering about you are not going to Him at all."[13]

Forget about yourself and concentrate on Him. Your real, born-again, newly created being will not come as long as you are looking for you. It comes as you seek first him and his kingdom.

The result will be many things added to you, to include discovery of one's true self. The Lord's Prayer does not read, "Let my self-kingdom come, let my self-will be done..."

Self-obsession is always unfulfilling and disappointing. Give yourself away, to God first, then to others. This theme runs throughout the New Testament.

In praying, give up your kingdom to be found in God's Kingdom.

---

[11] Galatians 4:19
[12] John 14:27; 15:11
[13] C.S. Lewis, *Mere Christianity*, 226.

12

PRAYING AND SELF-DENIAL

Whoever invented the Oreo cookie accompanied by a glass of ice cold milk should be escorted to the woodshed. It is logically impossible to eat just one. The statement, "I ate one Oreo cookie," is self-refuting. Just one taste of this deadly, evil union, and fat grows at the rate of one pound/cookie. Self-control runs and hides. Therein lies one of my problems. I must deny myself, for the sake of well-being.

Authentic praying is an act of self-denial. For God to speak his truth, direction, and life into me, I must press the "pause" button on my ideas. That is, I need to momentarily delete my cookies.

To listen requires speech-denial. Listening comes hard for those of us who, when you are talking, are already formulating what we will say to you.

Self-denial is learned behavior. I have learned much about it by engaging in lengthy times of praying. Praying has made me a better listener, to God and to others. In this chapter I will share thoughts I have about praying and letting go of the self.

To Pray Is to Let Go of Control

When I teach classes on prayer, I begin by sending my students out to do some actual praying. I usually have them use Psalm 23 as their meditative focus. When they return from praying I ask them, "What did God say to you?"

My experience is that thirty to forty percent of them don't get past verse 1a, "The Lord is my shepherd." This is because God asks them the question, "Am I really your shepherd?" Arguably, this is the basic question of one's spiritual life; viz., "Who do you belong to?"

Find out who, or what, you belong to, and place your trust there. To trust is, *ipso facto*, to let go of control. When we trust, ego-drivenness steps aside for other-sakeness. For example, if you are driving and see my foot edge towards the gas pedal, while my hand simultaneously materializes on the steering wheel, you will ask the obvious question – "Don't you trust my driving?" In that case, my answer would be, "No." By analogy, to trust in God means that he is the driver, and my embodied ego is along for the ride.

One biblical example is John 21:13-19. Jesus asks Peter the question, "Do you love me?" As Peter confesses his love for Jesus, Jesus says:

> I tell you the truth, when you were younger you dressed yourself and went where you wanted; but when you are old you will stretch out your hands, and someone else will dress you and lead you where you do not want to go.

Verse 19 tells us that "Jesus said this to indicate the kind of death by which Peter would glorify God." Then Jesus said to Peter, "Follow me!"

We are all in a control vs. trust situation. To trust is to stretch out your arms, allow a belt to be put around you, and be led where you would rather not go.[1] The alternatives are either "Dress yourself and go where you want to go" (control), or "Be dressed by someone else and go where they want you to go" (trust). To follow Jesus is to go where he leads. When someone becomes a follower of Jesus, they won't be leading themselves anymore.

Maturity, for the Christian, is learning how to be a "sheep." Counterintuitively, sheep are the victors in life, while wolves are defeated. Our

---

[1] See Jesus, in John 21:13-19. Henri Nouwen calls this maturity, and repeats it in many of his writings.

shepherd champions and feeds the sheep. Wolves lose the shepherd's support.[2]

An essential part of praying is being-shepherded. In praying, God directs me. Among other things, I pray to find out what God wants me to do. If the Lord is my shepherd, and I am his sheep who must hear his voice and follow, I need a trusting heart. Therefore, to pray is to trust, which means to let go of control.

A lot of this "control" thing is part of the kingdom of darkness. How so? For one thing, it's mostly illusory. We may think that we are in control of many things. Marketers tell us that if we buy their product, it will give us greater control over something. But the truth is that we mostly control nothing. We have no control over the weather, what other people think, time, the future, our past, and death. We have little control over sickness, the economy, our physical appearance, addiction, and our feelings. What, really, do we have control over? The TV controller? Maybe, but in some homes I doubt it.

The "I'm in control of things" attitude is an illusion. The thought that "I'm in control" may make me feel that it is so, but the feeling is non-indicative of any corresponding reality.

The only option, then, is that we must trust. But in what, or whom? In money? Governments? The self? Gerald May writes: "In our culture, the three gods we do trust for security are possessions, power, and human relationships. To a greater or lesser extent, all of us worship this false trinity."[3]

Some people are self-affirming control addicts. That is, in the act of control, the self is fundamentally affirmed. This makes praying impossible, since to pray *is* to self-deny and succumb to God.

The more controlling a person is, the more fearful they are. The problem comes when we become addicted to control, when most of life is actually out of our control. The control addict fearfully and not-so-wonderfully strives to gain control over essentially uncontrollable

---

[2] See Thomas Merton, *Conjectures of a Guilty Bystander*, vii. New York: The Abbey of Gethsemane, 1965.

[3] Gerald May, *Addiction and Grace*, 32.

circumstances. Like trying to control the hearts and minds of other people, which cannot be done. Yet the control addict tries, because they fear people who don't act, think, feel, or choose as they do. Such people are out of their control, and they don't like it.

God is not in our control. Some people don't like this.[4] While some Christians seem to think they can control God, the great truth is that God is sovereign. See the parable of the workers in the vineyard, where those who get hired last get paid the same as those who worked all day. The all-day workers cry out, "Hey, that's not fair!" To which the owner responds, "It's my money, right? I control it, and can do whatever I want with it."

God is in control, we are not. In some instances, we spin out of control. To have a heart that strives to gain control is counter to what's really going on in this world. What can we do?

The answer is: God desires, and is able, to transform (meta-morph) your controlling heart into a heart that trusts in him. Place yourself prayerfully in God's presence and God will, over time, accomplish this. As the change happens, your praying will be different.

Letting go of control is a form of denying the self. When this happens, praying becomes more conversational, and the primacy of the almighty self is defeated.

Praying and Fasting

One of prayer's companions is fasting. "Fasting" is a form of self-denial for the sake of more intensive God-reliance. We see this in Psalm 35:13-14.

> Ruthless witnesses come forward;
> they question me on things I know nothing about.
> They repay me evil for good
> and leave me like one bereaved.

---

[4] Especially, perhaps, moralistic therapeutic deists, who view God as the Great Butler in the sky whose reason for being is to please us and make certain we are "happy."

Yet when they were ill, I put on sackcloth
and humbled myself with fasting.
When my prayers returned to me unanswered,
I went about mourning
as though for my friend or brother.
I bowed my head in grief
as though weeping for my mother.

Old Testament scholar John Goldingay writes that "David's sadness was not yet fully bloomed until his body – in this case, fasting – was involved."[5] Scot McKnight says these verses assume "that merely to feel sadness is not enough; because we are physical creatures and not just minds and spirits, it would be odd not to express sorrow in (e.g.) abstention from food and then afflicting one's spirit and one's self.""[6]

The Judeo-Christian view is that we are embodied beings, not Cartesian spirits inhabiting a body like a driver in a car. What we do with our body affects our spirit.[7]

In fasting, we deny demands of our physical body for the sake of praying more intensely. Praying accompanied by fasting is a form of self-denial that focuses our spirit.

Prayer and Death

Death is the ultimate form of self-denial. Metaphorically, we speak of "dying to self," so that God might be first, and others second.

Often, when praying, I think about life and death. I have written in my journal that I want to finish well, and make a difference with my life. This is about leaving a legacy of God and Jesus, not some personal tribute where people remember me.

---

[5] In Scot McKnight, *Fasting: The Ancient Practices*, xiii. McKnight's book is an excellent summary of the practice of fasting. Nashville: Thomas Nelson, 2010.
[6] Ib.
[7] See, e.g., Dallas Willard's chapters "Spiritual Life: The Body's Fulfillment," and "St. Paul's Psychology of Redemption," in *The Spirit of the Disciplines: Understanding How God Changes Lives*. New York: HarperCollins, 1988.

At a conference I did one of the participants told me that God spoke to him and said, "Jason[8], death is not a big deal for me." That really struck me, especially since Jason has a brain tumor. Death is not a big deal for God? Correct.

Why not? I see two reasons.

First, because God is everlasting. God never began to be, and will never cease to be. God is a necessarily existent being who cannot not-exist. God, who never was born, cannot die.

Second, because God, in Christ, has conquered death on earth. All who are found in Christ shall live forever in the coming kingdom and age to come.

Death is no big deal for God, since: 1) God cannot die; and 2) death died. This has big-time implications for we mortals. We who are in Christ have died with him, and shall be raised in him. That being true, what's the fear of death about? Death has been swallowed up in victory. Therefore, dear brothers and sisters, stand firm. Let nothing move you.[9]

If death is no big deal, then by logical extension dying to the self is no big deal. I have had several prayer times where God has addressed self-denial, my physical death, and the death of others. Praying is the ultimate anti-avoidance, contra-denial activity.

Prayer and the Moment of Rescue

I heard from a friend who was doing a Prayer Summer challenge with me.[10] While taking their hour of prayer, God confronted them with some unrighteous behavior they were engaging in. It broke their heart in the right place. I found myself thinking, "This is good. Thank you, God, for doing this for my friend!"

I remembered an old television commercial for "Mennen Skin Bracer" after shave. A man is in a bathroom, looking at himself in a

---

[8] Not the person's real name.

[9] 1 Corinthians 15:54-58

[10] In the summers of 2013 and 2014 I challenged people to pray 30-60 minutes a day, 5 days a week, through the summer.

mirror. He finished shaving, took a bottle of Skin Bracer, poured some on both palms, and splashed it onto his face. Then a hand came out of the mirror and slapped his freshly anointed cheeks. The man said, "Thanks, I needed that!" That's how bracing and refreshing Skin Bracer was supposed to be. It woke the man up!

I have had many "Thanks God, I needed that!" moments while praying. God has pointed out something about me that is spiritually diseased. I write it down in my journal, using words like, "God, you have searched me out, and revealed something that needs to be removed." It could be pride, a bad attitude, hatred, lust, envy, covetousness, jealousy, a controlling spirit, lack of compassion, or resistance to God. These revelations of my inner garbage result in brokenness and grief.

In forty-six years of following Jesus, God has uncovered all these things and more, within me. This is good. When it happens (and it *will* if you continue to meet one-on-one with Him) it becomes another "Thank You, God" moment.

I know people who fear meeting with God because of this. They are like the person who delays going to the doctor because an illness may be discovered. To live under the illusion of health (also called "denial") is to be on a road to spiritual disaster.

While we may not like God telling us, "You are sick," we should be glad for the revelation of inner sickness when it is there. This is the beginning of its removal, by God. God never shows us our failure only to leave us in that miserable place. That would be like a doctor who diagnoses, but does not cure. When God shows us failure, it is always for our rescue. The revelation of personal fault *is* the moment of rescue from our false self.

This is not accompanied by condemnation. People do that; God does not. There is no condemnation for those who are in Christ Jesus.[11] Satan accuses. God rescues.

We may not have thought we needed saving. Then, as we meet with him for another praying hour, God the Great Physician identifies a spiritual cancer, operates, and bathes us with radiating, healing love.

---

[11] Romans 8:1

This breaks our hearts. We call it very good. We pray, "Thank You God, for rescuing me!"

True Solitude Peels Off the Mask

My spiritual life is a dialectical movement between solitude and community, solitude and community, solitude and community. The movement is: Solitude with God + *koinonia*, solitude with God + *koinonia*, and so on. I need both.

Ontologically, solitude comes first. In solitude, God purges my soul. This is good. I *experience* this, thus I know it, as a good thing. Without much time alone with God, community degenerates into pseudo-community, like masks at a costume party. In our solitude, God peels the mask away to reveal the true self. Then "you" go to the party, interact with other people, in authentic ways.

This is about your freedom, who God has made *you* to be, and who you *truly are* in Christ. As Thomas Merton has written, "The truest solitude is not something outside you, not an absence of men or of sound around you: it is an abyss opening up in the center of your own soul."[12]

True solitude is a condition of the heart. God morphs us until we have faces like Christ. In his presence we don't need the mask anymore.

---

[12] Thomas Merton, *New Seeds of Contemplation*, 80-81.

13

PRAYING AND REMEMBERING

Linda's mother suffered from Alzheimer's Disease for many years. This horrible illness caused her to slowly lose her memory. One result of her memory loss was an increase of fear.

One afternoon Linda, her mother Martha, her father Del, and I were shopping in a mall. At one point Linda and Del left for an hour to shop together, while I stayed with Martha. We sat together for a minute, and then she looked at me, her eyes filled with panic, and asked, "Where's Del?!"

"He's shopping with Linda. He'll be right back," I responded.

This put Martha at ease. But only for a few minutes. Forgetting what I had just said, Martha looked at me again, and asked, "Where's Del?"

"He's with Linda. He'll be right back."

This happened several times in an hour, with Martha forgetting, me reminding her, she calming down, then forgetting and filled with fear, asking "Where's Del?", and me reminding her again. Martha not only had forgotten what I said to her, she had forgotten a more basic truth, which was: in Del, she had a husband who would never, ever, leave her or forsake her. He was always by her side, Alzheimer's or not.

There is a "spiritual Alzheimer's disease" which results in forgetting the many times God has rescued and delivered us, provided for us, and been with us. Such forgetting breeds fear. The more one forgets the deeds of God in one's own life, the more one becomes fearful in the present moment.

The antidote to this is: *remembering.*

"Remembering" is huge in the Old Testament. The post-Exodus experience of Israel is grounded in remembrance. The Jewish festivals are remember-events, such as Passover, when the head of the household sits with his family and asks, "Why is this night different from all other nights?" In response, the past is recounted, and we hear again how God delivered their people out of bondage in Egypt. This remembering, reminding them of God's past faithfulness, brings fresh hope.

My spiritual journal functions as the written memory of the voice and deeds of God, in my life. I take time every year to re-ponder my journals. In doing so, I remember what God has done for me, how he has delivered me from bondage, and how he has answered many of my prayers. I re-read of past times when I was afraid, or worried, and then re-read how God came through, and my worry dissipated.

I *do* not, I *will* not, forget the deeds of the Lord in my life. The spiritual discipline of remembering brings renewed hope in the present, defeating the onset of spiritual Alzheimer's disease.

Here are some things I have remembered about the importance of remembering.

In Praying, Remember

Whenever I join the Lord at his communion table, I remember. In particular, I think of two things. First, I think of Christ on the cross, paying the price I should have paid, redeeming me, purchasing me out of bondage to sin and death. As I hold the bread I think of my forty-six years of Jesus-life, and my rescue. This runs deep in my soul. Like Moses said to the people, "Always remember this day. This is the day when you came out of Egypt from a house of slavery. God brought you out of here with a powerful hand."[1]

Secondly, I think of redemptive particulars of my life. I remember walking from my apartment early in the morning, alone, towards the campus of Northern Illinois University. I remember praying, "God,

[1] Exodus 13:3

now I know you are real. Save me! Jesus, inhabit me. If you do this, I will follow you the rest of my life." I remember that He did. He knows that I have.

I remember the day I was delivered out of Egypt. I give thanks to the God who rescued me! While praying, I think of the mighty acts of God in my life. Remembering is essential to my praying life.

Praying and Remembering as an Eschatological Event

I was born in Michigan's Upper Peninsula.[2] My parents moved to Rockford, Illinois, when I was a year old. That's where I lived for the next twenty years. The streets of Rockford were my holy ground. Whenever I return to Rockford I like to walk in my old neighborhood. I've done this many times, carrying my journal and camera with me.

We lived on a cul de sac. The address was: 3012 20th Avenue. Our phone number was 399-7931. These particulars, *minä muistan*.[3]

Adjacent to our house was 25th Street Park. I loved that park! I spent countless hours playing there with my friends. That was the late 1950s and 1960s. I have not forgotten.

I am thankful for my childhood. I could not wait for school to end and summer to begin! I had fun, adventure, and growth in a world without the Web. We had TV, but only three stations. Reception depended on which way the antenna on the roof was pointing. My father had to go on the roof to adjust the picture. I played from sun-up to sundown. I hear my mother's voice calling me in the dark - "John, it's time to come in!"

As I walk down 20th Avenue, my five senses recall. My parents are dead, but I smell my mother's cooking. We rarely ate out. For me that was no loss, since I'll eat from my parents' table any time. Mom loved to cook, and loved to watch us enjoy her creations. Her esteem came from providing and home-making. She taught me how to make mashed potatoes. I've never met a mashed potato that measured up to

---

[2] I was born in Hancock, Michigan.
[3] "I remember," in Finnish.

my mother's. In her cooking I encountered Platonic Forms, by which all shadowy, insubstantial culinary efforts were judged.

I walk to Rolling Green School, where I attended kindergarten through fourth grade. Then to Whitehead Elementary School, Jefferson Junior High School, and finally, to Rockford East High School. Whitehead and Jefferson were brand new when I was there. Now, they have aged. Everything here is older. I see the same trees, but they are bigger. And my parents are buried in a cemetery a few miles from here. And I am older.

One year my father brought home a small pine tree he dug up from the family farm in Michigan's Upper Peninsula. He planted it at 3012 20th Avenue. It was so small I could jump over it. Now, sixty years later, it's tall. I walk past, pluck a pine cone, and take it with me back to Michigan. One of these cones made it to my office. I left it there for years. On occasion I held it, and thought of my father and mother and family. It is good to do this. I will never forget where I have come from.

Remembering is sweet for me. I know that's not so for everyone, but it is for me. *Therefore, I remember.*

I remember loving, hard-working parents. I remember how they looked after me, and fed me, and clothed me. I remember my mother taking me to a store named Goldblatt's to buy a madras shirt and a pair of Levi's jeans. I remember my father, every winter, making an ice rink in our back yard. I remember every square inch of that small yard that I mowed and played in. I remember my mother making "pasties"[4] and fruit pies.

I remember my father hitting baseballs to me in the park. I remember my neighborhood friends, and every crack in the sidewalk on 20th Avenue. I remember going to our Lutheran Church, and having my father as a Sunday School teacher. I remember the smell of the brand new '55 Chevy dad bought - two-toned green. I remember our pet dog "Candy." I remember sharing a bedroom with my brother Mike.

I do not forget.

---

[4] When Finns migrated to Michigan's Upper Peninsula and worked in the copper mines they would carry these pastry-filled meat and vegetable pies with them.

Spiritually, "remembering" is foundational. Remembering is a core Judeo-Christian activity. This is not about "nostalgia." I don't dwell in the past, or long for a return to it. My many returns to walk in the old neighborhood are sacred. They are holy. "Holy" means: "set apart." A tiny, mundane piece of earth becomes the center of the universe, the place where God manifests his glory and presence.

Remembering, as essential covenant activity, is not really about the past. My memory-walk is a full-bodied eschatological event. To understand the future and to have hope, I must remember the past and where I came from. I am a hopeful person today because of my past, a childhood filled with days of expectancy. As I walk these earthly streets I think of the new heaven and new earth that is to come. It will be a safe, loving, playful, and adventurous place. My entire family will be there. I rejoice.

I remember Christ, and what God in Jesus has done for me. I remember the "rescue." I remember what the Lord has done. The Lord has done great things for me, and I am filled with joy.

Remembering creates expectation. Expectation concerns hope. Hope is future-oriented. As I pray, I remember the deeds of the Lord, in my life.

An Atheist Remembers and Tries to be Thankful to Something

Remembering is step one in the procession towards thanksgiving. But if there is no God to thank, the gratitude impulse is absurd. This is because there would be no culmination, no *objet de reconnaissance.*

Ronald Aronson, Professor of the History of Ideas at Wayne State University, wonders about this in his essay "Thank Who Very Much?"[5] The reason for the question mark is that, as an atheist, Aronson *feels* thankful. But on atheism there is no God to thank, so he wonders just *who* or *what* he should thank.

---

[5] Ronald Aronson, http://www.is.wayne.edu/raronson/Articles/TorontoStar.htm

Aronson believes a person can be thankful without either: a) belief in a God; or b) falling into existentialist absurdity. What's his alternative? He writes:

> Think of the sun's warmth. After all, the sun is one of those forces that make possible the natural world, plant life, even our very existence. It may not mean anything to us personally, but the warmth on our face means, tells us, a great deal. All of life on earth has evolved in relation to this source of heat and light, we human beings included. We are because of, and in our own millennial adaptation to, the sun and other fundamental forces.[6]

So? For Aronson, one can feel gratitude by "acknowledging one of our most intimate if impersonal relationships, with the cosmic and natural forces that make us possible." An atheist can show gratitude to larger and impersonal forces. This is because "we derive our existence from, and belong to, both natural forces and generations that preceded us, [thus] it is just possible that we will often feel connected [to such forces and generations], and often grateful."

Aronson says when we gather together with friends on one of those snuggly holiday nights, we are overcome by warm, happy feelings, even moments of well-being – "but to whom or to what?" Aronson's answer is: "Obviously, to natural forces and processes that have made our own life, and this reunion, possible."

OK. But I'll opt for the following dichotomy: either there is a God to thank, or we're left with Camus-ian absurdity.[7] Aronson's idea sounds like a spiritless animism (which is, of course, a contradiction). Thankfulness, if it is to have any meaning at all, requires inter-personality. I have felt innumerable moments of gratitude, but never felt like thanking the wall of my house for holding up the roof. Thanking

---

[6] Ib.

[7] For example, see Albert Camus, *The Myth of Sisyphus*. New York: Knopf, 1955.

"impersonal forces," no matter how "large" they are, is no different than walking outside and thanking your lawn for being green.[8]

To say "Thank you" only makes sense if there is, at least in principle, someone who can or could have responded, "You are welcome."

Aronson the atheist feels thankful. I do not doubt this. As an atheist, he doesn't want his thankful feelings to be absurd. But thanking impersonal forces strikes me as meaningless and sad, like thanking my stuffed teddy bear for loving me. The raw truth remains: No God = no ultimate meaning. Such is the logic of atheism, on which there is no one out there to thank.

Praying and Thanksgiving "With All My Heart"

Thanksgiving needs memory, whether long-term or short-term. A noticing, a recalling. I walk through the day and find myself saying, often, "Thank you, God." I take a deep breath, and then - instinctively – say, "Thank you, God, for life and the ability to breathe." I do not take this for granted. A lot of my journal entries record "Thank you, God" moments.

Psalm 9:1-2 reads:

> I will give thanks to you, LORD, with all my heart;
> I will tell of all your wonderful deeds.
> I will be glad and rejoice in you
> I will sing the praises of your name, O Most High.

Even though David the psalmist is oppressed by enemy forces, God showed up to defeat them. The acts of God elicit thanksgiving in David, with all his heart. His thanksgiving goes viral as David openly testifies to God's wonderful deeds. All this is in an atmosphere of gladness and praise. And remembering.

I have lists of God's wonderful acts and deeds, done to me. I have written some down in an email file which I continually send

---

[8] See Camus, Jean Paul Sartre, and a host of atheistic existentialists who write on the absurdity of moral and purposeful feelings.

back to myself. It's not that I am so e-barren that I need more mail. I just don't want to forget all that God has done for me. I call this particular e-file THANKFULNESS. I keep adding to the list of things I am thankful for, only to reply to myself with these things again and again, so as not to forget.

I re-read my thanks-list, and it produces offspring. In praying, I enumerate things I am thankful for, occasionally counting them on my fingers. And I give thanks to God.

Praying as Re-membering

Remembering is a spiritual discipline. Giving thanks is an act of praying, associated with something God has done for me.[9] Prayer-remembering is about the past. When that past is positive, it is accompanied by thanksgiving. I remember how God re-membered me, how God put me back together, when I was falling apart.

To re-member something is to "member again" that which has come apart. Pieces once together are rejoined. When this happens, the prevailing emotion is gratitude.

When I pray I am often re-minded of something that has "left my mind." God brings something to mind, and I am re-membered. This is good. It is clarifying and focusing when this happens. In praying, in the God-appointment, God puts pieces of life together again. God's Spirit achieves, in the act of praying, a great unifying.

I don't strive or work hard to re-member, since I can't put my pieces back together again. But, as I consistently meet with God, conversing in the slow-cooked prayer exchange, re-membering happens, by the Spirit. This is my constant experience.

This is good news and provides incentive to pray. All the king's horses and all the king's men couldn't put me back together again, but God has.

---

[9] Thanksgiving can also be eschatological; viz., thanking God for what he is going to do on the basis of what he has done in the past.

Praying and Potato Chips

There was a man in our church named Floyd. Floyd died several years ago. It was my privilege to do his funeral. When I met with Floyd's wife, Grace, she shared something I had never heard before. "Floyd," she said, "was a thankful person who was always thanking God for what he had been given."

Floyd had not come from a wealthy family. As I heard about him and his thankful heart, it reminded me of my mother who, as a young girl, sometimes received only an orange for a Christmas present, and cherished and savored it, and was thankful.

How deep did Floyd's heart of thanks run? "Whenever we had snacks, like potato chips," said Grace, "Floyd would stop, bow his head, and thank God as the bag of chips was passed to him."

"You're kidding me, right?" I said. "Floyd would give thanks, in front of everyone, for potato chips?!!"

"Yes. He was grateful to God for anything that came his way."

I thought: I'm not that thankful. I take too many things for granted.

"For granted" - to expect someone, or something, to be always available to serve you in some way without thanks or recognition; to value someone, or something, too lightly.

To "take something for granted" - to expect something to be available all the time, and forget that you have not earned it.

A "for granted" attitude *presumes*. A "for granted" attitude has a sense of *entitlement*. Like: "I am entitled to these potato chips."[10]

"For granted" - to fail to appreciate the value of something.

"Entitlement" - the belief that one is deserving of certain privileges. Like: "I deserve these potato chips."

Floyd, it seems, had no sense of entitlement, as if God owed *him* something. He didn't take provision, in any form, for granted. From that framework, giving thanks logically follows. And, in yet another "great reversal," God is deserving of, and entitled to, *our* praise

---

[10] To find healing for the entitlement disease see John Townsend, *The Entitlement Cure*. Grand Rapids: Zondervan, 2015.

and thanksgiving. God, for Floyd, was not some cosmic butler whose task was to wait on him, and make sure he was satisfied with the service.

The apostle Paul instructed us to "always give thanks for everything, in the name of our Lord Jesus Christ."[11] "For everything" is all-inclusive. Nothing exists outside the realm of "for everything." *Everything* is a gift from God, even my very life, even my eyes as I read this, and my breath as I inhale. If I gave thanks for *everything,* my gratitude would be unceasing.

If I realized how God-dependent I actually am, I would stop now and say, "Thank you." And then, in my next breath, I would say it again.

Praying on the "Thank God Ledge"

I watched a "60 Minutes" segment on TV that fully engaged me. It was on freestyle rock climber Alex Honnold's "free solo" of Half Dome, in Yosemite National Park.[12]

Half Dome is a nearly vertical, 2000-foot sheer granite wall. Alex climbs it without the assistance of ropes or a harness. It's just him, his hands, and his tennis shoes. It made me nervous watching him, even though I knew he survived. The shots of him clinging to the wall, with the trees and river a half mile below him, are astounding.

No one else in the world has done this. Perhaps no one else can. Alex's focus is amazing! One mistake and you are dead. No second chance. It's either perfection and completeness, or total failure. This sport is *unforgiving.* To conquer Half Dome, you have to be perfect.

Nine-tenths of the way up Half Dome there is a place climbers call the "Thank God Ledge."[13] It's a thirty-five-foot-long ramp, that is anywhere from five to twelve inches wide. If a climber can get himself on this piece of granite, he can jam his fingers into small cracks in the

---

[11] Ephesians 5:20

[12] "The Ascent of Alex Honnold," http://www.cbsnews.com/videos/the-ascent-of-alex-honnold/

[13] http://www.outsideonline.com/outdoor-adventure/climbing/rock-climbing/No-Strings-Attached.html?page=all

wall, and "take a break." The Thank God Ledge is a place of relief. It's a slim moment of respite, mercy, grace, and forgiveness.

Fortunately, when it comes to God, it's all about forgiveness. In Matthew 18 Peter comes to Jesus and asks, ""Lord, how many times shall I forgive my brother or sister who sins against me? Up to seven times?" Jesus answered, "I tell you, not seven times, but seventy-seven times.""[14] Which means: I am to keep forgiving others when they fail and when they fall. Why? Because I have been forgiven. Of much. I am to forgive others as I have been forgiven.[15]

Thank God that he is forgiving! His forgiveness is not narrow. God's love is wide.

In the 1970s I wrote a song called "How Many Times?" The words go: "How many times we all fall down, broken and bent by the wind. How many times his love comes down, lifts us up again." In the forgiveness of the cross God, has placed me on the "Thank God Ledge." When I experience his forgiveness, I am lifted to this place of beauty and rest. Here, there is restoration, and healing. When experienced and understood, it evokes praise. When I forgive others, I invite them to join me on this ledge. Unforgiveness lets people fall to their destruction. Forgiveness rescues.

There is plenty of room on Thank God Ledge. I'll be praying there, with others.

---

[14] Matthew 18:21-22
[15] Colossians 3:13

14

WHY I PRAY

This morning I received two e-mails from friends who have been desperately praying for answers from God. Today, they received those answers, and were blown away by this. One person wrote, "Why do I not expect this to happen?" Now, for the moment at least, they are motivated to pray more. God's loving responses to them motivate me to pray more.

In a few minutes I will walk to the back of our property, by the river, where there is an old table, and my praying chair. I'll bring my journal, Bible, and a cup of coffee... to meet with God for a while, and pray. I will pray for others, and I will listen to God speak to me. At this point in my life, I rarely leave these prayer times without feeling encouraged and strengthened.

Why do I do this? Why do I pray? The basic reason is: because Jesus did. Here's my reasoning.

1. Jesus is my Great Shepherd.
2. My Great Shepherd spent much time praying.
3. Therefore, I shall spend much time praying.

How do we know Jesus spent much time praying? Because "Jesus went out *as usual* to the Mount of Olives, and his disciples followed him."[1] What Jesus did there was:

---

[1] Luke 22:39

235

1) instruct his disciples to watch and pray.

2) pray, himself.

"As usual," Jesus went to the Mount of Olives, and prayed. "As was his custom." Praying was Jesus' customary way of doing life. If Jesus habitually did this, who am I, one of his followers, *not* to?

I read of a sign, supposedly on the Alaskan Highway, where the road turned from pavement to dirt. It read: "Choose your rut carefully. You'll be in it for the next hundred miles." Choose praying. Over time, it will become the habitual rut in which you live your life.

There are many reasons why I pray. In this chapter, I share some of them.

I Pray Because Jesus Prayed

The main reason I pray is because Jesus prayed.

1. I am a follower of Jesus.
2. Jesus prayed.
3. Therefore, I pray.

That's why praying matters. Jesus prayed. Not out of some religious obligation, but from a felt, compelling need to pray. Jesus prayed as if prayer accomplished things.

I am following in Jesus' knee prints today, and praying.

The Open Secret of Jesus' Ministry

Why did Jesus pray? He prayed to find out what the Father wanted him to do. He prayed to receive strength, and comfort. He and the Father were on a redemptive mission together. In times of praying, Jesus received marching orders.

Praying opens the door to the control room of the kingdom of heaven. In praying, I engage in God's kingdom activity. In praying, I gain discernment, and see how to separate kingdom activity from mundane activity. In praying, I become a relevant doer of the will of God.

Henri Nouwen wrote, "I have the sense that the secret of Jesus's ministry is hidden in that lonely place where he went to pray, early in the morning, long before dawn."[2] The open secret of Jesus' earthly ministry is that: he customarily prayed.

I Pray for God's Protection

One of my praying friends writes:

> In my alone time with God He is showing me that I must lean on Him especially now. He knows what I am going through. He understands the heartbreak and the pain of what is going on right now in my life. When I am alone with God I feel this incredible peace and comfort, even in the mist of not understanding why certain things are happening. He is teaching me that he is in control of all things and that I am going to have to trust him.

I received this note while preparing to preach on Philippians 4:4-7. In these verses we have four admonitions, plus a promise:

1. Rejoice in the Lord always.[3]
2. Let your gentleness be evident to all.
3. Don't be anxious about anything.
4. Pray in every situation, with thanksgiving.

Do such things, and "the peace of God, which transcends understanding, will guard your hearts and minds in Christ Jesus."

The word "guard" is a military term. Ben Witherington writes:

> Since the city of Philippi was at that time guarded by a Roman garrison, the metaphor would have been

---

[2] Henri Nouwen, *Spiritual Formation: Following the Movements of the Spirit*, 20-21.
[3] Note that ubiquitous Pauline word 'in'.

easily understood and appreciated by the Philippian readers. Paul is talking about a consequence of praying with thanksgiving. A sense of God's presence, peace, wholeness comes over the one praying, stilling and reassuring the heart about things and thus removing anxiety.[4]

My friend, who is going through a troubling time, is deepening her prayer life. She is experiencing the peace of God, enveloping her like an army of God's protection, as God promised.

I Pray Because God Guides Me

Out of the abiding-in-Jesus prayer relationship comes guidance, by the Holy Spirit. Directions are given. This is why Jesus spent time in prayer with the Father; viz., to find out what the Father wanted him to do. The call to action is the fruit of conversation with God.

Imagine this. God speaks to me, telling me to plant a vegetable garden that will produce food for hungry people. On hearing this, what do I do? I look for a plot of land to plant the garden in, and head to Lowe's to buy seeds.

I don't wait for more signs. I act on what God has told me to do. Such acting *is faith*. It may feel irrational and risky. Were it not so, it would not be faith. Faith is not epistemic certainty. My only certainty is that God will be with me. When I obey in faith, I grow in trust in God.[5]

Direction arises out of prayer-abiding in Christ. Jesus said if I abide in him I will bear much fruit. This includes acting in obedience, in faith. These two things I must do:

1) dwell tight with Jesus;
2) respond in faith when he gives direction.

---

[4] Ben Witherington, *Paul's Letter to the Philippians: A Socio-Rhetorical Commentary*. Grand Rapids: Eerdmans, 2011.

[5] See Alvin Plantinga's excellent chapter on faith as a form of knowledge, in *Knowledge and Christian Belief*. Grand Rapids: Eerdmans, 2015.

This is why precious little happens in some churches. Few take time to abide in Christ. "I don't have time to pray" is the blind mantra of the American Christian. And, if they do have time, few obey because of the risks. Jesus is a dangerous person who will take us out of our cocooned environments.

Jesus-following has the kind of dynamic we see when Jesus tells Peter to drop his fishing nets, and follow him. To follow Jesus is to leave nets behind. This is where many sing, "I have decided, not to follow Jesus. I'm turning back, I'm turning back."

To all who desire guidance from God, prepare to leave stuff behind so as to be guided. I need direction. In praying, God guides me. Everyone who spends time praying experiences this.

Purpose Comes Out of Praying Presence

I have a friend who loves to work in his large vegetable and flower garden. He talks about needing "garden time." I say to him, "That's your therapy."

Working and laboring for a purpose brings satisfaction. To work on a job worth doing is to potentially achieve a job well done. In praying, God gives work orders. In the praying war room with God, I receive his kingdom plans and purposes. Purpose clarifies, as I pray in the garden of God's presence.

Presence is prior to purpose. Purpose comes out of prayerful presence. In praying, I hear the call of God to "Go," or "Do." In this way my *doing* emerges out of my *being*.

From God's POV there is no such thing as a small call. To work at a task God has for me results in his plans being accomplished, and my emotional and spiritual needs being fulfilled. This even applies to small, seemingly insignificant tasks. I come home, and see dishes that need to be done, so I wash them. I love doing dishes. The *telos* or purpose for me is: this pleases Linda. When she gets home she notices. I like the thought of freeing up her life. I love Linda, and love sets people free. This is laboring with a greater purpose.

To work with purpose in life is to co-labor with God and his intentions. This is the heart of true prayer, which is: talking with God about what God and I are thinking and doing together. I want to come to the end of my life knowing God has worked through me to accomplish his desires. That is good. It is a way of loving God, and is therapy for my soul.

Laboring with no sense of purpose is a kind of hell.[6] It is boredom. "Boredom" is not having nothing to do; boredom is finding no meaning in what you are doing. Purposeless work produces inner agitation.

As a pastor, I am always meeting people who live purposeless lives and experience constant spiritual agitation. Jesus told his disciples, "Let not your hearts be agitated."[7] A washing machine has an "agitator." It thrusts the clothes back and forth, over and over again and again. Spiritually, "agitation is the useless and ill-directed action of the body. It expresses the inner confusion of a soul without peace… All this is the death of the interior life."[8]

To work for the goals of money, pleasure, or power, is to construct an agitator in the heart. It brings the death of the interior life. The antidote to this is: dwell, now, in Christ.[9]

In the praying relationship, I discover my work. This discovery arises out of a Christ-abiding connection. This is where the fruit grows, and the tasks are delegated. One's laboring becomes relevant, bringing peace and fulfillment to the soul.

Follow Jesus' command to abide in him. Allow him to shepherd your soul. A little bit of churchgoing won't help. A few mc-prayers won't either. Constant abiding will. Out of this Christ-dwelling comes not only his peace and joy, but life purpose.

I pray because I want my work to be purposeful.

---

[6] On the hellishness of purposeless work see Albert Camus, *The Myth of Sisyphus*.

[7] ταράσσω,*v* \{tar-as'-so} - to agitate, trouble (a thing, by the movement of its parts to and fro); to cause one inward commotion, take away his calmness of mind, disturb his equanimity. Greekbible.com.

[8] Thomas Merton, *No Man Is an Island*, 114-115. Orlando, Florida: Harcourt, 1983.

[9] See John chapters 14-16.

Praying Is Being Shepherded

Because the Lord is my shepherd I shall not be wanting.
- Psalm 23:1

In the act of praying, I surrender my heart to God's rule over my life. To pray is to surrender. This is one reason some do not have a prayer life. They are afraid of what God will ask of them. They are afraid of surrendering.

Sometimes a person asks for counsel, and I give them my sense of what God wants them to do. But they don't do it. Perhaps they only wanted me to tell them what they wanted to hear. Maybe they just wanted me to endorse their position. This is common in marriage counseling. If a marriage is failing, it doesn't take a rocket scientist to realize both husband and wife will need to do some things differently. Many do not want to hear this. If they refuse follow what I recommend, then I respond, "I am no longer your counselor."

When it comes to the counsel of God, what will he ask of me? He will require that I give *all* of myself to his reign and rule over my life. God wants to be my shepherd. He wants my full "sheep-ness" to follow after him, not just an arm or a leg, and not only on Christmas and Easter. Failure to follow the shepherd's leading means God is not, for all practical purposes, *my* shepherd.

In praying, I have found that God longs to shepherd me. My heart becomes Christ's home, a dwelling place where Jesus resides. The greatest leader the world has ever known now lives in me! Therefore, according to his nature, he leads me. In the intimate prayer environment the Father reveals his heart, desires, and plans to me. When we learn to pray like this "we discover the amazing consequences of surrendering our self-determination to God. It leads to peace inside ourselves that strengthens and encourages us to continue along the road of surrender to God."[10]

To pray is to surrender.

---

[10] James Houston and Dallas Willard, *The Transforming Friendship: A Guide to Prayer*, 44. Vancouver: Regent College Publishing.

I pray because God shepherds me.

Praying as the Antidote to Anxiety

I pray because I am less anxious when I do.

In Philippians 4, Paul commands Jesus-followers to "be anxious about nothing."[11] The biblical Greek word for 'anxious' is often used in contexts where persecution is happening. For example, where Jesus counsels his disciples, "When they arrest you, do not be anxious about what to say or how to say it."[12]

When Paul instructs the Philippians to not be anxious it's not like he's sitting on a beach in Cancun drinking piña coladas. He's in prison! The context is: persecution. The Philippian Jesus-followers were suffering under opposition from their pagan neighbors, just like Paul and Silas had suffered when among them.[13]

I know what it is to worry and be anxious. So I ask: how is it realistic to be told "Be anxious about nothing?" Paul's answer emerges out of the experiential reality of his rich, ongoing praying life. He writes, authoritatively: "Do not be anxious about anything, but in every situation, by prayer and petition, with thanksgiving, present your requests to God."[14]

When I don't pray, I am more easily filled with worries and fears. But as I do pray, God meets with me. For me, this has been huge!

In everyday prayer conferences with God I present requests to, and lay burdens before, him.[15] I have a Father God who loves me, in whom I trust. Where there is trust, there is neither worry nor anxiety. A person with a praying life grows in trust, and diminishes in anxiety.

For this result, I feel thankful. Our prayers should be accompanied "with thanksgiving." Paul believed "there is much to be said for praying

---

[11] Philippians 4:6
[12] Matthew 10:19
[13] Acts 16:19-24; Philippians 1:28-30
[14] Philippians
[15] See 1 Peter 5:7

in the right spirit or frame of mind."[16] I give thanks to God for removing anxiety and fear. Giving thanks to God is itself "a stress-buster."[17] John Wesley said that "thanksgiving is the surest evidence of a soul free from anxiety."[18]

This is significant for the Roman Philippians, since pagan prayers did not have thanksgiving. Roman prayers were often fearful, bargaining prayers, which were not based on a relationship with some god.

The antidote for worry and anxiety is praying, with thanksgiving. This is one of the reasons why I pray.

Praying and Burden-throwing

Yesterday afternoon I went to my solitary praying place at Sterling State Park on Lake Erie. I was carrying pages of burdens. I sat on the shores of the lake and read through these prayer requests that were sent to me. I prayed through them.

These requests included many cares and anxieties. In my mind I took every one of them and threw them on God, following 1 Peter 5:7, which directs me to "throw" [19] my cares and anxieties on him, because he cares about me

The word "throw" translates the Greek word *epiripsantes*[20]? It means "to throw upon," or "to cast upon." We see *epiripsantes* in Luke 19:35: "They brought it [the colt] to Jesus, *threw* their cloaks on the colt and put Jesus on it."

Anxieties work to "devour" me and eat my soul away. Unattended to, they are toxic to my heart. So, in my praying, I engage in care-casting. I throw burdens on Jesus, like a rider throws his saddle on a horse.

---

[16] Ben Witherington, *Paul's Letter to the Philippians: A Socio-Rhetorical Commentary.*

[17] Ib.

[18] Ib.

[19] [7]πᾶσαν τὴν μέριμναν ὑμῶν **ἐπιρίψαντες** ἐπ᾽ αὐτόν, ὅτιαὐτῷ μέλει περὶ ὑμῶν.

[20] ἐπιρίψαντες

The Amplified Bible reads: "Cast the whole of your care [all your anxieties, all your worries, all your concerns, once and for all] on Him, for He cares for you affectionately and cares about you watchfully."[21]

This is praying as constant detoxification. I do this each day, multiple times. Scot McKnight writes:

> Peter exhorts God's people to express a simple confidence in God's justice. By turning over our fears and worries to God, we express our trust in him and rely on him to bring about vindication and justice. The reason for turning over fears to God is because "he cares for you." [22]

Cares and anxieties are rooted in devil-inspired injustices meant to weigh me down, discourage me, and ultimately devour me. I therefore engage in regular deburdening as an act of world-rebellion, and a refusal to shoulder this world's injustices on my own.

I cast my cares on the LORD and he will sustain me; he will never let me be shaken.[23]

Praying Moves Me from Unreality to Reality

One of my Seminary students sent this note to me.

> Just as with anything else, once you get home [after a week of spiritual formation classes], its back to reality. I found myself drowned with so many things, whereas on campus I felt free as a jaybird. The hour of power prayer allowed me to abide in Christ. Although my physical body was starting to weaken, I focused on the elements of our spiritual formation class and it helps me to know

---

[21] 1 Peter 5:7, The Amplified Bible
[22] Scot McKnight, *The NIV Application Commentary:1 Peter*, paraphrased. Grand Rapids: Zondervan, 1996.
[23] Psalm 55:22, personalized.

that God is my comforter and my prayer life now is changed forever!

I wrote back:

> "Reality" is now going to be different for you. God desires to give you his reality in place of your unreality. You are moving from elements of unreality ("drowned with so many things") to freedom. There will be fruit, produced in you, as a result of a greater abiding in Christ. You are one of Jesus's great, praying persons!

Out of a life of abiding in Christ, expressed in a praying relationship with God, reality gets redefined. The really real stands out. The illusions of life vaporize like fog meeting the morning sun.

I pray, because praying moves me from unreality to reality.

Praying Breeds Love for Others

I preached yesterday morning out of 1 John 2:7-11. If I say I know God and love him, but hate my Christian brothers and sisters, I am a blind man walking in darkness. Since God has no fellowship with darkness (in him there is no darkness at all), I disfellowship myself in the act of hating.

These verses haunt me because I have hated other Christians. In my hatred I have *not* known, loved, or followed Jesus. Worshiping Jesus as Lord on Sunday morning while hating people on the side is just acting, and hypocritical. A Jesus-follower who hates others is a contradiction. Because "God so loved the world," right?

The antidote to my hate-filled heart is a Spirit-transformed, Jesus-shaped heart. So, I am praying for a heart of love. I want to look at others with the same compassion Jesus had. I want to love and forgive others from the heart, as he did when he hung on the cross. I want the freedom Jesus had from a spirit of victimization.

How can this happen? One way is *in the act of praying for others.* True praying breeds compassion. And togetherness.

Dietrich Bonhoeffer writes:

> A Christian fellowship lives and exists by the intercession of its members for one another, or it collapses. I can no longer condemn or hate a brother for whom I pray, no matter how much trouble he causes me. His face, that hitherto may have been strange and intolerable to me, is transformed in intercession into the countenance of a brother for whom Christ died, the face of a forgiven sinner. This is a happy discovery for the Christian who begins to pray for others.[24]

Now I'm thinking of an old Michael W. Smith song I used to sing.

> *Pray for me, and I'll pray for you*
> *Pray that we will keep the common ground*
> *Won't you pray for me and I'll pray for you*
> *And one day love will bring us back around*
> *Again*[25]

I pray because I am desperate to love as Jesus loves.

I Pray Because God Speaks to Me

One of my constant prayers is for God to raise my level of experience to the level of the historical biblical narrative. Otherwise, the alternative is dismal; viz., that I would understand the biblical narrative through the filter of my own experience. That would diminish the biblical text.

If the Jesus-life is only to be lived in mere human strength and ability, then I am not interested. I'm with theistic philosopher Dallas Willard as he writes:

---

[24] Bonhoeffer, *Life Together*, 86.
[25] Michael W. Smith, "Pray for Me"

It is worth reminding ourselves to read the biblical accounts as if what is described is happening to us. We must make the conscious effort to think that such things might happen to us and to imagine what it would be like if they were to happen.[26]

We must reaffirm our participation in biblical experience. What might this look like, especially when it comes to hearing God? Willard says that, in the biblical record, God addresses people in six ways. They are:

1. a phenomenon plus a voice
2. a supernatural messenger or an angel
3. dreams and visions
4. an audible voice
5. the human voice
6. the human spirit or the "still, small voice"[27]

I have experienced two, three, five, and six. It is my expectation that God will speak to me, today, in one of these ways. This alters how I pray.

I have access to God. Every Jesus-follower does, and can live with the expectation that God desires to, and will, communicate with them. Willard admits that "this will be difficult at first, for most people have become accustomed to thinking that God does such marvelous things only with other people."[28]

I pray because God communicates his love, direction, comfort, and strength *to me*, in many ways.

Praying Is Therapeutic

A good doctor examines their patient's total lifestyle before prescribing medications. Without lifestyle changes a pill may be a quick

---

[26] In Willard, *Hearing God: Developing a Conversational Relationship with God*, 119.
[27] Ib., 120-121
[28] Ib., 119

fix, masking underlying anomalies. If lifestyle choices are not made, the doctor will be unable to heal the sick person. If the person doesn't change their way of living, the results will be the same.

When someone asks for my help I prescribe lifestyle things that have brought me strength and relief. At the top of my counsel to every struggling Jesus-follower is: *Pray.*

"But... I don't have time to pray."

Then I can't help you.

Are you looking for a quick fix? Some drive-through "McHelp?" It's not going to happen. A life of actually praying, however, will sustain you. I have found that, in praying, God:

- meets me
- loves me
- directs my paths
- follows me in goodness and mercy
- empowers me
- fuels and feeds me
- encourages me
- answers my cries
- sets my feet on solid ground
- reminds me that I am His
- heals me
- delivers me
- clarifies my thinking
- fills me with hope
- astounds me
- graces me
- mercies me

In my world-weariness I run to God and pray. He becomes the therapist I need.

I Pray Because Peacemakers Pray

In his last words to his disciples Jesus said, "Peace I leave to you, my peace I give to you; a peace the world cannot give, this is my gift to you."[29]

I'll happily accept this gift. I experience it by abiding in him. A peacemaker dwells, not in the house of fear and war, but in the house of peace. In Christ, there is peace. I must connect with him who *is* my peace.[30]

How?

Try praying. Praying takes us into God's House of Peace. Arguably, praying is the main way of connecting yourself to God. Have an actual prayer life and receive the peace of God, as Jesus promised. Declare your identity and act accordingly. A peacemaker prays. In the act of praying, peace grows like fruit, as a gift.

> Prayer is the beginning and the end, the source and the fruit, the core and the content, the basis and the goal for all peacemaking. I say this without apology, because it allows me to go straight to the heart of the matter, which is that peace is a divine gift, a gift we receive in prayer.[31]

This is not mere theory. These words have existential and experiential content. To *not* have a life of abiding prayer is to live in the house of fear, where war breeds resentment and competition. I pray because God frees me from warring inclinations, and the fruit of peace grows in the soil of my heart.

---

[29] John 14:27
[30] Ephesians 2:14
[31] Nouwen, *The Gift of Peace,* 9

God-dependent People Pray

The day Jesus rescued me was my personal Dependence Day. I am a dependent. Therefore, I pray.

In the spiritual life dependence is good, independence is bad. The less a person has, the more God-dependent they are. There are exceptions to this, but I find this to be the rule.

"It is hard," Jesus said, "for a rich man to enter the kingdom of heaven."[32] By "kingdom" Jesus meant the rule, or reign, of God. It is hard for a rich man to come under the reign of God in their life. For these reasons.

Material possessions tend to give people the illusion of control.

If a person has money they have more control over elements and diseases; i.e., they have a roof over their head, food to eat, and access to health care.

People with lots of stuff spend their lives attending to their stuff - storing it, protecting it, cleaning it, etc. This takes lots of time, leaving less for God.

When material things become burdens, joy decreases. If you are wealthy and joyful for the right reasons (viz., the presence of God rules your being), then praise God. But there is arguably more joy in poor communities of South America than in the elite in America. The general rule is: the less stuff, the greater joy.[33]

When I was traveling and speaking in central India I discovered that people who wanted to receive prayer were numerically greater than what I find in the U.S. The same happened on my Kenya trip. When you have little food, shelter, and money, it is common to turn more to

---

[32] Matthew 19:23

[33] See Nouwen, *Gracias! A Latin American Journal.* New York: Harper & Row, 1983. Nouwen found more joy among the poor in South America than in the elite halls of Yale University where he taught.

God, because there's nowhere else to go. God-dependency is generally greater among the poor.[34]

Weakness breeds dependence. This is why when I am weak, then I am strong. The great Western illusion is that I am fundamentally non-dependent.

Over time a Jesus-follower's God-dependency should increase. The truth of how we are essentially God-and-other dependent is more clearly seen. The illusion that we are "in control" is broken in us. As a result, we may pray more.

An increasing prayer life is a sign of increased dependency on God. God-dependent people pray.

Prayer Looping: On Unceasing Praying

I cannot stop praying.

Last week Linda and I spend several hours together listening to "Serial," the radio series that went viral.[35] At the beginning of each show, and periodically throughout, the theme music played. It was this simple piano piece that became associated with the story of a young high school girl who was murdered. For days afterward I could not get this music out of my mind! It was unconsciously repeating, looping through my neural self, unceasingly.

Conscious repetition leads to unceasing consciousness. Paul's "unceasing praying" can be understood like this. The conscious dedication to intentional praying shapes us, by the Spirit, into constant pray-ers. Like the worship song that was repeated on Sunday morning sings in my heart on Monday morning, the praying I do day by day, week by week, and year after year, carves out a deep river in my heart that flows today. From much praying, comes praying without ceasing.

Apply this to 1 Thessalonians 5:16-18.

---

[34] But not always. Louis Brogdon, in *Hope On the Brink: Understanding the Emergence of Nihilism in Black America*, shows how the hopelessness of poverty, crime, and injustice in black communities is turning some away from God.

[35] https://serialpodcast.org/

"Rejoice always" (which emerges out of an intentional worshiping life).

"Pray without ceasing" (which happens as a result of choosing to pray consistently).

"Give thanks in all circumstances" (which happens as a result of a consistent choosing to be thankful).

"For this is the will of God in Christ Jesus for you" (This is God's "inclination" or "desire" (Greek *thelema*) for you; which is to say, this is God's very heart, produced in you and I.).

The rejoicing-praying-thanksgiving fugue contrapuntally loops through my soul, without stopping.

Praying Is Causally Efficacious

I pray because prayer works. If I thought prayer didn't work, I would not waste my time praying.

Prayer works by actually praying, a lot. To pray is to be in relationship with God. Deep interpersonal relationships communicate, a lot.

Praying "works." What does this mean? As I see it:

Praying brings me into relationship with God, experientially. I meet with God, in prayer.

I experience and sense the presence of God, with me. This is important because experience, not theory, breeds conviction.

I engage and co-partner with God in his redemptive mission. I experience God's guiding hand, and can empirically corroborate this.[36]

I have seen things happen and change as a result of praying. I have 3500+ journal pages as a testimony to this.[37] I can make a case for the causal efficacy of praying as co-laboring with God.

A life of praying recalibrates, daily, my heart to the heart of God.

---

[36] I have multiple accounts of this written in my 3500+ pages of journals over the past 40+ years. I have read countless stories of God's guidance from among the 3000+ students and pastors I have taught.

[37] BTW – I reject a B.F. Skinnerian philosophical naturalism that attempts to "reduce all mystery to knowledge." See Skinner, Beyond Freedom and Dignity.

A life of praying has changed me. For the better, I believe. Note: for the Christian theist "better" is understood in terms of the "best" that is Jesus.

A life of praying renders me less anxious, less fearful, and less lonely. Again, this is a palpable, existential, living reality.

Praying changes things and changes me. I experience brokenness within and see breakthrough without. Therefore, I pray.

The 4th-century theologian John Chrysostom, in a moment of joyful realization and remembering, wrote on the efficacy of praying:

> The potency of prayer hath subdued the strength of fire; it hath bridled the rage of lions, hushed anarchy to rest, extinguished wars, appeased the elements, expelled demons, burst the chains of death, expanded the gates of heaven, assuaged diseases, repelled frauds, rescued cities from destruction, stayed the sun in its course, and arrested the progress of the thunderbolt. Prayer is an all-efficient panoply, a treasure undiminished, a mine which is never exhausted, a sky unobscured by clouds, a heaven unruffled by the storm. It is the root, the fountain, the mother of a thousand blessings.[38]

I pray because prayer works.

DNA-Praying

I pray because I cannot not-pray.

It is common for me to wake up praying, and retire to bed at night praying. How did this happen to me? It is the end result of a life of disciplined praying.

This life began in 1977, when I forced myself to get away to a lonely place and pray, a half hour a day. I chose to pray, which means I acted on it. I prayed.

---

[38] John Chrysostom, *The Divine Liturgy of St John Chrysostom*.

The choice to pray and stay with it has morphed into DNA-praying. The choice to pray has become praying. If there is a choice now, it would be to choose not to pray. That would be hard to do, for I have become someone who cannot not-pray. I am a praying person. I am a person who would find it hard to not pray.

I am a disciplined pray-er. Jesus prayed, and I am one of his disciples. Spiritual disciplines create the environment in which in which a praying life can develop

Long ago I made the choice to pray at least a half hour a day. I chose to do my praying in the piano room of our house in East Lansing. I chose to accompany my praying times with Scripture meditation. I chose to keep a spiritual journal and write down what God was saying to me and doing in me. As a result of my choices I began to experience God meeting with me, speaking to me, strengthening me, guiding me, healing me. A life of uninterrupted praying began to develop.

I woke up today praying.

I Pray Because Everyone in the Bible Prayed

In the Old Testament people prayed

Abraham prayed. "Then Abraham prayed to God, and God healed Abimelek, his wife and his female slaves so they could have children again..."[39]

Isaac prayed. "Isaac prayed to the LORD on behalf of his wife, because she was childless. The LORD answered his prayer, and his wife Rebekah became pregnant."[40]

Jacob prayed. "Then Jacob prayed, "O God of my father Abraham, God of my father Isaac, LORD, you who said to me, 'Go back to your country and your relatives, and I will make you prosper...'"[41]

Moses prayed.

---

[39] Genesis 20:17
[40] Genesis 25:21
[41] Genesis 32:8-10

Moses then left Pharaoh and prayed to the LORD.[42] When the people cried out to Moses, he prayed to the LORD and the fire died down.[43] The people came to Moses and said, "We sinned when we spoke against the LORD and against you. Pray that the LORD will take the snakes away from us." So Moses prayed for the people.[44]

Samson prayed.[45]

Hannah prayed.[46]

Samuel prayed.[47]

David prayed. "Nathan hears from God and shares this with David. Then King David went in and sat before the LORD, and he said: "Who am I, Sovereign LORD, and what is my family, that you have brought me this far?"[48]

Elisha prayed.[49]

Hezekiah prayed. "In those days Hezekiah became ill and was at the point of death. He prayed to the LORD, who answered him and gave him a miraculous sign."[50]

Solomon prayed. [The Dedication of the Temple] "When Solomon finished praying, fire came down from heaven and consumed the burnt offering and the sacrifices, and the glory of the LORD filled the temple."[51]

Ezra prayed. "So we fasted and petitioned our God about this, and he answered our prayer."[52]

---

[42] Exodus 10:18

[43] Numbers 11:2

[44] Numbers 21:7

[45] Judges 16:28

[46] 1 Samuel 1:10-13

[47] 1 Samuel 7:5

[48] 2 Samuel 7:18

[49] 2 Kings 6:17-20

[50] 2 Chronicles 32:34

[51] 2 Chronicles 7:1

[52] Ezra 8:23

Nehemiah prayed. "When I heard these things, I sat down and wept. For some days I mourned and fasted and prayed before the God of heaven."[53]

Job prayed. "After Job had prayed for his friends, the LORD restored his fortunes and gave him twice as much as he had before."[54]

Psalms – the word "prayer" is used thirty-four times in the Psalms.[55]

Isaiah prayed.[56]

Jeremiah prayed.[57]

Elijah prayed.[58]

All the prophets prayed.

Jonah prayed. "From inside the fish Jonah prayed to the LORD his God."[59]

Daniel prayed. "Then these men went as a group and found Daniel praying and asking God for help."[60]

The early church prayed.

> They all joined together constantly in prayer, along with the women and Mary the mother of Jesus, and with his brothers.[61] And: They devoted themselves to the apostles' teaching and to fellowship, to the breaking of bread and to prayer. Everyone was filled with awe at the many wonders and signs performed by the apostles... Every day they continued to meet together in the temple courts... And the Lord added to their number daily those who were being saved.[62]

---

[53] Nehemiah 1:4
[54] Job 42:10
[55] In the Psalms we see David as a prayer fanatic.
[56] Isaiah 33:2 ff.
[57] Jeremiah 12:1-13
[58] 1 Kings 18:36
[59] Jonah 2:1
[60] Daniel 6:11
[61] Acts 1:14
[62] Acts 2:42; 46-47

And:

> On their release, Peter and John went back to their own
> people and reported all that the chief priests and the
> elders had said to them. When they heard this, they
> raised their voices together in prayer to God.[63]

"Peter was kept in prison, but the church was earnestly praying to
God for him."[64]

Peter prayed.

> About noon the following day as they were on their
> journey and approaching the city, Peter went up on
> the roof to pray. He saw heaven opened and something
> like a large sheet being let down to earth by its four
> corners.[65]

Paul and Silas prayed.

> About midnight Paul and Silas were praying and singing
> hymns to God, and the other prisoners were listening
> to them. Suddenly there was such a violent earthquake
> that the foundations of the prison were shaken.[66]

Paul prayed.

> "God, whom I serve in my spirit in preaching the gospel
> of his Son, is my witness how constantly I remember
> you in my prayers at all times...[67] And: Be joyful in
> hope, patient in affliction, faithful in prayer."[68]

---

[63] Acts 4:23-24
[64] Acts 12:5
[65] Acts
[66] Acts 16
[67] Romans 1
[68] Romans 12:12

257

Paul counseled Jesus-followers to "Devote yourselves to prayer."[69]

Jesus prayed.

Jesus was often found praying, in various contexts; e.g., in the synagogue, in lonely places, etc.

Jesus spent time in solitude. "Jesus began his ministry by spending 40 days alone in solitude and prayer."[70]

"Before choosing the 12 Jesus spent the entire night alone in the desert hills praying."[71]

"When he heard of John the Baptist's death Jesus "withdrew from there in a boat to a lonely place apart.""[72]

"After feeding the 5000 he dismissed the crowd and "went up into the hills by himself" where he prayed."[73]

After a long night of work, "in the morning, a great while before day, he rose and went out to a lonely place."[74]

After healing a leper, Jesus "*often* withdrew to the wilderness and prayed."[75]

Before his time on the cross he went alone to the Garden of Gethsemane and prayed.[76]

Jesus went out as usual [as was his custom] to the Mount of Olives, to pray…[77]

If the God-followers in the Old Testament prayed,
if the early church prayed,
if Peter prayed,
if the apostle Paul prayed,

---

[69] 1 Corinthians 7
[70] Matthew 4:1-11
[71] Luke 6:12
[72] Matthew 14:13
[73] Matthew 14:23
[74] Mark 6:31
[75] Luke 5:16, emphasis mine
[76] Matthew 26:36-46
[77] Luke 22:39

and if Jesus took habitual solitary times of praying out of his own need to be in contact with the Father,

should I do any less?

If we don't have time to pray, who do we think we are, God Almighty?

Prayer Is My First Resort

I still struggle with attitudes that are not Christlike. This morning, while praying, I confessed some things to God. I asked God to get at the root of my attitudinal disease and extract it out of my heart. "Heal me, O God," is one of my constant prayers.

I pray for God to help me do what I cannot do myself. I left self-healing techniques behind decades ago. I do read to gain greater understanding of my troubledness. But my real help comes from the Lord, maker of heaven and earth, to include me.

This is different from "Do your best, and God (hopefully) will do the rest." "When life is divided into "our best" and "God's rest," we have turned prayer into a last resort to be used only when all our own resources are depleted."[78]

When I am struggling, my first resort is to pray.

Prayer Is the Glue that Enables My Freedom

I hear of so much violence through the media that my heart easily becomes desensitized to it. But not this week. I can barely hear of what happened to James Foley.[79] My heart aches, it longs, as I see his parents and brother expressing their grief and talking about their loss. Their love, grace, and lack of vindictiveness make the whole thing harder for me. Had they responded with the common world-default "eye for an eye" philosophy, I would be hating instead of grieving. Pure, unpolluted grief does not hate, but loves.

---

[78] Henri Nouwen, *The Only Necessary Thing*, 93

[79] James Foley was an American journalist in Syria who was abducted and headed by Isis.

The Foleys talked with Pope Francis.

> "Pope Francis, like Jesus, loves, like Jim. He understood Jim's heart," Diane Foley said of her son, who "was able to draw strength from prayer" during his capture. She said love and compassion had drawn her son to cover the plight of the people in Syria, which has been embroiled in a violent conflict for the past several years... "We must stand together," Foley said. "Good and love and all that is free in the world must be together to fight the evil and the hatred."[80]

Fight evil with good and love. That is correct. There is no other way. Love your enemies and pray for those that behead you.

Jim Foley was a Jesus-follower who prayed.

> "Foley was a devout Christian who, unlike most journalists I've known during my almost four decades in the field, was unapologetic about his heart for social justice and the inspiration he found for his beliefs in the New Testament."[81] When held captive in Libya in 2011 Jim said that "prayer was the glue that enabled my freedom, an inner freedom first and later the miracle of being released during a war in which the regime had no real incentive to free us."[82]

Jim and fellow prisoner Claire "prayed together out loud. It felt energizing to speak our weaknesses and hopes together, as if in a

---

[80] http://www.reuters.com/article/us-iraq-security-pope-idUSKBN0GM0R220140822

[81] http://www.lohud.com/story/money/personal-finance/taxes/david-mckay-wilson/2014/08/22/james-foley-beheading-victim-had-deep-christian-faith/14468129/

[82] "Journalist Jim Foley Turned to Prayer for Strength." http://www.ncregister.com/daily-news/journalist-james-foley-turned-to-prayer-for-strength/

conversation with God, rather than silently and alone."[83] Jim said "I'd pray to stay strong. I'd pray to soften the hearts of our captors. I'd pray to God to lift the burdens we couldn't handle. And I'd pray that our Moms would know we were OK."

At his life's end on earth James Foley was dressed in orange, and a hooded killer decapitated him. One writer concludes, "This time, God did not answer James Foley's prayers. This time, James Foley was not delivered from evil."

But God did, and Jim was. The root of evil lies in the human heart. Jim was delivered from what Thomas Merton referred to as inner "seeds of destruction," and Paul Tournier called "the violence within." As Jesus was free even as he was brutalized, Jim did not succumb and drink from the sickspring of evil. Jesus "loved them to the end." This is the message that comes through Jim's life and family, and simultaneously crushes and gives hope.

Elisabeth Scalia writes: *"Prayer is a subversive means of freedom*, at once consoling, engaging and efficacious throughout time and space. It has power, and that power holds, when everything else falls apart."[84] Prayer is the glue that enables my freedom, and holds me together when everything else is falling apart.

Why I Believe Prayer Works (I Lay My Google Down)

James 5:16 states that "the prayer of a righteous person is powerful and effective." I believe this. I believe prayer is powerful and effective. Here are some preliminaries, before I give reasons in support of this claim.

---

[83] "Jim Foley: Beheading Victim Had Deep Faith." http://www.lohud.com/story/money/personal-finance/taxes/david-mckay-wilson/2014/08/22/james-foley-beheading-victim-had-deep-christian-faith/14468129/

[84] "Jim Foley, Martyrdom and the Subversive Freedom of Prayer." http://www.patheos.com/blogs/theanchoress/2014/08/21/james-foley-martyrdom-and-the-subversive-freedom-of-prayer/

1. I define prayer as talking with God about what we are thinking and doing together. *Prayer is a relationship with God that I have.* When I claim that prayer works I have this definition in mind.

2. My reasons for believing in prayer's efficaciousness form an inductive, not deductive, argument. I present reasons to believe, or why I see it as rational to believe, that prayer is powerful and effective. (Logically, I'm using abductive reasoning, or inference to the best explanation.) Can this be doubted? Of course. Any inductive argument is subject to doubt, more or less. In the same way, the inductively arrived-at claim *Prayer does not work* can logically be doubted. (Note: If one begins with the claim *God does not exist*, then it deductively follows that *Prayer does not work.*)

3. I present why *I* believe prayer works. I think it is important to state it this way. I lay my omniscient God-substitute Google down, and speak for myself. (Note: This is why I also value meeting face-to-face over coffee with people who don't believe what I believe. Thanks to all of you who have done, and do this, with me. I have learned from you.)

In 1977 I began a practice of getting alone and praying for several hours every week. I have maintained that practice, to this day. I believe the question, "Does prayer work?", can only be answered by those who have committed themselves to a life of praying.

I have kept journals recording my prayer life since 1977. My journals total over 3500 pages. I have had many incidences where the best explanation for an event, as far as I can tell, is that it is an answer to my prayers.

So, I have much *personal experience* with praying. This is important to me because of a deep philosophical belief I have, which is: *experience, not theory, breeds conviction.*

I'm going to be praying today, and tomorrow. I would not pray if I thought it did not work. (This reason is by *via negativa*.) It is important for me to say this. I don't expect my experience to convince others. But this *is* my experience, just as you have your experiences; therefore,

I stand convinced. Call this an existential reason, without which I have no idea why I would pray (To religiously fake it? To impress others?).

I have taught praying to many people. My estimate is that I have taught at least 3500 pastors and Christian leaders about praying. 1500 of them have engaged in six weeks of praying, one hour a day, five days a week. They have kept journals recording their prayer experiences. They have sent their journals to me. I have read them. These students have been, literally, from all over the world. A few have invited me to their countries to teach prayer to their people and colleagues. I have a broad, deep, data base of people who committed themselves to actually praying. These people tell of experiences and events that deepen my already-held conviction that prayer works.

I have studied, and taught, the history of prayer and praying. I am familiar with the praying lives of many historical figures. The end result of my studies has been to inspire me to continue to pray.

Scholarly, empirical studies of prayer and praying support my existential belief in the veridicality of praying. Such as, to cite but two, *Testing Prayer: Science and Healing*, by Candy Gunther Brown; and *The Psychology of Prayer: A Scientific Approach*, by Bernard Spilka and Kevin Ladd.

I have read countless counterexamples to my belief that prayer works. I've read innumerable atheistic (and other) arguments claiming that the statement *Prayer works* is false. I began reading this counter-literature in 1971, as an undergraduate philosophy student. (Beware - philosophy makes you read opposing ideas!) I have little sympathy with atheists who have never had a praying life and, out of their non-engagement, believe they have falsified the claim that prayer works. Their theoretical arguments, which are logical manifestations of their worldview, do not dissuade me. I have also read many books by, e.g., ex-theists who claim to have prayed like I have but found no reciprocity. I am sympathetic towards these testimonies. But note this: since *my* personal testimony is to the efficacy of praying, absence-testimonies do not persuade me any more than my testimony persuades an ex-believer.[85]

Jesus believed praying works.[86] I believe Jesus is God incarnate. Therefore, *I* believe praying works.

A major portion of my adult life has been spent immersed in Christological studies. I remain convinced that Jesus is who he claims to be.[87] Note the pronoun 'I'. *I* know why *I* believe praying works. Obviously I *do* believe praying works, since I continue doing it. Here *personal knowledge is important* (see Kierkegaard, and Michael Polanyi).[88]

I believe prayer works because I believe a personal God exists. If I did not believe this I would not pray, period. My praying life is a function of (is in direct proportion to) my belief in God.

I have a deep, experiential, and philosophical belief that, not only does God exist as a personal agent, but God is good, God loves me, and God is working all things together for good.[89] Because I am certain, as well as happy, that I am not the all-knowing, all-loving God, I know I do not have full epistemic access to what God is doing. I have prayed for things that, from my POV, seem unanswered. At this point my properly basic belief in God helps me trust that my prayers are not going unheard.

---

[85] Absence-testimonies are examples of what philosopher Charles Taylor has called "subtraction stories." See Taylor, *A Secular Age*, and James K. A. Smith's. commentary *How (Not) to Be Secular: Reading Charles Taylor*

[86] For a greater understanding of why Jesus believed this, see Charles Kraft, *Christianity with Power: Your Worldview and Experience of the Supernatural*, especially the chapter entitled "Jesus Had a Worldview."

[87] Note: my Christological studies are historical and textual studies. Some of my critics mistake me for a religious fundamentalist, which I am not. Ironically, these critics are usually themselves hermeneutical fundamentalists.

[88] See especially Michael Polanyi on "tacit knowledge," in *Knowing and Being: Essays by Michael Polanyi*.

[89] I am defining "good" is in relation to God's plans and purposes (no, this does not lead us to the "Euthyphro dilemma").

The Canary

A friend from Brazil asked me - "Do you remember the first miracle you saw and what was it like?" I do. It was like this.

I was five years old. My mother came in my bedroom and told me that our pet canary had died. The birdcage was in another room. I went, followed by my mother, and saw the canary. It was on its back lying on the floor of the cage. It was not moving. I was crying.

I went to my bedroom and was sobbing and praying "God, please make my canary live!" I can't remember how long I was doing this. My mother came into my room and said, "John, come with me and look!" I followed her to the room where our dead canary lay. I was afraid to go and have to see it again. We went into the room and there was the canary, sitting on its swing, like nothing had happened.

I went back to my room, happy, and after a few minutes it was like this sad incident never happened.

Here's what I know. 1) My mother and I saw the canary on the cage floor, on its back, legs pointed skyward, not moving. We were eyewitnesses of this. 2) I prayed, asking God to bring my canary back to life. 3) Minutes later we saw the canary alive and sitting on its swing. (More eyewitness testimony.)

Was the canary really dead? I can't prove this. We didn't check its heartbeat. Did it die and come back to life? That's what mother and I thought. Again, I cannot prove this. But what I do know is that 1-3 above are true.

I know one more thing. On that day a little boy believed that God can raise the dead, and that his prayers were heard by God.

15

THE NEED FOR PRAY-ERS

I travel around the world teaching people to pray. I spend time calling Christian pastors, leaders, and laity to a life of praying. I've taught prayer retreats in the busyness of Singapore, Vancouver, and New York City. I've led prayer conferences for leaders on the Deccan Plateau in India, the mountains of west Kenya, the jungles of Brazil, and the steamy Caribbean island of Trinidad. I have spoken to countless university students about prayer. I am committed to being another agent of renewal, as God allows himself to work through me.

There is a close relationship between praying and renewal. We will never see global renewal until urban renewal happens. We'll not experience urban renewal until renewal in the Church happens. And we cannot expect to see Church renewal until individual leaders and pastors walk in renewal. Call this the power of the individual, praying person. Renewal is needed. Renewal begins with one follower of Jesus, praying. It begins with you, abiding in Christ, praying, listening, and obeying.

> Every spiritual awakening of significance from the beginning of Acts to the powerful Welsh revival early in [the 20ᵗʰ century] had its roots in prayer. The awakenings under John Wesley, Jonathan Edwards and Charles Finney were first of all revivals of prayer. These religious leaders openly declared that prayer was the

basis for all that happened in these world changing revivals.[1]

Where there is no ongoing personal and corporate renewal, the people "are too busy to pray." Therefore, "the greatest challenge facing the church today is that of motivating people to pray."[2]

I feel no pressure about this. It's all up to God. Only God can motivate people to pray. I can pray that he does, for we need praying people in such a time as this. This is you, if you have come this far in my book.

How Many People Pray?

Bernard Spilka and Kevin Ladd's excellent book *The Psychology of Prayer: A Scientific Approach* is necessary reading for anyone who wants to study the phenomenon of praying. How many people pray in America? Spilka and Ladd conclude:

- As many as 97% of Americans pray, and some 57% indicate that they pray one or more times each day.
- A Princeton University study found 74% of men and 86% of women rely on prayer when faced with a problem.
- Countless prayers go unreported.
- Citing Robert Wuthnow, far more Americans pray than engage in other religious activities, including any other private or public religious behavior.[3]

What I make of this is:

Prayer is mostly accepted as efficacious by Americans. That is, Americans mostly believe that there is a God, to whom we can communicate.

---

[1] In Stanley Grenz, Prayer: *The Cry for the Kingdom*, 4.

[2] Ib. Note: If you are looking for a very good book on praying read Grenz. But remember that reading a book on prayer without having a praying life is like reading books on swimming without ever jumping in the pool.

[3] Bernard Spilka and Kevin Ladd, *The Psychology of Prayer: A Scientific Approach*, 3.

This empirical fact can provide the needed spark to touch off prayer movements that issue forth in people who have praying lives (different from only praying when facing a problem). I see the broad acceptance of praying as providing kindling to ignite a prayer fire. I view myself, and others like me, as holding a match.

My concern is how we are defining "praying." My approach is that, by "praying," I am looking for a significant prayer life. By "significant prayer life" the model, for Christians, is the "as usual," habitual, praying life of Jesus. With this definition, I would expect Spilka and Ladd's numbers to be reduced.

The *General Social Survey* Spilka and Ladd refer to also showed that, as odd as it sounds, some atheists said that they pray. Recently, a former atheist told me of a time he prayed, out of desperation. And in his case the God he did not believe in did a miracle (his own words), and answered his prayer.

The More Westernized a Person Is, the Less They Pray

When encouraging people to pray, as conversation-with-God, I often hear the following expressed by Westernized Jesus-followers: "I don't have time to pray thirty-sixty minutes a day, five days a week." However, if the Jesus-follower is from a Third World country, like ancient Israel during the time of Jesus, they do have time to pray. What's going on?

The more Westernized a person is, the less they take time to meet and talk with God. The less Westernized a person is, the more they take time to meet and talk with God. I estimate that 80% of European and North American pastors and Christian leaders do not have a significant prayer life.[4] By this I mean that they do not take time to actually pray. By "taking time" I mean more than saying a blessing over dinner, or

---

[4] This figure comes from teaching spiritual formation and prayer to 3500 pastors and Christian leaders since 1977 (Northern Baptist Theological Seminary) to the present (Payne Theological Seminary), and in conferences, retreats, and seminars around the U.S. and the world.

multi-tasked praying. By "significant" I mean something like Jesus did, habitually.

The statistics flip for pastors and leaders who are from Third World contexts. Eighty percent of them have a significant prayer life. When they attend my prayer and spiritual formation classes they already have a quantitative praying life. They pray... a lot. European and North American clergy, on the other hand, find themselves "too busy to pray." They find it a struggle to fit in times of actual praying. Why is this so?

The reasons Westernized Christians don't significantly pray and Third World Christians do are:

1. SENSE OF NEED: More access to human helping agencies lowers the desperation level. When I was, e.g., teaching and speaking in India, the lack of access to medical care, education, jobs, etc., was massive. One could only turn to God, in prayer. So in India I found pastors who were praying people. *The less felt need there is, the less one prays; the more felt need there is, the more one prays.*

2. NEED TO CONTROL: Westernized Christians live under the general cultural illusion that they are in control of life; Third World, non-westernized Christians live in a cultural milieu where human control is minimal at best; hence, they appeal to God (or gods, or spirits) for help. *The more one feels in control of life, the less one prays; the less one feels in control of life, the more one prays.*

3. TIME: The more stuff a person has, the less they pray. This is because much of their life is dictated by their possessions, which demand time organizing, protecting, arranging, storing, repairing, cleaning, cultivating, displaying, flaunting, wearing, etcing. Stuff demands time. On the other hand, the fewer possessions a person has, the more actual time they have to pray. *The more stuff one has, the less one has time to pray; the less stuff one has, the more one has time to pray.*

The typical European and North American Jesus-follower may have little felt need. They may have submitted to the illusion that they control things, and are likely afflicted with the burnout-busyness that follows. As these three elements converge, the God-relationship is virtually gone.

The good news here is that forty percent of my students acquire a lifelong prayer habit as a result of my classes. So, twenty percent increases to forty percent.

Two Reasons People Don't Pray

Over one hundred years ago James Ryle came "to the conclusion that the vast majority of professing Christians do not pray at all."[5] James Houston suggests that Ryle "would say the same thing of the church in the West today."[6]

We've all heard people say the words "I don't have time to pray," or "I just can't find time to pray." Why not? Two reasons for this are: 1) unbelief; and 2) an incomplete view of prayer.

Unbelief is one reason for a prayerless life. If praying means talking with God about what God and I are doing together, then how could anyone pass up daily opportunities to meet, one-on-one, with the Maker of Heaven and Earth? I can assure you that, if the President of the United States (or any country's President) wanted to meet with me today, I would stop typing this entry, say "Excuse me, I have a meeting with our President," and leave. I would somehow discover time to meet with the most powerful leader in the world. You would not be able to keep me away from it! And, I would go with awe and trembling.

Multiply this unlikely earthly scenario several times and we have the matter of praying as meeting with the all-powerful, all-knowing, omnibenevolent, necessarily existent, Creator of all things. In praying, Almighty God invites me to conference with him, to enter into conversation with him concerning many things, to include the Kingdom Mission. If I can't find time for this, it may be because I don't believe.

---

[5] In Houston, *The Transforming Power of Prayer: Deepening Your Friendship With God*, 16.
[6] Ib.

A second reason Christians don't actually pray is because they may have been taught an incomplete, one-sided theory of prayer. This is the idea of praying as only "asking" or "petition." This is found, e.g., in the theology of Karl Barth, who so much emphasized the "Wholly Otherness" of God that God was viewed as experientially distant. We're left with talking *to* him more than *conversing with* him. We come to God mostly with requests. And, we especially approach this distant God when we're in trouble.

I know there's more to Barth than this. But this was his emphasis. I once invited a well-known Reformed Barthian scholar to speak in a class I was teaching on prayer at Northern Baptist Theological Seminary. He had just published a book on prayer, and graciously accepted my invitation. His presentation was excellent, but his Barthian emphasis was too much on speaking *to God* and not enough on hearing *from God*. If I thought the probability of God speaking to me was small this would discourage me from praying.

I like how Anglican theologian Kenneth Leech writes about this. Leech says:

> Many people see prayer as asking God for things, pleading with a remote Being about the needs and crises of earth. sometimes these pleas produce a response; often, they do not. So prayer is seen in essentially functional terms - is it effective or not? Does it produce results?... But in order to pray well we need to disengage ourselves from this way of thinking.[7]

Too much focus on the effectiveness of prayer will miss the relationship with God. God becomes some far-away object from whom to "get results."

How can I help people who "can't find time to pray" because they don't believe God will respond? My view is that only God can change their hearts about this. I don't force this on people. I can create

---

[7] Kenneth Leech, *True Prayer*, 7. New York: Morehouse, 1980.

opportunities and contexts for people to encounter God. When I send students out to pray, as an assignment for my seminary courses, some become believers in a God who has much to say to them. This is exhilarating. These students write to thank me for helping them acquire a prayer life that can last for a lifetime.

Churches Without Prayer Are Like KFCs Without Chicken

Last summer Linda and I were driving through northern Indiana on the expressway. We stopped at a rest plaza to eat. Linda ordered a salad, and I went to Kentucky Fried Chicken. I was in line with two other men, one in front of me, the other behind me. The man in front ordered a four-piece chicken meal. The woman said, "I'm sorry, sir, but we are out of chicken."

I was stunned. The man behind me asked, "Did she just say they are out of chicken?"

"Yes."

The man and I then slowly walked away, feeling like Gregor Samsa, who awoke to discover he was a beetle.[8]

Imagine a church where people do not have time to pray. They say they believe in prayer, but don't act on this belief, for whatever reason. This is an ecclesiastical nightmare. It would leave nonbelievers very confused.

To *believe in prayer* is not the same thing as *to pray*. "Believing in prayer" without praying counts for nothing. A prayerless church does not really believe in prayer, for to "believe in prayer" but not have time for it is to not believe in prayer. "Living without prayer is the result of going to bed with all the attitudes of a modern secular society."[9]

Much of today's prayerlessness among professing Jesus-followers is due to practical unbelief. For how could anyone rationally refuse the offer of ongoing conversation with God? How does the following make sense?

---

[8] From Franz Kafka, *The Metamorphosis*.
[9] James Houston, *The Transforming Power of Prayer*, 15

1. God, Maker of heaven and earth, wants to talk with me.
2. Therefore, I don't have time to do this.

There is no logical claim of inference from premise one to the conclusion.

These are cultural observations. They won't motivate people to pray. Feelings of guilt rarely change behavior. What's needed is re-conversion and *Aufklarung*.[10]

Imagine an unbelieving church. This would be a church without wisdom, power, or love. A disconnected church. The dark church. The hollow church. The church without influence. The ghettoized church. The unsalted church. The empty cathedrals in Nietzsche's "Parable of the Madman."[11]

Needed: More Deep, Praying People

What is most needed today are more *deep* people. People with *wisdom* and *discernment*. Pondering, meditative people.

Deep people are stable. They have an inner strength that cannot be uprooted during cultural storms. Shallow-rooted people are surface people who uncritically surf and skim over an Internet-life of disconnected data.

Here is Henri Nouwen writing on spiritual depth.

> Trees that grow tall have deep roots. Great height without great depth is dangerous. The great leaders of this world - like St. Francis, Gandhi, and Martin Luther King, Jr., - were all people who could live with public notoriety, influence, and power in a humble way because of their deep spiritual rootedness. Without deep roots we easily let others determine who we are. But as

---

[10] Aufklarung – "enlightenment," in the Kantian sense that woke Kant from his "dogmatic slumber."

[11] Friedrich Nietzsche, "The Parable of the Madman," from *The Gay Science*. New York: Vintage, 1974.

we cling to our popularity, we may lose our true sense of self. Our clinging to the opinion of others reveals how superficial we are. We have little to stand on. We have to be kept alive by adulation and praise. Those who are deeply rooted in the love of God can enjoy human praise without being attached to it.[12]

People who habitually pray grow roots deep into the banks of the river that flows from the throne of God.[13]

The Power of Prayvailing

Yesterday morning I spent time teaching our church's second through fifth graders. I asked them a question: "What do you think I do as a pastor?" A lot of the kids responded, giving answers such as...

"You preach."

"You do weddings."

"You do funerals."

"You spend time with people you love."

"You play games with kids."

"You get to have a wife."

"You drink coffee in the church kitchen."

"You meet with people in your office in Panera Bread."

"You help people who have problems."

What great answers! All of them are true. I especially like the last one. I love helping people with problems.

After spending time with these kids I went into the church sanctuary and preached a sermon on 1 John 5:16, which reads: "If you see any brother or sister commit a sin that does not lead to death, you should pray and God will give them life." If I see a Christian brother or sister messing up I am not to judge them, condemn, finger-point, post their mess-up on Facebook, slander, or gossip about them. I am not to view

---

[12] Henri Nouwen, *Bread For the Journey*, April 5. New York: HarperOne.

[13] See Psalm 1.

myself as above them while tanning in the glow of my superiority. What I am to do is pray for them, with a promise.

I pray for my fallen friends. I am on their rescue team.

One biblical Greek word for 'pray' is *aiteo* (αἰτέω), which can be translated as:

- to ask
- to beg
- to crave
- to desire
- to require
- to command

These words dial up the intensity.

I remember getting off the airplane in Mumbai, India, walking out of the terminal in the 4 A.M. darkness, only to be surrounded by begging children. One was, maybe, 12 years old. His teeth were brown and rotting. The children were touching me, pleading for money. I remember their eyes. When you pray for a brother or sister in need your eyes should look like this, before God. This is praying as craving something; viz., the rescue and saving of people you love.

This is travailing praying. To "travail" is physical or mental work that is sometimes painful. The word is used of a woman in labor about to give birth to her baby. We see travailing praying in Colossians 4:12-13, where Paul writes of Epaphras, who is "always laboring earnestly for you in his prayers, that you may stand perfect and fully assured in all the will of God." Epaphras is filled with *deep concern* for his Christian brothers and sisters.

Travailing praying has two foci:

1. Love for the followers of Jesus.
2. Concern for what darkness is doing to them.

Sin crushes people. Sin separates us from God and destroys friendships, families, and marriages. We cannot love and help people if we do not have compassion for them, and concern about the ramifications of wrongdoing in their lives. The foundational attitudes required to rescue people are love and concern.

I like helping people who have problems. Many of my brothers and sisters are falling and failing. Who will travail over them in prayer? We are promised that, if we do, *God will give them life.* The prayer of travail is for God to create an opening to bring forth a measure of life and growth. Travailing prayer brings prevailing in the weak person's life. Travailing praying effects prevailing. Call this *prayvailing.*

What if we went after our stumbling brothers and sisters by prayvailing? What would the environment in our churches look like? They would be safe places. They would be rescuing places. Loving and healing places. There would be new levels of holiness and unity. Fault-finding and gossip would unavail, intercession, love, and life would prevail. Wholeness would return, and we would be what God has always intended for them. The Church is to be a great, prayvailing, rescuing community.

This is the power of prayvailing people. It begins with love for one another. It takes sin and wrongdoing seriously. It knows the power of praying for others in the community. Heaven's gates are opened. And God gives us life!

The Importance of Praying Parents

If parents pray, it is likely their children will pray. The converse also seems true: if parents do not pray, it is likely their children will not pray. The latter may cause difficulties, since some scholars believe "religiousness is first manifested at ages 2 or 3"; hence, there seems to be an innate propensity towards the transcendent.[14]

Spilka and Ladd conclude:

- Close identification with one's parents sets the stage for a child's initial religious understanding of prayer (in early stages primarily from the mother).

---

[14] See Bernard Spilka and Kevin Ladd, *The Psychology of Prayer*, 65

- Concepts of God come later, along with prayerful practices learned from parents.

  The influence of high and low religious parents was especially evident in the responses of the 3- and 4-year-olds.

  "Respondents who came from religious homes had a definite concept of prayer and an understanding of what was desirable when praying."[15]

Praying to Have My Mind Changed about Praying

Prayer is conferencing with God about what God is thinking and doing. In praying I enter God's kingdom; i.e., in the act of praying I come under the dominion of God. This seems important for followers of Jesus to do, right? The good news is: you and I have time to do this. You have time to pray today if...

> ...you had time to attend to your technology
> ...you spent time texting people
> ...you watched TV
> ...you spent time wondering how to spend your time
> ...you were bored
> ...you spent time "doing nothing"
> ...you "wasted time"
> ...you shopped
> ...you read something today

To confess "I don't have time to pray" mostly means, "I chose not to use my time to pray." I don't wish to guilt-manipulate you into praying. But I believe, as an observation, that non-praying Jesus-followers (that's an oxymoron, right?) have no desire to meet one-on-one with God, since if they did they *would* meet with God.[16] Desire without discipline is an illusion.

---

[15] Ib., 66

[16] As Thomas Merton said, desire without discipline is an illusion.

I have time to pray. Only God can change my heart about who and what I love and how I will spend my time. Change my heart, O God. Make me a praying person.

The Deep Praying Life of Martin Luther King[17]

As we remember Dr. Martin Luther King's great speech that changed our nation, I am reflecting on my understanding of him. When I first read Martin Luther King's "Letter From Birmingham Jail" I was deeply moved. How beautiful and eloquent, how persuasive and biblical it is. I remember thinking how I rarely heard the media talk about King's deep faith in Jesus while they applauded his civil rights actions. But only a spiritually deep person could write the kind of letter King wrote.

Dr. King had a deep praying life that formed the foundation for his social activism. It would be a great mistake to speak of Dr. King's activism without looking at his indebtedness to the God he encountered in prayer.

When King accepted a request to lead African-Americans during a bus-boycott in Montgomery, Alabama, he began to receive death threats. One night, after yet another such threat, King began to doubt his decision.

As the threats poured in, his fears increased for his wife, Coretta, and their infant daughter, Yolanda. He wondered how he could relinquish his role as the boycott leader without appearing a coward.

Then something happened that King would talk about for years afterward. He bowed over his untouched cup of coffee, and prayed aloud in desperation. King said he heard an "inner voice" that addressed him by name, and encouraged him to stand up for justice.[18]

Yes, King was a brilliant orator. But he also had a deep prayer life.[19] After the kitchen experience, King felt a special divine companionship,

---

[17] I wrote this article for our local newspaper, on the occasion of Martin Luther King, Jr.s birthday.

[18] See Lewis Baldwin, *Never to Leave Us Alone: The Prayer Life of Martin Luther King, Jr.*

[19] Note how our media ignores this. Our annual celebration of King's birthday has reduced him to a mere secular hero.

or what he called cosmic companionship, and this sustained him. Fear left him and he was assured that if he continued to stand up for justice and righteousness, God would be with him.

Deep prayer and meditation preceded King's writing his brilliant "Letter." Such words only come out of a deep soul, one that spends much time in the presence of God and in dialogue with God. God spoke to King, and King was in a place to hear.

Today's "too busy to pray" people who want to do great things for God without dwelling daily in God's intimate presence should not wonder why they are not part of The Revolution.

16

A CALL TO PRAYING

When I shut up the heavens so that there is no rain, or command locusts to devour the land or send a plague among my people, if my people, who are called by my name, will humble themselves and pray and seek my face and turn from their wicked ways, then I will hear from heaven, and I will forgive their sin and will heal their land. Now my eyes will be open and my ears attentive to the prayers offered in this place. I have chosen and consecrated this temple so that my Name may be there forever. My eyes and my heart will always be there.[1]

X was a great, gifted preacher who traveled the world to bring his message of hope in Christ. He was a seminary student in my Spiritual Formation class. X was so sought-after that he had an agent who arranged his preaching engagements.

I assigned X to pray an hour a day, for six weeks. After two weeks X contacted me. He said, "I am sorry Dr. Piippo. I am so busy traveling the world preaching that I just cannot find time to pray an hour a day."

I told X: "I would never invite someone to preach in my church who didn't have time to pray an hour a day."

X got angry with me.

Allow me to defend myself. Just as I wouldn't invite someone to teach swimming who never had time to get into the water, I am

---

[1] 2 Chronicles 7:12-14

uninterested in listening to prayerless preachers guide me in paths of righteousness, much less my church family. I don't need to hear from voices of inexperience.

X contacted me six months later. God spoke to him through another person, and called him to pray. I was told that X took a year off from preaching so as to return to the dwelling, praying life. Then, with this established, he preached. I would have loved to hear his first sermon!

In this chapter I am calling you to pray. This is why I have written this book.

Recalibrating Prayer

It is good to return to square one and remember why we are praying people. Let's recalibrate and re-tune our minds to the basics. Here are some of the salient points, as I see things. Here is why I pray.

Prayer is a relationship with God. To pray is to communicate, to converse, with God.

This means that *to pray* is *to be in relationship with God.*

To pray is *to conference with God.* The subject of the God-conference is: *what I (the praying person) and God are thinking and doing together.* To pray is to collaborate with God. This is why Jesus prayed.

To pray is to accept the invitation to the God-conference. The "prayer room" is the control center of the universe; viz., the presence of God. Jesus-followers are invited to enter into this room, this place, which is essentially a place of the heart.

Praying involves speaking to God, and listening to God speak to me. The ability to do this is gained by actually praying, by having a prayer life.

Prayer brings a deburdening. In prayer, I bring my burdens to God, and cast them upon him (1 Peter 5:17). In prayer, I find healing. My healing is not merely for me, but is for the sake of God and his kingdom. Everything is for his name's sake.

Prayer brings direction for life. The direction God gives me is kingdom-oriented. God is about the 24/7 business of establishing his rule and reign. God directs me in paths that lead to him.

In the ongoing activity of prayer, I experience formation and transformation into Christlikeness (Galatians 4:19). Prayer is the connection whereby I gain more and more of the mind of Christ and the heart of Christ. To pray is to change.

1) Jesus prayed. 2) Therefore, I pray.

Or: 1) Jesus needed to pray. 2) Therefore, I need to pray.

Or: 1) I want to pray. 2) Therefore, I pray.

The desire to pray grows in the activity of praying. The more I pray, the more I desire to pray. My experiences with the God who is there compel me to pray.

Only God can give this. I am praying this for you, as out of obedience you go to lonely places, and pray.

Pray That You Would Pray

I had just finished preaching a Sunday morning sermon at Faith Bible Church in New York City. FBC is a Chinese church, and my message was translated into Mandarin. When I was done a man came forward and asked me to pray for him. He was a government worker from China. China's government is atheist, and discourages its workers from expressing religious inclinations.

He could not speak English, so an interpreter told me: "He wants you to pray for him."

"I would be glad to. How can I pray for him?"

"He wants you to pray that he would believe in God."

I never had a prayer request like that before. It was clear to me that God was pursuing this man, that very moment. A. W. Tozer writes, "We pursue God because and only because, He has first put an urge within us that spurs us to the pursuit."[2]

The urge within spurs us to the pursuit. Those that desire, pursue. On that morning in New York City a Chinese government worker was going after God. This is how it is with prayer. Those that desire God go

---

[2] In Richard Foster, *Prayer*, 71.

after the conversation. A person who heart-wants to pray, prays. That's how it is with urges and desires.

This is why I don't think we can make people pray. Making people feel guilty that they don't have a prayer life will not result in them having a prayer life. This is because it's all about desire, or what Tozer called the "urge." You cannot command or force this.

In my seminary classes I assign students to pray. I have seen, occasionally, that in fulfilling the assignment a student gets a prayer life, for life. A desire, an urge for relationship with God, is placed within them. One student who viewed praying as just another class requirement acquires a fire for praying. And they pray. They find time for this. They just do. That's the way it is with anything you love.

Richard Foster writes: "Here is the beautiful thing: finding God only deepens and heightens the pursuit. One taste of obedience and we want more. "O taste and see that the LORD is good," invites the Psalmist (Ps. 34:8)."[3] Pray that you would pray.

Ten Minutes of Praying

Prayer is talking with God about what we are thinking and doing together. By "we" I mean: God and I. Praying is talking and listening, to God.

If you are struggling to find time to do this in a focused way, I recommend beginning with Ten Minutes of Praying. Lay aside the guilt-producing thought, "But it's only ten minutes, and that doesn't seem like much." I predict that, if you begin this today, and continue it for the rest of your life, you will change, dramatically, into greater and greater Jesus-likeness.[4] And, you will experience times when ten minutes turns into an hour with God. You will experience God so powerfully that *chronos* will fade into *kairos*.[5]

---

[3] Ib., 71-72

[4] See Galatians 4:19

[5] *Chronos* is the Greek word for clock time; *kairos* is the Greek word for "it is God's time."

Henri Nouwen writes: "You need to set aside some time every day for active listening to Jesus, if only for ten minutes. Ten minutes each day for Jesus alone can bring about a radical change in your life."[6]

Nothing Can Stop You from Praying Today

(Lt. Cmdr. Edwin "Ned" Shuman III died at age 82 on December 3, 2013. The *New York Times* had his obituary.[7])

It was Christmas, 1970. Lt. Commander Edwin Shuman, plus forty-two American soldiers, were being held as prisoners of war in the notorious Hanoi Hilton in North Viet Nam. The prisoners wanted to hold a church service, but their guards stopped them, and so the seeds of rebellion were planted.

Shuman orchestrated the rebellion. He knew he would be the first to face the consequences. For leading his companions in prayer, he was beaten in a torture cell.

After the beating Shuman asked the soldiers, "Are we really committed to having church on Sunday?" Fellow prisoner Leo Thorsness said that Shuman "went around the cell pointing to each of us individually. When the 42nd man said yes, it was unanimous. At that instant, Ned knew he would end up in the torture cells."

On the next Sunday Shuman stepped forward to lead the prisoners in prayer. The guards quickly removed him, along with the next four ranking officers. "The guards were now hitting P.O.W.'s with gun butts and the cell was in chaos." Then the sixth-ranking senior officer began, "Gentlemen, the Lord's Prayer." This time, they finished it. The guards had yielded.

Everett Alvarez Jr. was the first American pilot captured in the Vietnam War when his Navy plane was shot down in 1964. Shuman's defiance and refusal "was contagious," said Mr. Alvarez, who was in another cell during the first prayer service. "By the time it got to the

---

[6] Nouwen, *The Only Necessary Thing: Living a Prayerful Life*, 89.

[7] http://www.nytimes.com/2013/12/25/us/edwin-a-shuman-iii-former-prisoner-of-war-who-defied-hanoi-hilton-guards-dies-at-82.html?hp&_r=2&

fourth or fifth cell," he said, the guards "gave up." He said the prisoners were also singing patriotic songs."

Shuman was held at the Hanoi Hilton for two more years. Thorsness, an Air Force pilot and Medal of Honor recipient, wrote in his memoir:

> From that Sunday on until we came home, we held a church service. We won. They lost. Forty-two men in prison pajamas followed Ned's lead. I know I will never see a better example of pure raw leadership or ever pray with a better sense of the meaning of the words.[8]

During his time in the prison camp Shumann "spent 17 months in solitary confinement. On one occasion, when he violated regulations, he was beaten for hours with a whip."

Commander Shuman was freed in March 1973 as part of a mass release of remaining P.O.W.'s. He retired from the Navy as a captain 11 years later. His commendations included the Silver Star for his resistance to brutal treatment.

He returned to North Vietnam in 1991 as part of a three-week humanitarian medical mission, mainly out of curiosity about what had become of it. "I didn't view this as a healing process," he told The Baltimore Sun on returning. "I never had a nightmare." He said that he liked the Vietnamese people, whom he found to be hardworking."

About his experience Shuman said,

> I have often compared ocean racing in bad weather with being a prisoner of war, an environment with which, unfortunately, I have some experience. Harsh conditions, cramped quarters, bad food and diverse personalities. Instead of the guards beating on you, mother nature takes over. You can't get out so you make the best of it. It's a character-builder.

Nothing can stop you from praying today.

---

[8] In Ib., from Shuman's obituary.

I will build my church, and the gates of hell shall not prevail against it.[9]

The Reason for the Biblical Urgency of Praying

2 Chronicles 7:14 is an "if…, then" example of God giving a promise to help and heal, on the condition of his people humbling themselves and praying. Such as: "If you clean your room, then I will take you to the movie." Which means: On the condition of your room being cleaned by you, you will be taken to the movie by me. But, if you do not clean your room (if that condition is not met), then I will not take you to the movie. The logic looks like this:

1. If you clean your room, then I will take you to the movie (given no other extenuating circumstances).

2. I did not take you to the movie (given no other extenuating circumstances; e.g., perhaps you did clean your room but an unexpected emergency prevented me from taking you to the movie).

3. Therefore, you did not clean your room.

In 2 Chronicles we read:

> *If* my people, who are called by my name, will humble themselves and pray and seek my face and turn from their wicked ways, *then* I will hear from heaven, and I will forgive their sin and will heal their land.

God desires to hear from heaven, forgive the sins of the people, and heal the land. But God will *not* do so if the condition is unmet. This implies that our prayers have causal power in bringing about the desires of God. Greg Boyd writes that when God "decided to populate the creation with free agents, he gave each human various units of "say-so." We each have a certain amount of power to affect what comes to pass by our choices."[10]

---

[9] Jesus, in Matthew 16:18
[10] Greg Boyd, http://reknew.org/2014/07/analogies-for-understanding-prayer/

Greg believes that "God set aside a vast reservoir of "say-so" that is accessed only by communicating with him. Because of how central this objective is for God, he covenanted with himself to release this "say-so" only if his people pray...."

It seems that there are many things God would like to do but will not, unless his people align their hearts with his in prayer. "This explains the incredible urgency Jesus and rest of the Bible attaches to prayer."[11]

Does the following argument help explain what is happening in our world today?

1. If my people humble themselves and pray, then I will forgive their sins and heal their land.
2. I have not forgiven their sins and healed their land (though I [God] desire to).
3. Therefore, my people have not humbled themselves and prayed.

Desperately needed in these times: followers of Jesus who align their hearts with his, and pray as he did.

One Hour with Psalm 23 and God

In a few hours I will have the opening session of my Spiritual Formation class at Payne Theological Seminary. Twenty-five Master's students are enrolled. After introductions, I will send the students out to pray for an hour, using my Psalm 23 handout. Here it is.

One Hour with Psalm 23 and God

Take ten minutes to go alone to a quiet place to meet with God. When I dismiss you go quietly – don't talk with anyone.

Don't take anything with you except for this piece of paper. Do not go to your room or car or office. Do not make a phone call or do any shopping. Do not do any "church work." God wants to break you of the illusion of your indispensability.

---

[11] Boyd, Ib.

When you find your quiet place stay there for 60 minutes. Your purpose: To meet with God. The idea is: You need God in your life. You need God to speak to you, to minister to you, to direct you, to counsel you, to confront you, to empower you.

During this hour keep a spiritual journal. A spiritual journal is a record of God's voice and activity in your life. During this time when God speaks to you or reveals Himself to you, write it down.

Use Psalm 23 for your meditation. Biblically, to meditate is to ponder something. Meditation is repetitive. Like a cow chewing its cud, the food God gives us is more easily assimilated to our heart. Your purpose in this is not to get "sermon material." Your purpose is not to exegete Psalm 23. Instead, be exegeted yourself by the Holy Spirit.

If your mind wanders, write down where it wanders to. Your mind will not wander arbitrarily, but will always go to something like a burden, a hope, or a fear. I feel that one's wandering mind is a barometer of one's true spiritual condition.

After the hour return to our meeting place.

Psalm 23

The LORD is my shepherd, I shall not be in want.
He makes me lie down in green pastures,
He leads me beside quiet waters,
He restores my soul.
He guides me in paths of righteousness for his name's sake.
Even though I walk through the valley of the shadow of death,
I will fear no evil,
For you are with me;
Your rod and your staff,
They comfort me.
You prepare a table before me in the presence of my enemies.
You anoint my head with oil;
My cup overflows.
Surely goodness and love will follow me
All the days of my life,

And I will dwell in the house of the LORD
Forever.

I'm Praying Again Today

7:30 AM. I'm at the computer. Linda just woke up. She came downstairs and into the room where I am sitting. I greet her. She does the same to me. We hug. "Good morning." "How did you sleep last night?" We share some details. We look at one another. We attend; we listen. But of course! How rude not to do this.

Linda asks, "How are your eyes this morning?" Last night my eyes were stinging before I went to bed. "Fine," I tell her. She cares about me. She asks questions, about me. I feel important to Linda. I *am* important to her, as she is to me. She is more important to me than any person in this world. I communicate with her, not out of duty, but out of love and compassion and interest.

We ask each other, "What is your schedule today?" We sync and coordinate. We are a team. We are teammates on the Great God Mission.

I'm meeting with God today. "Good morning, God." God cares about me. I love God. How rude not to greet him. God and I are in a long-term relationship. I talk with him, not out of religious duty, but out of thankfulness, love, wonder, and amazement. God is more important to me than anyone or anything in this universe. And, I am important to God. I am one of God's much-loved sons.

I'm praying again today. Praying is me and God, God and I, talking about what we are up to.

"God, what are we doing together today?"

"John, you know about the tragedy that recently happened. Attend to it, and I will be with you, and with them. I will tell you what to say and what not to say. My peace will accompany you."

"Yes Lord..., thank you... be with this family in their great loss..."

God is my Shepherd. He guides me. He strengthens me. He loves me. He wields me. Therefore, I am praying.

17

QUESTIONS ABOUT PRAYING

I'm a Parent and Have Little Time to Get Alone with God

One of my blog readers sent me a personal response to my post, "Praying Is Ontologically Antecedent to McPraying."[1] They wrote:

Dear John,

I haven't commented in a long time, however I felt compelled to comment this time. First of all, I can appreciate what you are trying to say. I also appreciate that you do not discredit what you have termed "Mcprayer."[2] On the whole I think I can agree, however I just felt the need to add some of my thoughts, lest some of my friends lose hope altogether.

Just as a marriage goes to different seasons, so does our relationship with God. For instance, when a married couple has young children, they are not going to have long periods of quiet time together. However, they do need some time together, and this is where many marriages fall apart; viz., because they don't get any free time during this period. It may just be one date night together once a month, or twenty minutes after the children have gone to bed. The couple has to adjust, and learn to get the most value out of what little quiet time they have together,

---

[1] http://www.johnpiippo.com/2013/08/mcprayer-and-prayer-prayerlife.html. I have their permission to post it, with my response.

[2]

and the rest of the time learn to be together with their children while doing their necessary tasks.

I think the same would go for a full-time mother and wife's relationship with the Lord. To ask anymore of her would be to ask the impossible. She can be single-minded in how she cares for her family, and worship the Lord as she raises her children to follow his ways. As her children grow up, and her responsibilities change, she can adjust her time of quiet devotion to both her husband and the Lord accordingly.

My other thought is this. Sometimes I find it more helpful to occupy my hands with a mindless task such as washing the dishes, or taking a shower, while praying. I actually find it easier to listen. I have heard similar testimony from others, including Mark Virkler, who specializes in teaching people to hear God's voice. He emphasizes journaling as a method to facilitate listening. One benefit is that it gives the hands and mind a focused occupation, and therefore we are less likely to wander.

In the end I still agree with you that some amount of solitude, quietness, and quality time, are necessary to nurture and sustain any relationship, especially our relationship with the Lord.

I'm open to any thoughts you have on what I have just said. Thank you for allowing me the opportunity to share.

-E

My response:

Thank you E for sharing this with me. Here are some things I am thinking about this.

1. I agree with you that life brings certain events that make it more difficult to take extended prayer times with God. When one of our sons was in a medical emergency situation that lasted for months, it was harder to find alone time with God. Linda and I were constantly in the hospital at our son's side. And, of course, we prayed a lot while we were there.

2. In general, Linda and I encourage parents to continue to carve out time together, without the kids. This will benefit the kids,

since what they most need are a spiritually healthy mom and dad who love each other. Linda and I did this by having a regular Friday night "date," which we have never stopped. I think the same kind of thing can be done with God. I encourage busy people to begin by finding five to ten minutes a day to get alone with God. If someone does, this I believe God will meet them, and will help them break free from any busyness that is unneeded.

3. The antidote to spiritual burnout is time with God. I see pastors burning out who have taken little or no time with God. I see this with busy parents too. My calling is to help people find or recover or rediscover that "quiet place" with God.

4. I encourage "busy people" to step back and evaluate their busyness. Our world system does not promote solitude, and offers us continuous servings of more things to do and more things to buy, all in the name of "happiness." I think many people could find more one-on-one time with God (the kind of time Jesus took) if they looked closely at their "doing." I believe that, in a Christian's spiritual life, one's "doing" should come out of and be determined by one's "being." First, meet with God. Then, do.

5. Are you familiar with the spiritual classic *The Practice of the Presence of God,* by Brother Lawrence? In this book Lawrence prays while he washes dishes. That is good. But my understanding of this is that he lived in a monastery, where there was a foundation of a lot of solitary praying that undergirded and fueled his praying while he was doing tasks.

6. I am familiar with Mark Virkler. Many years ago we had him for a weekend at our church. I think journaling can, as you say, facilitate listening to God. I know it does for me!

Finally, you write, "In the end I still agree with you that some amount of solitude, quietness, and quality time are necessary to nurture and sustain any relationship especially our relationship with the Lord."

I think we are in basic agreement about this.

Thank you so much E for writing me. I hope these thoughts of mine make sense.

Blessings to you this day as you continue to draw close to Jesus, J.P.

God Seems Absent from Me

A friend told me that God's presence seems to have withdrawn from them. They cried as they shared this.

This person is a Jesus-follower who, for many years, has lived in a near-constant experiential sense of God-with-them. Now, God seems to be far from them. They know intellectually that God is with them, but currently lack experiential reality of this.

What can we make of this? Here are some of my thoughts, which are not all directly related to this one person's spiritual desert.

That God is with his followers is a truth that is not necessarily related to one's experience of God-with-us. For example, I know that my wife Linda always loves me. Her love for me is constant, as is mine for her. But I do not always experience her love for me. The lack of such experience does not cause me to doubt that she loves me, and loves me now.

I think the same of God. I have had many experiences with God. I've also had many times when I lacked God-experience. While I often want more God-experience than I have, this does not cause me to wonder why I don't feel God as powerfully as I have at other times.

None of us experiences pure, unfiltered, face-to-face God-encounters. All our God-encounters are "see-through-a-glass darkly" events. Yes, some claim more immediate (= unmediated) God-encounters. My own belief is that even purported unmediated God-encounters (such as certain Christian mystics report, Meister Eckhart among them) are still mediated events. Some are more so than others. God-experiences are, more or less, proximal. I am not expecting full-blown unmediated face-to-face God moments, and thus am not disappointed at the lack of them.

The Psalms contain *Deus absconditus* moments (the "hidden God"; God as experientially hidden from us). Psalm 10 complains of God's hiding - "Why, O Lord, do you stand far off? Why do you hide yourself in times of trouble?" Ps. 30:7 expresses sadness that, after a time when the psalmist felt secure, he then felt God went into hiding: "When I felt secure, I said, 'I will never be shaken.' O Lord, when you favored me, you made my mountain stand firm; but when you hid your face, I was dismayed.'" Ps. 44 expresses outright ticked-offness at God's hiding, suggesting that God is morally irresponsible: "Rouse yourself! Why do you sleep, O Lord? Awake, do not cast us off forever! Why do you hide your face? Why do you forget our affliction and oppression?" Part of the noetic framework of Judaeo-Christian theism *is* experiencing the absence of God.

My personal history (forty six years) of brief and extended times of sensing God's presence makes me confident that God is with me, near me, and dwells within me, even when I am not experientially aware of this. Even when I do not feel God, I know God is near me, even within me, by his Spirit. I do not find myself doubting this. Indeed, this is more of a reality for me today than ever.

John 20:29 may be instructive here. Jesus says, "Have you believed because you have seen me? Blessed are they who, not seeing, believe." This implies that Jesus-followers who believe, even without perceptual experience of him, have something, perhaps an existential certitude, that needs no empirical proof of the reality of God-with-them and God-for-them. Jesus applauds this kind of faith and trust.

I am thinking of Henri Nouwen's distinction of a "ministry of presence," and a "ministry of absence." Persons who engage in redemptive activity know that there is a time to be *with* people, and a time to *not be with* people. The difference between the two is a matter of discernment. Sometimes, even often, the best thing for a person we are helping is to *not* be with them. Perhaps this is also how it is with our Redeemer God and us, with God knowing the difference. This may be related to the soul-making theodicy of Michael Murphy (via John Hick) in his "Deus Absconditus."[3]

The "hidden God moment" *par excellence* is surely Jesus' cry of, "Why have you forsaken me?" Uttered from the cross, it expresses (I think) a total absence of God as a result of bearing this world's sins. Sin makes a separation from relationship with God; Jesus' experience of abandonment was absolute. Sometimes, therefore, our sin causally effects, in a negative way, our sense of God's presence.

Is "experiencing God" equivalent to "feeling God?" I think not. I see "experiencing God" as the broader class within which "feeling God" is a subset. Thus one may *experience* God without *feeling* God (the relationship is asymmetrical). This is a broad sense of "knowing" that includes yet is more than "feeling." In this regard I am interested in two sources I am currently reading: 1) the work of Paul Moser, especially his idea of "filial knowledge" found in "Cognitive Idolatry and Divine Hiding"[4] and The Evidence for God[5] and 2) James K.A. Smith's Pentecostal epistemology in his brilliant *Thinking in Tongues*.

When you are a Jesus-follower and are suffering, or are in need of rescue, you want God to come out of hiding and show up. At such times the feeling-absence of God seems painful. Yet if "knowledge" is more than feeling, then you can *know* God is with you in the absence of feeling. That, too, can be an experience if we understand that experience is not reducible to feeling *simpliciter*.

Therefore, pray anyway.

How Do I Know if God Has Answered My Prayer?

A former student sent me this question about prayer: "How do we know God is behind the things we ask God for that happen to us? It seems rather simple-minded to attribute everything to God just because we prayed for it."

---

[3] In Daniel Howard Snyder, *Divine Hiddenness: New Essays*. New York: Cambridge, 2002.

[4] In Ib.

[5] Especially chapter 4, "Personifying Evidence for God."

My thoughts are:

Saying, "God answered this prayer for _____," has inductive probability, not deductive certainty. This does not mean we have no claim to "know" that God answered our prayer. Most of what we know is gained inductively, rather than deductively.[6]

We must distinguish this from existential certainty. I may experience no doubt, while at the same time admitting that there is only inductive logical certainty.[7]

When I pray for X and X happens, it makes me think that God has answered my prayer. If, e.g., I pray for $100 to pay my electric bill lest I be kicked out of my apartment, and $100 unpredictably arrives in the mail, then I will think, "God answered my prayer for $100." Still, my certainty is only inductive. I have had many answers to prayer over the years like this, recording a number of them in my journals.

X must be something in line with God's will and desire for us to claim "God answered my prayer for X." If, e.g., "X" is evil, then the arrival of evil is surely not something that God is behind.

Our discernment about what God is, and is not, behind (re. our prayers) grows with increasing intimacy with God, and much praying. An ongoing prayer-as-relationship-with-God is needed.

The best way to answer this question is by engaging in a life of personal praying, and adding corporate discernment with a group of Jesus-followers who have praying lives.

How Can I Pray When I Have Doubts?

Someone asked me about feelings of doubt they have when they are praying. What do we do with our doubts?

---

[6] In logic, inductive knowledge is probableistic knowledge; deductive knowledge is logically necessary knowledge. All scientific conclusions, for example, are arrived at inductively. For example, I know that the earth orbits the sun, but only inductively (a very strong inductive argument can be made to support this claim).

[7] James K. A. Smith's book *Thinking in Tongues* is helpful here. Grand Rapids: Eerdmans, 2010.

My response:

I think "doubt" is more like an emotion than it is like a choice. Emotions are not chosen. Emotions are feelings, and feelings cannot be chosen. Anger, for example, is the emotion we feel when one of our expectations has not been met. The unmet expectation gives rise to our emotion of anger. I think doubt is like this; viz., an emotion.

Descartes, in his *Meditations*, famously provides us with his method of "systematic doubt." Cartesian doubt is methodical doubt; "doubt," as a method. Descartes chose to doubt everything he could, even those things he felt most certain of. He writes: "how could I deny that I possess these hands and this body." If he did, people would consider him insane. Descartes did not really doubt that he had hands and a body. He simply claimed such things *could* be doubted. And if they *could* be doubted then we do not have, regarding them, absolute certainty.

This is intellectual, philosophical "doubt." It is "logical doubt." *Could* I doubt that I am now sitting in this chair, using my hands to type out these words on my laptop? Is it at all *possible* that I am not doing these things which seem so certain to me? Yes, it is possible that I am not doing these things, with these hands. But one can engage in Cartesian, intellectual doubt, while having no existential doubt at all.

Existential doubt is not chosen. It comes on a person like a mood. Like an emotion. Because it is not chosen, we are not morally responsible for it. This is important to understand.

Recently, someone talked with me about guilt they were feeling because they doubted something in relationship to God. This happened while they were praying. "Is God angry with me because I doubted?" they asked. My immediate answer was, "Not at all." You didn't choose to doubt. Something happened to you, and it provoked the emotion of doubt in you."

God knows about your doubt, and he can handle it. A reading of the Psalms would show a number of instances where the psalmist openly shares a doubt with God. For example, there is doubt fueling the series of questions at the beginning of Ps. 13.

How long, LORD? Will you forget me forever? How long will you hide your face from me? How long must I wrestle with my thoughts and day after day have sorrow in my heart? How long will my enemy triumph over me?

We see the same in Psalm 22: "My God, my God, why have you forsaken me?" Why are you so far from saving me, so far from my cries of anguish?"

Here is doubt that God is near, or that God even cares. These feelings are real, and many have experienced them. They are not the result of a moral choice for which one is half responsible.

In John 20 the disciples say to Thomas, "We have seen the Lord!" Thomas's response is, "I doubt it." He says, "Unless I see the nail marks in his hands and put my finger where the nails were, and put my hand into his side, I will not believe." A week later, when Jesus comes to him, he lets Thomas touch and feel his side, and gain the empirical proof Thomas needed. Jesus did not freak out because Thomas doubted.

God doesn't enter a panic room when you or I doubt. I think "doubt" is part of our human condition. The more one cares and knows about a certain subject, the more susceptible they are to doubts. For example, I don't find myself doubting if the Dallas Cowboys will win their next game, for the reason that I'm not a Cowboys fan and know nothing about them. But I do have doubts about some of my favorite sports teams because I have care for them, and have some knowledge about them. Care and knowledge always give rise to doubt.

Doubt is universal, and finds a home in every worldview. Every person has a worldview. Every person who understands their own worldview and is passionate about it will, at times, have doubts about it. Questions arise, no matter what the worldview. In this sense doubt is normal, and part of our human condition.

There are groups where one is not allowed to doubt. These include cults. And certain families. I have seen Christian parents scold their child for doubting something about God, even God's existence. This will only serve to drive a child away from God.

One must discern which doubts to entertain, and which to not sweat over. Some doubts are reasonable; many others are not. But initially they come as emotions, even if provoked by intellectual things (which sometimes happens). So it is that Jesus-followers can have, and will have, doubts. "Doubt" does not mean "unbelief." In doubt there can be a sense of wonder. The emotion of doubt can empower study and creativity.

As you engage with God in prayer you may - you likely will - experience the emotion of doubt. God is not angry with you about this. Like Thomas, it might even turn into an occasion to touch his side.

Why Isn't Everyone Healed When I Pray?

Over the years I've seen people healed of emotional and physical illnesses. One of them was my grandmother. She lived with my family six months out of every year when we were growing up. When she was in her mid-eighties she was diagnosed with breast cancer. She decided not to have it medically treated. The cancerous tumors in her breasts grew. My mother used to bathe her, and visually and physically felt and saw these tumors.

Grandma knew she was going to die. She had lived a long life, and was ready to leave this world for the better one. She even bought the dress she wanted to be buried in.

When Grandma had spent what we assumed would be her last six months in our home, she went to live with my aunt and uncle, who cared for her during the next six months. One day my aunt called. She told my mother that, while bathing Grandma, she noticed that the tumors did not appear to be there. My mother could not believe this, yet wanted to believe it. Mom personally traveled 400 miles to visually inspect Grandma and confirm this.

Grandma lived for 12 more years, and bought two or three more dresses to be buried in (because styles change). She died at age ninety-seven. What happened? How can we explain this? I, and my mother, concluded two things:

1. Grandma once was cancer-filled, and then one day the cancer was gone.
2. God healed Grandma.

I've heard of, and personally seen, other things like this.[8]

I've also prayed for people who have not been healed, at least as far as I can tell. Which raises the question: Why? Why do I not see everyone healed when I pray for them?

I've thought long and hard about this over the years. I don't have all the answers. I don't think I can, given my quite-limited point of view, expect to have all the answers. Nonetheless, when I am asked this question, here's how I respond.

1. Sickness and disease are not caused by God. God hates sickness and disease.
2. Sickness and disease are in this world because we live in, as Jesus referred to it, "this present evil age." We live in a fallen world that's ruled by Satan, who is called "the Prince of this world."
3. Some diseases are part of living in this fallen world. The entire world is crying out for redemption (release) from this bondage.
4. The "age to come" in all its fullness is not our present reality. So, my physical body wastes away even as my spirit is being renewed.

Why did God create a world like this? Why a world where such suffering was even allowed? For me the answer is this:
- God is love. That is, God, in His essence, IS love. God cannot not-love.
- Therefore love is the highest value for God.
- God created persons (and spiritual beings) out of love.
- Genuine love is only possible if created agents have free will.
- Therefore God gave created agents free will.

[8] See, e.g., Eric Metaxas, *Miracles*. Also Craig Keener, *Miracles: The Credibility of the New Testament Accounts*.

- This is risky, since free will implies that one can choose to not love God.

From God's end, giving his created agents (that's us) free will is worth it. This is because God is love, and love is the highest value for God. Much of this world's suffering happens because of people exercising free will to hurt themselves and others.

This is no mere theory, no abstraction from reality. It is an explanation of reality. As a pastor, I've been around a lot of death and dying, to include in my own family, even my son David. How do I continue to find hope in such a world?

My understanding of what Jesus taught about the kingdom of God provides answers for me. Jesus talked about "the age to come," a time when will be no sickness, no struggle, no tears. When God invaded earth in the form of a person, the "age to come" invaded this present evil age. Jesus once said that, "If you see me cast out demons by the finger of God, you can know that the kingdom of God is in your midst." That is why I pray for the sick to be healed today, and will continue to do so.

I am part of a faith community. This makes a huge difference. I know people (even Christians) who would never pray for someone to be healed. In a faithless community one should not be shocked that healings are not seen.

Sometimes a deeper spiritual healing is needed. Some illnesses are, at root, spiritual and emotional. I have found that, for example, a person who lives for years with bitterness towards others, and refuses to forgive others, can be especially subject to physical illnesses. The account of Jesus' healing the lame man let down through the roof (Mark 2:1-12) implies that the forgiveness of the man's sins had some connection with his ability to pick up his mat and walk.

Don't lay blame on the person who is sick. When Jesus prayed for sick people he never blamed them for their sickness. For example, Jesus rejects his disciples' assumption that the blind man in John 10 was blind because either he or his parents must have sinned.

Persist in prayer. When some sick people are not healed through prayer, it may simply be because we haven't prayed long enough to bring the healing to completion.[9]

How Can I Build More Prayer Time into My Life?

One of my former seminary students asked,

> Do have any suggestions that would allow me to develop a greater consistency in my prayer life? I pray, but not every day. Sometimes I allow life situations get in the way. I work full-time, go to school, and struggle to find time to pray.

My response was:

If you cannot do an hour of praying[10], then scale back. How about ten to fifteen minutes a day? Let this time be focused.

My experience is that if someone can build ten to fifteen with God into a day, there will be times when God so moves upon that person that the time will extend.

Begin with Psalm 23, and spend a few weeks with these verses. They never grow old!

---

[9] In Francis MacNutt's classic book *Healing* he gives *11 reasons why people may not be healed*:

1. Lack of faith
2. Redemptive suffering
3. False value attached to suffering
4. Sin
5. Not praying specifically
6. Faulty diagnosis (is it inner healing/ physical healing/ deliverance that is needed)
7. Refusal to see medicine as a way God heals
8. Not using natural means of preserving health
9. Now is not the time
10. Different person is to be instrument of healing
11. Social environment prevents healing taking place

[10] I assign my seminary students to pray one hour every day.

Then, use John chapters 14-15-16.

Then, go to Matthew chapters 5-6-7.

Go slow. Slow-cook in these verses.

And be prepared and ready. For what? For God to move upon you, and within you. Remember - He loves you!

Prayer and Neuroscience - Some Resources

A former student asked for resources referring to praying and brain studies. Here are a few I suggested to them.

Neuroscientist Andrew Newberg (U of Pennsylvania) is doing major research in this area.[11]

University of Montreal neuroscientist Mario Beauregaard is working in the area of spirituality and neuroscience.[12]

Candy Brown, prof. of religious studies at Indiana University, is working in areas of science and prayer - see her book *Testing Prayer*. See also here.[13]

See Ladd and Spilka, *The Psychology of Prayer: A Scientific Approach* – especially chapters 6 and 7.

Finally, New Testament scholar Joel Green is working in the area of neuroscience - see his excellent book *Body, Soul, and Human Life*.

If God Already Knows the Outcome, Why Pray?

If God already knows what I am going to pray before I pray it, why do so?

---

[11] http://www.amazon.com/s/ref=nb_sb_noss_1?url=search-alias%3Daps&field-keywords=andrew+newberg

[12] http://www.amazon.com/Spiritual-Brain-Neuroscientists-Case-Existence/dp/0061625981/ref=sr_1_3?s=books&ie=UTF8&qid=undefined&sr=1-3&keywords=mario+beauregard

[13] . - http://www.docvadis.es/jorge-cordero/document/jorge-cordero/estudio_de_los_efectos_terap_uticos_de_la_oraci_n_de_intercesi_n_proximal_en_discapacidades_auditiva_y_visual_en_la_zona_rural_de_mozambique/fr/metadata/files/0/file/Study_of_the_Therapeutic_Effects_of_Proximal.5.pdf

Because: This is about a relationship, not a religious ritual. Think of a loving parent who already knows what their child is going to say, and allows them to say it without interrupting.

This is about us, being real and authentic in that relationship. Like a loving parent is proud of their child's transparency before them. "We must lay before Him what is in us, not what ought to be in us," wrote C. S. Lewis.[14] To put it another way, we must trust God with what God already knows.

As you pray, you can trust God with what he already knows.[15]

What Does It Mean to Ask for Anything in Jesus' Name?

I was talking with someone about John 14:13-14, where Jesus says, "I will do whatever you ask in my name, so that the Son may bring glory to the Father. You may ask me for anything in my name, and I will do it." My friend asked: "How are we to understand these words? Surely it doesn't mean we can pray for just anything and God will comply!"

Here's my response to them.

1) In context, Jesus says, "I am in the Father and the Father is in me." This is Trinitarian stuff, the perichoretic union of mutual indwelling and interpenetrating and co-inhering. *Peri-choresis* means to dance in a circle (from "peri'" [around], and "choresis" [dance; cf. Plato's use of this word as "cosmic dance" in the Timaeus]. In the Godhead we have the Big Dance of Everlasting Relationship. Jesus' words about "asking anything" are understood in this Trinitarian context.

2) Jesus invites anyone who puts their faith in him to the Big Dance. This is huge! David Crump of Calvin College states its hugeness when he writes[16]: "Divine union is at the heart of the Gospel of John. Jesus

---

[14] C. S. Lewis, *Letters to Malcolm: Chiefly on Prayer*, 22.

[15] It is not true that if God knows what you are going to pray, then you have no choice in it. To think so is to commit a fallacy in modal logic. See what I have written here: http://www.johnpiippo.com/2010/04/compatibility-of-divine-foreknowledge.html

[16] http://journals.cambridge.org/action/displayAbstract;jsessionid=2013E8CFD5445AC727FEDF80EB361629.tomcat1?fromPage=online&aid=521852

is the one sent from the Father to lead his people into a provocative, new terrain of perichoretic union with God" (slightly edited by me). The Father comes to make his home in us. Jesus is the Vine, the Father is the gardener, and we are the branches. What we say and what we do now comes from unity with the Godhead.

3) Understand points 1-2 above, and you will understand praying as: talking with the Godhead about what *we* are thinking and doing together. Real Prayer comes out of the Big Dance. N. T. Wright, in his commentary on John, writes:

> Praying 'in Jesus' name', then, means that, as we get to
> know who Jesus is, so we find ourselves drawn into his
> life and love and sense of purpose. We will then begin
> to see what needs doing, what we should be aiming at
> within our sphere of possibilities, and what resources
> we need to do it. When we then ask, it will be 'in Jesus'
> name', and to his glory; and, through that, to the glory
> of the father himself (verse 13). But, when all this is
> understood, we shouldn't go soft on that marvelous
> word *anything*. He said it, and he means it.[17]

When we are in spiritual sync with Jesus, anything we ask in prayer will concern what he is thinking and doing. Within this context my understanding is that God, by his love and grace, is open to suggestions.

What Do I Do When I Hear from God?

"I have a question regarding personal prophecy and need some advice about it. I am minding my own business and out of nowhere comes a voice saying "Thus says the Lord" followed by Scripture. What am I to do with this?"

My response was:

To help understand the ideas of New Testament prophecy and hearing from God I read books on the subject. The best scholarly book

---

[17] N.T. Wright, *John for Everyone*, 64. Ouisville: Westminster, 2002.

on prophecy to read is Wayne Grudem's *The Gift of Prophecy*. Jack Deere's little book on prophecy[18] is excellent, as are Mike Bickle's *Growing In the Prophetic,* and Jim Goll's *The Seer.* Another great book is Dallas Willard's *Hearing God.*

I am certain God has much he wants to say to his children every day. You are one of God's children. Thus God has much to say to you today.

When this happens to me:

1. I write it in my journal. I have had some impressions that seemed to be from God that have led me to fast and pray until I got an answer. There's sometimes a sense of the level of importance that's made me think, "I need to seek God about this."
2. I take alone-times with God, asking, "God, show me what this means. If it's something you want to say to me I'm open to it."
3. I have some people I run things like this by. I trust their discernment. They personally spend a lot of one-on-one time with God and, therefore, hear from God. We talk together about these things.
4. Keep spending much time with God. Abide in Jesus. That's the place where his sheep hear his voice.

What If I Don't Feel Like Praying?

I set aside times to pray. If you are new at this I suggest praying thirty minutes a day, 5 days a week.

What if you don't feel like praying? Pray anyway. Choose to pray anyway, because to pray is to engage in relationship with God.

Think of it like this. I talk with Linda every day, multiple times. Whether or not I feel like talking with her is irrelevant, because we are married. Because I love her, I mostly feel like talking with her. But my communication with Linda is not proportionate to any feelings I have.

It is important to pray when you don't feel like it. The person who only prays when they feel like it is not a praying person any more than

---

[18] Jack Deere, *The Beginner's Guide to the Gift of Prophecy.* Ventura, CA: Regal, 2003.

a person who practices the guitar only when they feel like it is a serious guitar student. We are not to allow feelings to determine whether or not we will actively stay in relationship with God.

Henri Nouwen writes:

> It is very important to remain faithful to these times and simply stick with our promise to be with God, even if nothing in our minds, hearts, or bodies wants to be there. Simple faithfulness in prayer gives the Spirit of God a real chance to work in us, to help us be renewed in God's hands and be conformed to God's will.[19]

A praying person is a faithful person.
Choose to pray today. If you do, I expect feelings will come.

---

[19] Nouwen, *Discernment*, Kindle Locations 496-500

18

PRAYER AND DEATH: A NOTE TO MY DYING FRIENDS

All my friends are dying. This is for you.

I won't be here in a hundred years. I won't be here in fifty years (I'd be 116, the oldest person on earth!). How about twenty-five years from now? I'll be ninety-one. If I last that long the end will be near. Life will then be moment by moment, breath by breath.

The question is not *will* I die, but *when I die will I be ready?*

Let's be basic. One day, you are out of here. Maybe you'll have a funeral, maybe not. Some of this depends on *how* you expire. (Some years ago I read physician Sherwin Nuland's *How We Die*.[1] It's sobering.)

Maybe there will be friends and loved ones at your funeral. You could outlive them all, in which case no one will mourn your passing. Or, perhaps, you made things so miserable for others that you fill the coffin, friendless. Even all your Facebook friends have unfriended you.

I have seen this happen. I once got a call asking if I would do a funeral for a total stranger because no one was interested in doing it, and no family would be there. I declined, due to other circumstances.

Perhaps you will be martyred for following Jesus. It is happening as I write these words.

---

[1] Sherwin Nuland, *How We Die: Reflections of Life's Final Chapter.* New York: Random House, 1993.

The point is: you and I are inextricably finite and fragile. We are contingent beings who have come into existence and will pass out of it. Yes, I believe there is life after life after death.[2] Still, one day we shall exit this present darkness. It is good to acknowledge this. It is bad to live in denial of this (or shall I say, "die-nial?")

Life is best lived when death is acknowledged. So, no immortality complexes allowed! Adolescents have immortality complexes. Mature adults do not.[3] Live life in the awareness of death. This focuses and prioritizes things.

Readiness for death begins *now*. Not in some morbid, gothic sense. We don't have to wear black, get skull tattoos, and wear dark, dripping makeup. That's not readiness for death. True readiness is living day by day in spiritual renewal. Look at Paul's perspective: "Therefore we do not lose heart. Though outwardly we are wasting away, yet inwardly we are being renewed day by day."[4]

Avoid this: "Though my spirit is wasting away, I am spending thousands of dollars on my extreme makeover day by day." Have you seen pictures of sixty-seven-year-old men with the physiques of body builders and the faces of post-Halloween pumpkins? In moving towards death, outwardly waste away, gracefully. You will not successfully wage war against this. Focus on inward renewal. Exercise spiritually unto godliness.

Live life for something greater than your own appearance, for God's sake!

Envision your obituary. You want it to read differently than this: "He loved gardening, enjoyed vacationing in Florida, ate everything in sight, was an avid Tigers fan, and tried to do everything on his 'bucket list'." How about this instead: "He kicked the bucket list and lived for a greater purpose."

---

[2] This is N.T. Wright's scholarly and, I think, accurate way of expressing it in his *Surprised by Hope: Rethinking Heaven, the Resurrection, and the Mission of the Church.*

[3] See the work of Elizabeth Kubler-Ross on youthful immortality complexes.

[4] 2 Corinthians 4:6

I believe in the historical resurrection of Jesus. This is huge for me! While not having yet experienced my own death (not possible), I've lost loved ones, including my son David, my parents, Linda's parents, and her two sisters. In all of these events I have had great hope.[5] I have been brought to a place where *I know my Redeemer lives, and one day I shall enter fully into his presence.* Remember, my brothers and sisters, death has lost its sting.

Some have the opportunity to think long and hard about death. They are those who know, for medical reasons, that unless God miraculously intervenes, they won't be here much longer. Others have no opportunity to do this. They appear well. Then they drop dead, or are gunned down in a movie theater. I'm not sure which is better. Regardless, death-prep begins today. What we do today prepares us for the inevitable.[6]

How we think about death is important. German philosopher Martin Heidegger believed the answer to the question of death is the solution to the meaning of life. How a book begins and ends is important. The same can be said for a piece of music. Or a sermon. Or a life. Do not forget the ending part. Paul, in Philippians 1:21, wrote: "For to me, to live *is* Christ and to die *is* gain." Therefore, finish strongly.

If you are reading this, then you have not expired. You read; therefore, you are. I suggest you…

…get alone before God in the place where heaven and earth intersect.

Slow down in your heart.

Close your eyes.

Take a few deep breaths.

---

[5] I am so grateful that, when I became a Jesus-follower, I was introduced to resurrection studies through William Lane Craig. Bill was one of my campus pastors and apologetic-philosophical mentor. And then there was John Peterson, who was my other campus pastor. John married Linda and I. He introduced me to C.S. Lewis and other apologetic material. From that beginning my Jesus-resurrection-studies have not ceased. My doctoral dissertation was on Wolfhart Pannenberg's use of metaphorical language in describing the historical resurrection, found in his brilliant *Jesus: God and Man*. Fast-forward to the present and I see 40 years of engagement in resurrection studies to include, more recently, N.T. Wright's *The Resurrection of the Son of God*.

[6] See Henri Nouwen, *Our Greatest Gift*.

Pray, thinking about the following:

You are alive! Thank God for it.

Are you facing problems today? You are alive to face them.

Do you have friends? You are alive to "friend" them today.

If you are a parent, behold your children.

Are you a spouse? There is your wife; there, your husband.

Enemies? They are your great love-opportunity. Instead of wishing they were dead, thank God they are living.

Celebrate life, whether abased or abounding, now.

Gratefully, live to consider such things.

In the face of death put on the full armor of God.

And pray in the Spirit on all occasions with all kinds of prayers and requests. With this in mind, be alert and always keep on praying for all the Lord's people.[7]

---

[7] Ephesians 6:18